Walker

MW01480808

LightFoot Guide
to the
Via Francigena

Edition 3

Vercelli
to
St Peter's Square, Rome
836 Kilometres

About the Authors

We are two very ordinary people who quit the world of business and stumbled on the St James Way during our search for a more viable, rewarding alternative to our previous lifestyle. Since then we have completed four pilgrimages, one of which was particularly tough and finally prompted us to create Pilgrimage Publications and the LightFoot guide series. We have no religious beliefs, but share a 'wanderlust' and need to know about and contribute to the world we occupy.

Pilgrimage Publications is a not-for-profit organisation dedicated to the identification and mapping of pilgrim routes all over the world, regardless of religion or belief. Any revenue derived from the sale of guides or related activities is used to further enhance the service and support provided to pilgrims.

The ethos of Pilgrimage Publications is based on 4 very basic aims:
* *To enable walkers, cyclists and riders to follow pilgrim routes all over the world.*
* *To ensure LightFoot guides are as current and accurate as possible, using pilgrim feedback as a major source of information.*
* *To use eco-friendly materials and methods for the publication of LightFoot guides and Travel Books.*
* *To promote eco-friendly travel.*

LightFoot guides are designed to enable pilgrims to enjoy the best, while avoiding the worst, of pilgrim travel.

Also by Babette Gallard and Paul Chinn

Riding the Milky Way 2006

Riding the Roman Way 2007

Reflections - A Pictorial Journey Along the via Francigena 2008

LightFoot Guide to the via Francigena - Canterbury to Besançon 2008/9/10

LightFoot Guide to the via Francigena - Besançon to Vercelli 2008/9/10

Companion to the via Francigena (a historical and cultural companion to the Guides)

LightFoot Guide to the Three Saints Way - Winchester to Mont St Michel 2008

LightFoot Guide to the Three Saints Way - Mont St Michel to St Jean d'Angely 2008

Tracing Yesterday Using Today's Technology

LightFoot Guides are designed to enable everyone to meet their personal goals and enjoy the best, whilst avoiding the worst, of following ancient pilgrimage routes. Written for Walkers, Cyclists and Horse Riders, every section of this LightFoot guide provides specific information for each group.

The authors would like to emphasise that they have made great efforts to use only public footpaths and to respect private property. Historically, pilgrims may not have been so severely restricted by ownership rights and the pressures of expanding populations, but unfortunately this is no longer the case. Today, even the most free-spirited traveller must adhere to commonly accepted routes. Failure to do so will only antagonise local residents, encourage the closure of routes and inhibit pilgrims following on behind.

Revised editions of this guide will be published each year, but everyone is advised to refer to the relevant update page on the Pilgrimage Publications website - changes will be listed as soon as they are received.
Please let us know about any changes to the route or inaccuracies within this guide book - mail@pilgrimagepublications.com

Reliable directions! Such a huge difference. The authors show their expertise in particular when they guide the walker away from the Way Marks, as their recommendations are almost always superior to the official option. The maps - accurate, reliable, and (particularly important to me) provide a lot of detail for the surrounding area, making it easier to correct a mistake if you do make one. No need to also purchase the Topofrancigena - this guide has you covered. The altitude chart is also quite handy. It is clear that this guide is as up-to-the-moment as a guide can get. Making a guide is hard enough - annual updatesthat provide the details this guide does is a massive commitment. I definitely want to reiterate once more my gratitude for the books. I wouldn't have had the great experience that I had in September-October without them, and I probably wouldn't be planning on a student trip for next summer.
Dave Whitson walked the via Francigena, using the LightFoot Guides, in 2009.

Our special thanks go to:
Barbara Edgar, for her tireless and ever vigilant proof-reading.
William Marques, Confraternity of Pilgrims to Rome, for his help and support.
François Louviot, President Association Via Francigena Français, for his support and offer of accommodation information.
Adelaide Trezzini for her contribution to the development and mapping of the via Francigena route.
Openstreetmap: The maps in this book are derived from data (c) Openstreetmap (http://www.openstreetmap.org) and its contributors and are made available under the Creative Commons agreement (http://creativecommons.org/licenses/by-sa/2.0/).

CONTENTS

This book traces the Via Francigena from Vercelli to St Peter's Square. You will find an introductory section followed by 28 chapters, each of which covers a segment of the route.
Each chapter contains:

      A route summary
      A cultural and historical overview of the region
      Detailed Instructions
      Map
      Altitude Profile

Instructions

The entire route has been GPS traced and logged using way point co-ordinates. On this basis, it should be possible to navigate the route using only the written instructions, though a map is provided for additional support and general orientation. Use of a compass is recommended.

Each instruction sheet provides:

  Detailed directions corresponding to GPS way point numbers on the map
  Verification Point - additional verification of current position
  Distance (in metres) between each way point

Each map provides:

  A north/south visual representation of the route with way point numbers
  Altitude Profile for the section
  Icons indicating places to stay, monuments etc. (see Map symbols)
  Relevant signs to look out for along the route
  Map reference number/s for the section

Accommodation Listings:

Accomodation prices are based on one double room per night - accurate at the time of entry, but subject to change. For simplicity, the listing is divided into 3 price bands:

B1 0-20 €   **B2** 21-50 € **B3** 51-70 €

In general there are no listings above 70€ per night, unless nothing else is available in the area. Prices may or may not include breakfast and some establishments charge a tariff for dogs. In general, dogs are not welcome in Youth or Religious Hostels. Similarly, the general rule for accommodation in Religious Houses is that reservations must be made 24 hours ahead of arrival. The title 'Parish Accommodation' is used where it is in a church hall with minimal facilities. At the end of this section you will also find details of churches and religious organisations either in or near towns along the route.

Look out for the PR - Pilgrim Recommended - in front of listings

The route is under constant development by many agencies and volunteers and unfortunately not always within an overall framework of signing or routing principles. As a result you may find that the instructions conflict with some signposting. It has been our goal to find a route for walkers that is a compromise between attractiveness, historic authenticity and practicality. We anticipate that horse-riders and cyclists (mountain bikers) will primarily follow the pedestrian route, however we have created some alternatives where there are particular problems for these groups. We have also suggested walkers alternatives when we feel the full route will be either too long or too difficult for some people. Road-bikers may find some parts of the pedestrian route acceptable but overall they are encouraged to plan their routes from an appropriate road map.

It is unfortunate that there is no single set of signs that follows the route from beginning to end. Signs are also inconsistent in frequency and type and prone to stop in mid-stage e.g. at the boundary of a commune. As a consequence you may find that the instructions in the guide will from time to time conflict with the signing that you find on the ground. It is up to you to decide whether to follow the signs or the instructions. However, we constantly work to ensure that the instructions will not let you down throughout the entire route.

The maps include a series of icons indicating the facilities that can be found in each town on the main route or within reasonable reach of the main route. The text for each stage gives complete descriptions of the facilities with address and contact details. We have included an icon for food stores and cafés for the areas outside of Italy. In France for example, there are many long stretches of the route with very limited opportunities to find food and drink. In Italy cafés and food stores are much more frequent and are typically found in all but the very smallest villages and as a result we have elected to exclude these icons there in favour of more map detail. The maps show towns and roads within a corridor of about 5 kilometres on either side of the main route. This is provided to help with orientation, but also to allow pilgrims that have gone off-piste to find their way back to the main route.

Each instruction is numbered where the numbers coincide to the GPS Waypoints for those that have downloaded these data. Each instruction is accompanied by a verification information - a description of a nearby feature to give you confidence in your route, the distance in metres to the next Waypoint, an approximate compass direction and Altitude. A compass and a watch will help you make best use of the data. Our experience is that most walkers maintain an average of around 4k.p.h. on level ground or 200metres every 3 minutes - remember to add time for climbing and descending, some people suggest allowing 1 hour for each 300metres of altitude difference. You may find it useful to time your progress against the Waypoint distance in the first few sections after which you will quickly develop your own sense of speed and distance.

The maps all conform to the north up standard with the direction of travel, for those heading to Rome, normally from top left to bottom right - South-Eastwards. If you are travelling in the summer months then you will find the sun in the South-East at about 9am.

To give as much information as possible we have tried to expand the maps to fill the pages of the books. Unfortunately this means that the map scale is variable map to map but will be consistent within each map.

LightFoot Tracker

The Via Francigena has the benefit and also the drawback of being less well developed than the Saint James Way. The sense of adventure of travelling a less well developed way and the escape from commercialism is very positive, however the smaller numbers also reduce the opportunity of those wonderful meetings with pilgrims from other backgrounds, with whom you are able to share experiences and often make new friendships.

Today, it is possible that you could follow one day behind or ahead of another group and still meet no other pilgrim on the entire journey. Or spend a night in the same town as another group and be unaware of their existence. We feel that these are lost opportunities and would like to let you know of some work we are doing to develop a few computer tools to help improve this situation.

1. A planning program that will enable you to quickly calculate your likely stop-over points and arrival dates based on your preferred rate of progress, departure date and rest or sight-seeing stops.

2. The facility to publish your plan and appropriate contact details on the internet in a visual form - probably using google earth.

3. The facility to review the plans of others and spot possible cross-over points - again using google earth facilities - giving you the opportunity to schedule a meeting or even find travel partners.

4. A simple process to record your progress along the route and display the progress to others to allow ad hoc meetings.

5. A database of completed journeys with details of age, pack-weight and rate of progress, that can be used to advise future pilgrims.

As a further stage we would like to bring our accommodation data into this environment to facilitate, budgeting and advance booking.

We will keep registered purchasers of the books up to date with progress on these developments through www.pilgrimagepublications.com and our periodic newsletter. We would also welcome your ideas for related functions.

Currency: **Euro**. Standard banking Hours: 08.30–13.30 and 14.30-16.00, Monday to Friday. Closed on Sundays.

Post Offices - Standard Opening Hours: 08.30-19.30 and 13.45-18.30, Monday to Friday. Branches in smaller towns and villages close for an hour, 13.00-14.00.

Phone booths that still accept coins are hard find. If you're planning to use a public phone purchase of a telephone card is recommended.

Numbers beginning with 800 are free.

170 - English-speaking operator.

176 - International Directory Enquires.

12 - Telephone Directory Assistance Number

112 - *Carabinieri* (national-level police who also perform military police duties)

113 - Emergency Police Help Number (also ambulance and fire)

115 - Fire Department

116 - A.C.I. (Italian Automobile Club) road assistance.

118 - Medical Emergencies

Note: Italian telephone numbers can include 4, 5, 6, 7, or even 8 digits, so don't automatically assume you have the wrong number if it looks strange. Since December 1998, calls to land lines in most cities, but not all, and all other points in Italy must include a leading '0' regardless of whether the call originates within or outside of Italy. However, the leading '0' is not required with mobile phones. The '0' is shown as (0) throughout the guide, in order to draw your attention to this potential confusion.

Basic Business Hours 08.00-13.00 and 16.00-19.00, Monday to Friday. Shops in smaller towns may close on Saturday afternoons and Monday mornings.

Visting **churches and religious sites**. Most churches are open in the early morning for Mass and close around noon, opening up again at 16.00 and closing at 19.00 or 20.00. In some remote places, churches only open for early morning and evening services. Opening hours for museums are generally Tuesday to Saturday, 09.00 to 19.00 with a midday break.

All EU citizens are eligible for free **health care** in Italy, if they have the correct documentation. Non EU Citizens must arrange personal health insurance.

Traditionally **Italian food** consists of lunch (*pranzo*) and dinner (*cena*) starting with *antipasto* (literally before the meal), a course consisting of cold meats, seafood and vegetables. The next course, *primo*, involves soup, risotto or pasta, followed by *secondo* - the meat or fish course, usually served alone. Vegetables - *contorni* - are ordered and served separately. Pizza is now a worldwide phenomenon, but Italy remains the best place to eat it.

Italian ice cream (*gelato*) is justifiably famous and available in every conceivable flavour.

Public Holidays - August, particularly during the weeks either side of *Ferragosto* (August 15) is a difficult time for travellers, because many towns are deserted, with shops, bars, hotels and restaurants shut.

Italian **hotels** fall into a number of categories, though the difference between each is gradually decreasing.

Locanda - historically the most basic option, but now tending to charge more for 'traditional' facilities.

Pensione, albergo or hotel - prices vary greatly between tourist hotspots and rural areas. Expect an additional charge for breakfast.

Hostels usually charge 15€. Virtually all hostels (excepting Religious Hostels) are members of the International Youth Hostel Association and you'll need to be a member.

Agritourismo - basically an upmarket B&B in a rural area and usually a working farm (see Travel tips for more information)

Camping in Italy is popular and the sites are generally well equipped.

The Basics in Italy

ENGLISH	ITALIAN	ENGLISH	ITALIAN
Sunday	Domenica	one	uno
Monday	Lunedi	two	due
Tuesday	Martedi	three	tre
Wednesday	Mercoledi	four	quattro
Thursday	Giovedi	five	cinque
Friday	Venerdi	six	sei
Saturday	Sabato	seven	sette
January	Gennaio	eight	otto
February	Febbraio	nine	nove
March	Marzo	ten	dieci
April	Aprile	eleven	undici
May	Maggio	twelve	dodici
June	Giugno	thirteen	tredici
July	Luglio	fourteen	quattordici
August	Agosto	fifteen	quindici
September	Septembre	sixteen	sedici
October	Octobre	seventeen	diciassette
November	Novembre	eighteen	diciotto
December	Dicembre	nineteen	diciannove
today	oggi	twenty	venti
yesterday	ieri	thirty	trenta
tomorrow	domani	forty	quaranta
in the morning	alla mattina	fifty	cinquanta
in the afternoon	nel pomeriggio	sixty	sessanta
in the evening	nella sera	seventy	settanta
now	ora	eighty	ottanta
later	piu successivamente	ninety	novanta
at midday	al mezzogiorno	one hundred	cento
at one o'clock	un in punto	on the other side of	dall'altro
bus	vettura	on the corner of	sul angolo di
bus stop	arresto di bus	next to	vicino a
bus station	autostazione	behind	dietro
car	automobile	in front of	davanti
train station	stazione di treno	before	prima
what time does it arrive/leave?	quando arriva/va?	after	dopo
how many kilometres	quanti chilometri?	under	sotto
how many hours	quante ora?	to cross	alla traversa sopra
on foot	à piedi	where?	dove?
the road to	la strada a	when?	quando?
near	vicino	how many/much?	quanto?
far	lontano	why?	perche?
left	sinistra	at what time?	a quando?
right	destra	a room for one/two person/people	una stanza per una gente/persona due?
straight on	dritto		

Cycling Vocabulary

ENGLISH	ITALIAN	ENGLISH	ITALIAN
to adjust	regolare	to lower	abbassare
axle	asse	mudguard	parafango
ball bearing	cuscinetto a sfere	pannier	borsa
battery	batteria	pedal	pedale
bent	inclinazione	pump	pompa
bicycle	bicicletta	puncture	foratura
brake cable	cavo freno	to raise	sollevare
brakes	freni	to repair	riparare
broken	rotto	saddle	sellino
bulb	lampadina	to screw	avvitare
chain	catena	spanner	chiave
to deflate	sgonfiare	spoke	raggio
frame	telaio	to straighten	assettare
gears	marce	stuck	bloccato
grease	grasso	tight	stretto
handlebars	manubri	toe clips	fermapiedi
to inflate	gonfiare	tyre	pneumatico
inner tube	camera d'aria	wheel	ruota

Equine Vocabulary

ENGLISH	ITALIAN	ENGLISH	ITALIAN
Farrier	Veterinario	Stirrup	Staffa
Mane	Criniera	Saddle pad	Sella imbottita
Tail	Coda	Brush	Spazzola
Horse	Cavallo	Hoof-picks	Curasnette
Mare	Giumenta	Horse shoe	Stivali da equitazione
Foal	Puledro	Helmet	Elmetto
Gelding	Cavallo castrato	Hat	Cappello
Stallion	Stallone	Gloves	Guanti
Head	Testa	Boots	Stivali
Eyes	Occhi	Walk	Passo
Ears	Orecchie	Canter Trot	Galoppo Trotto
Nostril	Narici	To limp	Zoppicare
Withers	Garrese	Saddle	Sella
Croup (rear)	Groppa	Girth	Sottopancia
Neck	Collo	Bridle	Briglia
Hay	Fieno	Oats	Avena
Legs	Zampe	To unsaddle	Dissellare
Hoof	Zoccolo	To girth	Assicurare la sella
Tack	Bardatura	To loosen the girth	Allentare il sottopancia
Lame	Zoppo	To shorten	Accorciare

Pilgrim and Travel Sites

www.Pilgrimstales.com	PILGRIM TALES publishing is passionate about inspiring others with the possibility of discovery, understanding and peace through travel
www.pilgrimstorome.org.uk	Practical information for the pilgrimage to Rome
www.theexpeditioner.com	THE EXPEDITIONER popular travel-themed webzine featuring articles about travel, music and film.
www.eurovia.tv	EUROVIA serves as a platform made by pilgrims, for pilgrims. Everybody is welcome to share their experiences with others, and to contribute their views and opinions. Other pilgrims are always grateful to receive useful tips
www.camminideuropageie.com	An Italian, Spanish, French collaboration
www.culturalroutes.ch	CULTURAL ROUTES OF SWITZERLAND deals with cultural routes in Switzerland and as such has information about the Via Francigena through that country. At time of writing it is in German and French only
www.francigena.eu	EUROPEAN ASSOCIATION webpage. In Italian. Has photos and maps of the route in Italy though they may not have enough detail for walkers
www.giovannicaselli.com/francigena/italy.htm	VIA FRANCIGENA - HIGHWAY TO HEAVEN Website of Giovanni Caselli. In Italian.
www.groups.yahoo.com/group/viafrancigena/	VIA FRANCIGENA YAHOO DISCUSSION GROUP A lively discussion group with a large amount of useful information.
www.pelgrimswegen.nl	DUTCH ASSOCIATION OF PILGRIMS TO ROME Site in Dutch
www.canterbury.gov.uk	CANTERBURY CITY COUNCIL
www.csj.org.uk	CONFRATERNITY OF ST JAMES providing a wealth of information about the many pilgrim routes to Santiago de Compostela in Spain as well as general guidance and advice to pilgrims. It is well worth visiting if this is your first pilgrimage.
www.sixtina.com	ITALIA SIXTINA A French booking service for lodging in convents and monasteries.
www.stjamesirl.com	IRISH SOCIETY OF THE FRIENDS OF ST JAMES The site of the Irish equivalent to the CSJ.
www.francigena-international.org	INTERNATIONAL ASSOCIATION OF VIA FRANCIGENA publishes maps of the route in walking stages as well as route instructions and accommodation lists.
http://www.osun.org/francigena-pdf.html	Files, brochures, articles and on the Via Francigena.
http://vfpilgrims.blogspot.com	Excellent site, full of information, run by a VF pilgrim

Useful Links

General

French Tourist Board, 178 Piccadilly, London W1J 9AL Tel: 0044 (0)9068 244 123
info.uk@franceguide.com http://uk.franceguide.com

French Youth Hostelling Association, FUAJ - National Centre Office, 27 rue Pajol, 75018 Paris Tel: 0033 (0)1 44 89 87 27

AIG, NATIONAL BOARD, 44, via Cavour - 00184 ROMA Tel: 0039 06 4871152
info@ostellionline.org
AIG, TRAVEL SECTION, 48/50, via Farini - 00184 ROME Tel: 0039 06 48907740
info@ostellionline.org

Swiss Youth Hostels, 14 Schaffhauserstrasse - 8042 ZÜRICH Tel: 0041 (0)44 360 14 14
bookingoffice@youthhostel.ch

IGN Maps http://ign.fr

Swiss maps available from Kümerley+Frey www.swisstravelcenter.ch

Further Reading

Europe's Monastery and Convent Guest Houses	Kevin J. Wright
The Art of Pilgrimage	Phil Cousineau
Have Saddle Will Travel	Don West
The Essential Walker's Journal	Leslie Sansone
Pilgrimage to Rome in the Middle Ages: Continuity and Change (Studies in the History of Medieval Religion)	Debra J. Birch
The Age of Pilgrimage: The Medieval Journey to God	Jonathan Sumption
The Pilgrim's France - A Travel Guide to the Saints	James & Colleen Heater
Along the Templar Trail	Brandon Wilson
Via Francigena - Impressions of a Pilgrimage	Publisher: Eurovia
The Christian's Guide to Rome	S.G.A Luff
Rome: a pilgrim's companion	David Baldwin (Catholic Truth Society, London)
In Search of a Way: two journeys of spiritual discovery	Gerard Hughes
Pilgrim-Diary, Nikulas of Munkathvera: the Road to Rome	Francis P. Magoun
In Search of a Way	Gerard W Hughes
Sigeric's Journey to Rome	Heather Burnley

Useful Links and Recommended Reading

Map Legend

 Restaurant

Café

Accommodation

Food store

Camping Site

Tourist Information

Railway Station

Equestrian Centre

Historical Monument

Airfield

Abbey/Cathedral

Church

Viewpoint

 Main Route Way Point

  Alternate Route Way Point

 Via Francigena Main Route

 Via Francigena Alternate Route

Motorway or major highway

   Main Road

Minor Road

Railway Track

Canal

River

 Area of Water

Large Town

The Route

Vercelli
to
St Peter's Square, Rome
836 kilometres

"Let your mind start a journey thru a strange new world. Leave all thoughts of the world you knew before. Let your soul take you where you long to be...Close your eyes let your spirit start to soar, and you'll live as you've never lived before."

Erich Fromm

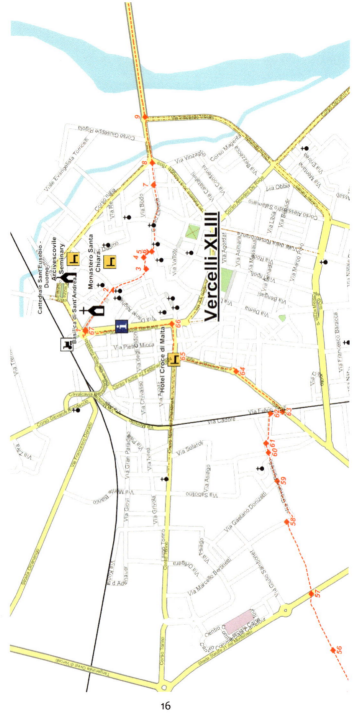

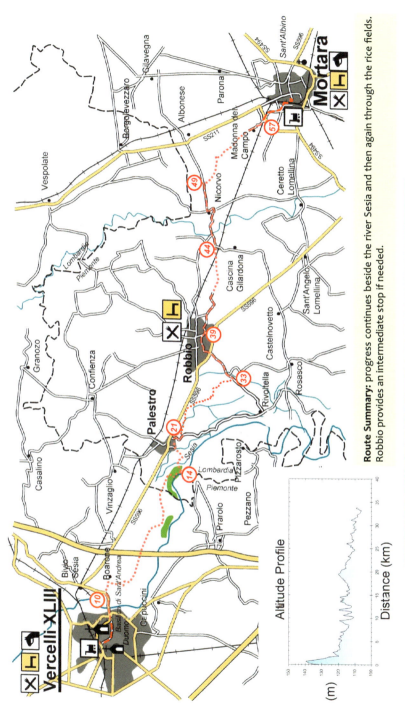

Route Summary: progress continues beside the river Sesia and then again through the rice fields. Robbio provides an intermediate stop if needed.

Mortara

Vercelli XLIII

Altitude Profile

(m)

Distance (km)

Sant'Albino

SS494

SS596

Parona

Madonna del Campo

57

Albonese

Nicorvo

49

Borgolavezzaro

Gravellona

Vespolate

SS211

Ceretto Lomellina

Sant'Angelo Lomellina

44

Cascina Gilardona

SS596

Castelnovetto

Rosasco

39

Robbio

Rivoltella

33

Lombardia Piemonte

Palestro

21

Sesia

SS596

Confienza

Granozo

14

Lombardia Piemonte

Pizzarosto

Prarolo

Pezzano

Casalino

Vinzaglio

SS596

Boaronte

Basilica di Sant'Andrea

Duomo

Cappuccini

10

Bivio Sesia

Distance from Canterbury: 1247km   **Distance to Rome:** 836km

Ascent: 31m   **Descent:** 42m

Vercelli to Mortara 33.9 km

Way Point N°	Way Point Distance (metres)	Total Distance (kilometres)	Directions	Verification Point	Compass	Altitude (metres)
47.001	0	0.0	From the roundabout in front of the railway station – piazza Roma – take via Galileo Ferraris	Pass the basilica of Sant'Andrea on the left	SE	125
47.002	300	0.3	At the crossroads continue straight ahead	No Entry, towards church	SE	138
47.003	300	0.6	Bear left into piazza Cavour go straight ahead keeping to the right side of the piazza		E	138
47.004	80	0.7	Cross the piazza and bear right on via F. Crispi		SE	139
47.005	50	0.7	Shorty after turn right	Remain on via Crispi	S	139
47.006	40	0.8	At the end of the road turn left	Piazza San Paolo and then Corso Libertà	E	140
47.007	400	1.2	At the mini-roundabout at the end of Corso Libertà continue straight ahead	Piazza Modesto Cugnolio, via Francigena sign beside the kiosk ahead	E	131
47.008	150	1.3	At the roundabout continue straight ahead, direction Pavia	Cross bridge over waterway	E	129
47.009	300	1.6	At roundabout go straight ahead, direction Pavia (SS11)	Cross over the Sesia river bridge	E	127
47.010	1000	2.6	After bend to the left on the main road, turn right on the small road Strada del Boarone	Via Francigena sign	SE	124
47.011	400	3.0	At fork, bear right towards the river and follow the dyke under the motorway	VF sign	SE	121

Way Point N°	Way Point Distance (metres)	Total Distance (kilometres)	Directions	Verification Point	Compass	Altitude (metres)
47.012	5400	8.4	Continue straight ahead - please add to the cairn beside the sign	Roma 720km	SE	114
47.013	1800	10.2	Keep straight ahead parallel to river		SE	112
47.014	200	10.4	Turn left, at right angle to river		E	110
47.015	200	10.6	Go straight ahead over wooden bridge		E	113
47.016	300	10.9	At track crossroads turn right		SE	116
47.017	300	11.2	At T-junction turn left towards the village of Palestro		NE	114
47.018	600	11.8	Turn right at the edge of Palestro on SP56 - via Garibaldi	VF sign	E	117
47.019	300	12.1	Cross bridge and proceed straight ahead	VF sign	SE	119
47.020	90	12.2	Turn right direction Rosasco on via Rosasco	VF sign	S	118
47.021	400	12.6	On the crown of the bend to the right, turn left onto partially visible grass track	Towards trees	NE	112
47.022	110	12.7	Turn right on the embankment	Trees to the left	E	112
47.023	400	13.1	The embankment narrows and becomes a footpath	Beside rice field	SE	116
47.024	200	13.3	Follow the sign to the left		NE	116
47.025	70	13.4	Turn right on the track		E	117
47.026	300	13 7	At the junction continue straight ahead		SE	120
47.027	600	14.3	Take the left fork	Trees to the right	SE	116
47.028	200	14.5	At the end of the path beside the trees turn right on the track		S	118
47.029	200	14.7	Follow the sign to the left and immediately turn right	Tracks zig-zags around fields	SE	118

Way Point N°	Way Point Distance (metres)	Total Distance (kilometres)	Directions	Verification Point	Compass	Altitude (metres)
47.030	1200	15.9	Enter into a private property and at the junction after the cascina Bosco dei Cani turn right		S	116
47.031	190	16.1	At the next farm turn left		SE	114
47.032	200	16.3	At the crossroads continue straight ahead		S	113
47.033	600	16.9	At the T-junction with the tarmac road turn left on the road		NE	115
47.034	400	17.3	Straight ahead direction Robbio		NE	115
47.035	1400	18.7	At crossroads with the SS596 proceed straight ahead into Robbio centre		N	117
47.036	300	19.0	At crossroads, after passing building material yard, turn right	VF sign, via Rosasco	E	118
47.037	400	19.4	At crossroads proceed straight ahead	VF sign, direction Mortara	E	120
47.038	300	19.7	At traffic lights bear right direction Mortara	Via Mortara, pass church on the left	SE	120
47.039	200	19.9	Turn left onto via Roggetta	VF sign	E	119
47.040	400	20.3	Crossroads with major road straight ahead beside the sports ground	VF sign, tarmac road emerges onto gravel track	SE	118
47.041	1000	21.3	Bear left after crossing a small bridge	VF sign	E	115
47.042	600	21.9	Fork right passing large concrete barn on the right	VF sign	E	116
47.043	1100	23.0	Bear right at fork	VF sign	E	114
47.044	1300	24.3	At junction with road turn left - SP157	VF sign, irrigation ditch on the right	E	112

Way Point Nº	Way Point Distance (metres)	Total Distance (kilometres)	Directions	Verification Point	Compass	Altitude (metres)
47.045	300	24.6	Road forks, bear left over bridge	VF sign	NE	111
47.046	190	24.8	At T-junction turn right direction Nicorvo on SP 6	VF sign, towards mobile-phone mast	E	111
47.047	1300	26.1	At T-junction in Nicorvo turn left. **Note:** VF signs point both left and right, but the route to the right has been blocked	Direction Cilavegna	N	114
47.048	200	26.3	In the centre of Nicorvo with the bell tower on the left, turn right direction Mortara	VF sign, via Albonese	E	115
47.049	1400	27.7	Turn right onto the part grassed track between rice fields	VF sign	S	112
47.050	300	28.0	Bear left at fork in track	VF sign	SE	111
47.051	500	28.5	Cross the gravel track and continue on the grass track	Large red farm on the right	E	113
47.052	700	29.2	Turn right to cross over concrete bridge	VF sign	SE	110
47.053	400	29.6	Continue straight ahead at crossroads in track	VF sign	SE	111
47.054	600	30.2	Bear right at T-junction in track	VF sign	SE	111
47.055	800	31.0	Bear right at T-junction in track	VF sign	SE	108
47.056	200	31.2	Proceed straight ahead and pass through the village of Madonna del Campo	VF sign, walled gardens on both sides of the road	SE	112

Way Point N°	Way Point Distance (metres)	Total Distance (kilometres)	Directions	Verification Point	Compass	Altitude (metres)
47.057	800	32.0	Continue straight ahead across the railway tracks. **Note**: the route ahead includes an underpass under the main railway line. Riders are recommended to bear left at this point and then turn right at the junction with the main road into the centre of the Mortara and the end of the section	VF sign, towards apartment buildings on the horizon	SE	108
47.058	400	32.4	At the junction continue straight ahead	Concrete barn on the left	S	109
47.059	600	33.0	At the junction bear left towards the railway and the prominent apartment block	Via A. da Cantiano	SE	107
47.060	400	33.4	At the rear of the railway sidings turn right	Keep railway on the left	S	105
47.061	170	33.5	In the square beside a water-tower continue straight ahead into the No Through Road	Keep railway close on the left	S	108
47.062	200	33.7	Take the pedestrian tunnel under the railway and continue straight ahead on the far side		NE	109
47.063	200	33.9	Arrive in Mortara centre in front of the railway station	Beside fountain		108

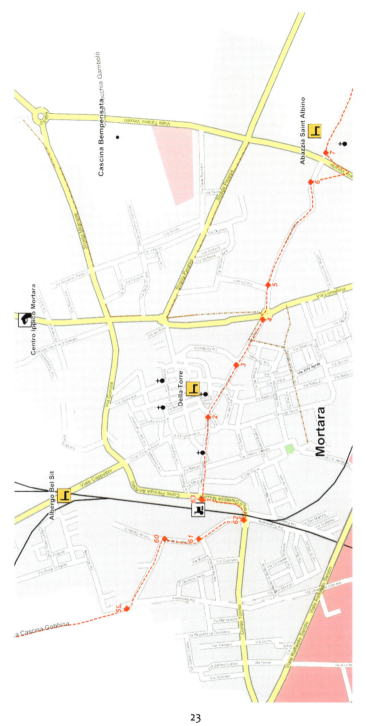

Mortara Town Map

Hotel/B&B	Price
Agriturismo Oasi delle Cicogne, Via Tenuta Broccone - 27038 ROBBIO Tel: 0039 (0)384 672673 www.centroippicomortara.it	B2
Moderno, 1/5, via Mazzini - 27038 ROBBIO Tel: 0039 (0)384 670367	B2
PR Bel Sit, 58, viale Capettini - 27036 MORTARA Tel: 0039 (0)384 98169	B2
Della Torre, 7, via Contrada Della Torre - 27036 MORTARA Tel: 0039 (0)384 90775	B2

Religious Hostel	Price
Oratorio Parrocchiale, piazza S. Stefano - 27038 ROBBIO Tel: 0039 (0)340 670436	Donation
Francesca & Gianmario Grosso, Via Roma 16 - 27020th NICORVO Tel: 0039 (0)384 524024 Mobile: 338 3785706 Mobile: 0321 668526 Mobile: 313 8083303 www.guidafrancigena.it www.comune.nicorvo.pv.it	Donation
Abazzia Saint Albino, viale Tiziano Vecellino - 27036 MORTARA Tel: 0039 (0)384 295327 Mobile: 0039 347 7194503	Donation

Equestrian

Centro Ippico Mortara, 433, via Parona Cassolo - 27036 MORTARA
Tel: 0039 (0)384 295988

Useful Contacts

Doctor

Studio Crosio Dr. Luigi, 45, via Roma - 27036 MORTARA Tel: 0039 (0)384 93342

Veterinary

Clinica Veterinaria Citta' Di Mortara, Strada per Cascina Cassagalla - 27036
MORTARA   Tel: 0039 (0)384 93330

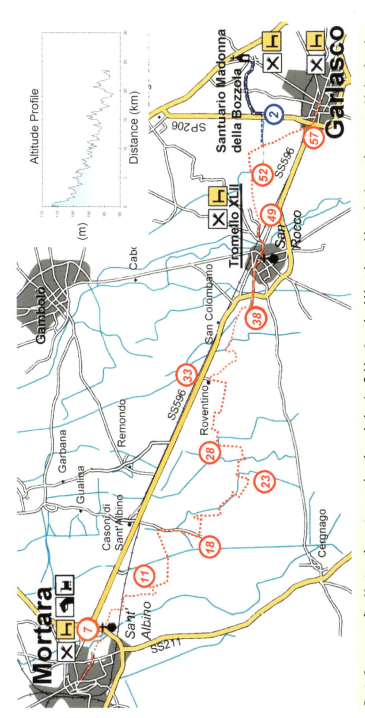

Altitude Profile

(m)

Distance (km)

Route Summary: after Mortara the route meanders through the rice fields. Care should be taken with navigation as the countryside has few clear landmarks, before Tremello. In the event of getting lost in this section, turn North and follow the SS596 towards Pavia. It is also possible to visit Santuario Madonna della Bozzola by taking the Alternate Route.

Mortara to Garlasco 23.6 km

Way Point N°	Way Point Distance (metres)	Total Distance (kilometres)	Directions	Verification Point	Compass	Altitude (metres)
48.001	0	0.0	From the railway station in Mortara go straight ahead on Corso Garibaldi	Railway station directly behind	E	108
48.002	400	0.4	Beside the town hall (municipio) bear right	Corso Cavour	SE	111
48.003	300	0.7	Continue straight ahead on Corso Cavour	Direction Sant'Albino	SE	111
48.004	200	0.9	At the roundabout go straight ahead	Via Sant'Albinio Alcuino, towards water tower	E	109
48.005	170	1.1	Continue straight ahead to join the cycle track	Water tower immediately to the left	SE	106
48.006	500	1.6	Bear right on the cycle track and take tunnel under the main road (SS494) and then immediately left	Parallel to the main road	SE	104
48.007	300	1.9	Turn right on the gravel track	Immediately pass the Abbazia Sant'Albino on the right	SE	105
48.008	600	2.5	At the junction bear right	Towards the railway track	S	104
48.009	200	2.7	Cross over the railway and turn left	Railway immediately on the left	SE	104
48.010	1200	3.9	At the T-junction beside irrigation channel turn left		NE	102
48.011	140	4.0	Take next right. **Note:** the former route via the villages of Casoni di Sant'Albino and Remondo is straight ahead rejoining this route at Roventino		S	104
48.012	500	4.5	At the junction just before the farm turn left		E	104

Way Point N°	Way Point Distance (metres)	Total Distance (kilometres)	Directions	Verification Point	Compass	Altitude (metres)
48.013	600	5.1	Continue straight ahead	Cross canale Cavour	NE	103
48.014	600	5.7	Continue straight ahead	Towards the clump of trees	E	103
48.015	150	5.9	At the T-junction turn right	A broad white road	S	105
48.016	500	6.4	At the crossroads continue straight ahead	Close to fishing reserve	S	103
48.017	200	6.6	At the junction continue straight ahead	Towards the farm	S	101
48.018	400	7.0	At the junction turn left on the track	Just before cascina Barza	E	102
48.019	300	7.3	At the junction continue straight ahead between trees	The track ahead will bear left and then right	NE	102
48.020	400	7.7	At the junction turn right		SE	101
48.021	1100	8.8	At the junction continue straight ahead	The track ahead will bear left and then sharp right	S	99
48.022	500	9.3	At the junction turn left		SE	98
48.023	500	9.8	Turn left	After crossing irrigation canal	N	100
48.024	300	10.1	Turn right	After crossing another irrigation canal	SE	102
48.025	600	10.7	In front of a fence for a private property turn left and take the track on the far side of the canal		NF	98
48.026	110	10.8	Take the right fork		E	100
48.027	200	11.0	At the junction turn left and follow the irrigation channel	Ignore the turning towards the farm buildings	N	100

Way Point N°	Way Point Distance (metres)	Total Distance (kilometres)	Directions	Verification Point	Compass	Altitude (metres)
48.028	600	11.6	At the T-junction turn right	After crossing irrigation canal	E	98
48.029	300	11.9	At the T-junction turn left	After crossing irrigation channel. The path ahead will turn sharp right	NE	98
48.030	200	12.1	Continue straight ahead	Cross the embankment and follow the irrigation channel	SE	98
48.031	500	12.6	At the junction turn left	Pass the cascina la Sciandola to the right and then another embankment	E	97
48.032	800	13.4	Turn left on the broad white road	Towards a group of houses	N	96
48.033	400	13.8	Pass through the cascina Roventino after the arch turn right	After the turn keep the farm buildings close on the right and then follow the irrigation ditch	SE	98
48.034	1200	15.0	Pass through a clump of trees and at the T-junction turn left		N	101
48.035	300	15.3	At the junction turn right	Parallel to the main road	E	99
48.036	300	15.6	Cross the Langosco canal and continue straight ahead		E	100
48.037	300	15.9	At crossroads proceed straight ahead	Towards cascina S. Vincenzo	SE	98
48.038	700	16.6	At the T-junction turn left		E	97

Way Point N°	Way Point Distance (metres)	Total Distance (kilometres)	Directions	Verification Point	Compass	Altitude (metres)
48.039	80	16.7	At the junction where the track becomes tarmac continue straight ahead on the wooded path. **Note:** at the next Way Point there is a crash barrier and dangerous road crossing to negotiate. Riders should turn right here and then left at the T-junction and follow the road into the centre of Tromello		E	97
48.040	200	16.9	Cross the main road (SS596) and continue straight ahead on the track	Towards the village	E	95
48.041	400	17.3	At the crossroads continue straight ahead on the tarmac road	Via Ronchi dei Legionari	E	94
48.042	300	17.6	At the junction with the via Crispi continue straight ahead		E	96
48.043	120	17.7	At the T-junction turn right on via Cavour	VF signs	SE	96
48.044	400	18.1	In Piazza Campegi turn left	Via Giovanni Mussini, café on the left	NE	97
48.045	180	18.3	At the traffic lights turn right	Via Guglielmo Marconi, direction Garlasco	SE	96
48.046	300	18.6	After crossing the bridge turn left	Towards Borgo S. Siro	NE	95
48.047	190	18.7	After crossing the railway turn right	Via Cascinino , VF sign	E	94

Way Point N°	Way Point Distance (metres)	Total Distance (kilometres)	Directions	Verification Point	Compass	Altitude (metres)
48.048	300	19.0	At the end of the tarmac continue straight ahead on the unmade road		E	93
48.049	110	19.2	Take the right fork on the track		E	93
48.050	500	19.7	At the crossroads with the white road continue straight ahead		E	94
48.051	600	20.3	At the junction continue straight ahead		E	96
48.052	200	20.4	Continue straight ahead	Cross canale Cavour	SE	99
48.053	1000	21.4	Recross canale Cavour and continue straight ahead. **Note:** the official route proceeds to Garlasco, it is possible to turn left here to take the Alternate Route to Santuario Madonna della Bozzola where accommodation is also available		S	97
48.054	300	21.8	Bear left shortly at the junction	Via Grassano	SE	95
48.055	500	22.3	Continue straight ahead on the track		S	93
48.056	300	22.6	Continue straight ahead on the tarmac	Cross the railway	SE	94
48.057	300	22.9	At the T-junction with the main road turn left and continue straight ahead towards the centre of Garlasco	Via Tromello, towards bell tower	E	94
48.058	700	23.6	Arrive piazza de la Repubblica, Garlasco	In front of the church of S. Maria Assunta		96

Note: the Alternate Route bypasses Garlasco ending at Santuario Madonna della Bozzola

Way Point N°	Way Point Distance (metres)	Total Distance (kilometres)	Directions	Verification Point	Compass	Altitude (metres)
1	0	0.0	Turn left beside the canal, keeping water on right	VF sign	E	97
2	700	0.7	Cross over road and bear left on track with canal on the left	VF sign	N	94
3	300	1.0	Fork right away from the canal	VF sign	E	97
4	200	1.2	Fork right to proceed between trees	VF sign	E	97
5	400	1.6	Turn left to cross over the small aqueduct and then right to proceed with the water on your left as you cross over the bridge	VF sign	E	95
6	900	2.5	Arrive in the piazza in front of the Santuario Madonna della Bozzola	VF sign		97

Hotel/B&B	Price
Margherita, via Don Minzoni, 2 - 27026 GARLASCO Tel: 0039 (0)382 822674	B2
Duca di Tromello, 4, via Cesare Battisti - 27020 TROMELLO Tel: 0039 (0)382 86494	B2

Religious Hostel	Price
Parrocchia s. Martino Vescovo, 1, via Branca - 27020 TROMELLO Tel: 0039 (0)382 86020	Donation
Santuario Madonna della Bozzola - 27026 GARLASCO Tel: 0039 (0)382 822428	Donation

Alternate Route from canale Cavour to Santuario Madonna della Bozzola 2.5km

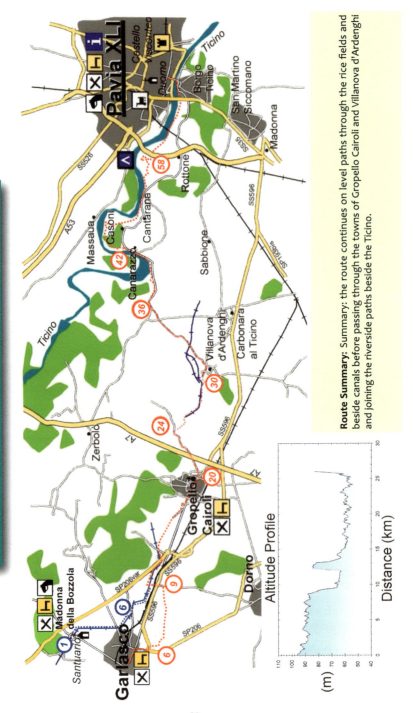

Garlasco to Pavia 26.1 km

Altitude Profile

Distance (km)

(m)

Route Summary: Summary: the route continues on level paths through the rice fields and beside canals before passing through the towns of Gropello Cairoli and Villanova d'Ardenghi and joining the riverside paths beside the Ticino.

Distance from Canterbury: 1305km

Distance to Rome: 778km

Ascent: 100m

Descent: 113m

Way Point N°	Way Point Distance (metres)	Total Distance (kilometres)	Directions	Verification Point	Compass	Altitude (metres)
49.001	0	0.0	From the church of S. Maria Assunta continue along the main road towards Pavia	Corso Cavour	E	96
49.002	200	0.2	At the traffic lights continue straight ahead on the main road	Corso Cavour	SE	95
49.003	300	0.5	Turn right towards Voghera on via Dorno	Beside petrol station	S	94
49.004	400	0.9	At the traffic lights cross the road and turn left, direction A7	Via Leonardo da Vinci , SP206	E	92
49.005	170	1.1	Cross the canal and turn right on the unmade road	Via Albera, canal on the right and industrial buildings on the left	S	92
49.006	300	1.4	Beside the bend in the canal turn left on the track		E	93
49.007	180	1.6	Continue straight ahead	Over irrigation channels	E	90
49.008	700	2.3	Continue straight ahead	Ignore the turning to the right	E	88
49.009	1000	3.3	At the T-junction beside the farm turn left	Pass farm buildings on the right	N	90
49.010	200	3.5	At crossroads with the SS596 continue straight ahead on the unmade road	Cross the tarmac road and the railway	N	92

Way Point Nº	Way Point Distance (metres)	Total Distance (kilometres)	Directions	Verification Point	Compass	Altitude (metres)
49.011	300	3.8	Cross the canale Cavour and immediately turn right - Alternate Route rejoins from the left	Canal-side path with canal on the right	SE	91
49.012	1000	4.8	At the crossroads with the SP206 cross the road and continue on the track beside the canal	Canal on the left	E	89
49.013	300	5.0	At the crossroads continue straight ahead	Canal on the left	E	88
49.014	200	5.3	Fork right away from the canale Cavour on lower track direction Gropello Cairoli	VF sign	SE	89
49.015	1000	6.3	Continue straight ahead at the junction	Pass behind the cemetery	SE	89
49.016	200	6.5	Fork left on the track	Avoid tarmac road to the right	E	88
49.017	300	6.8	Cross the canal and turn right	Keep canal on the right	S	87
49.018	190	6.9	At the junction with the main road turn left on the road and enter Gropello Cairoli	Via Marconi, towards bell tower	SE	90
49.019	200	7.1	Continue straight ahead through the centre of the town	Pass chiesa Parrocchiale S. Giorgio on the right	SE	91
49.020	600	7.7	Pass the church of San Rocco (in centre of main road) and immediately bear left	Viale C.B. Zanotti, sign for Centro Hippico Sant'Andrea	E	86

Garlasco to Pavia 26.1 km

Way Point N°	Way Point Distance (metres)	Total Distance (kilometres)	Directions	Verification Point	Compass	Altitude (metres)
49.021	600	8.3	On leaving the town continue straight ahead on the bridge over the motorway	Pass telephone mast on the right	E	88
49.022	300	8.6	After crossing the bridge bear left	Strada del Morgarolo, keep factory on the right and motorway on the left	NE	84
49.023	400	9.0	Continue straight ahead	Pass beside Centro Hippico Sant' Andrea	NE	76
49.024	600	9.6	At the junction turn right	Direction cascina Morgarolo, No Through Road sign ahead at the junction	S	66
49.025	160	9.8	On the entrance to the farm turn left, over the canal and then immediately right between buildings	Proceed with canal close on the right	SE	66
49.026	300	10.1	Take the left fork	Between two irrigation channels	E	65
49.027	190	10.3	At fork bear right	Keep irrigation channel close on right	SE	65
49.028	700	10.0	After crossing a bridge bear left	Keep irrigation ditch close on left	E	64
49.029	600	10.7	At T-junction turn right, away from the irrigation channel	Bridge on the left at the junction	SE	64
49.030	140	10.8	At fork bear left into Villanova d'Ardenghi	Taking the tarmac road, uphill between trees	E	64
49.031	400	11.2	Continue straight ahead through the town	Via Pollini	SE	83

Way Point N°	Way Point Distance (metres)	Total Distance (kilometres)	Directions	Verification Point	Compass	Altitude (metres)
49.032	200	11.4	At crossroads turn left	Via Roma	NE	84
49.033	1300	12.7	Continue straight ahead on the tarmac road	Ignore the turning to the left, pass casina Caselle on the right	NE	64
49.034	1500	14.2	At crossroads continue straight ahead	VF sign	NE	63
49.035	400	14.6	Continue straight ahead on the raised road.	Large farm on left, cascina Gaviola	E	59
49.036	400	15.0	Shortly after the bend to the right, descend from the embankment and take the path on the left. **Note:** to avoid potentially wet ground, cyclists may wish to remain on the road for the 8.8km to the ponte coperto in Pavia		SE	60
49.037	300	15.3	Turn right to follow the water-course		E	59
49.038	700	16.0	Continue straight ahead on the path with the river Ticino on the left		E	59
49.039	300	16.3	Continue straight ahead on the riverside path		NE	58
49.040	600	16.9	Take the right fork, climb the embankment and continue straight ahead	Keep the river to the left	NE	62
49.041	200	17.1	Shortly after, bear left to leave the embankment and return to the riverside path	Village of Canarzzo on the right of the embankment	NE	60

Way Point N°	Way Point Distance (metres)	Total Distance (kilometres)	Directions	Verification Point	Compass	Altitude (metres)
49.042	300	17.4	Cross a car park and at the T-junction turn left and then bear right	Path branches away from the road	N	60
49.043	200	17.6	Take the left fork	Right fork leads to farm buildings	NE	60
49.044	700	18.3	Continue straight ahead	Ignore the turning to the beach on the left	E	56
49.045	500	18.8	At the T-junction turn left	Signpost	E	61
49.046	200	19.0	Turn sharp right on the white road	Away from the river	SW	58
49.047	100	19.1	Continue straight ahead		S	60
49.048	180	19.3	Leave the white road and bear left on the track		S	60
49.049	300	19.6	Continue straight ahead	Ignore the turning towards the river	S	58
49.050	500	20.1	Continue straight ahead on the riverside path		E	60
49.051	140	20.3	Continue straight ahead	Pass beside a restaurant	E	59
49.052	1500	21.8	At a T-junction in the woods turn right	Pass small lake on the left	E	59
49.053	600	22.4	Take the left fork	Towards the river	NE	59
49.054	110	22.5	After a short distance take the turning to the right	The path quickly begins to bear left	N	58
49.055	200	22.7	At the next junction turn right		E	58
49.056	100	22.8	At the end of the path bear right on a white road		SE	60

Garlasco to Pavia 26.1 km

Way Point N°	Way Point Distance (metres)	Total Distance (kilometres)	Directions	Verification Point	Compass	Altitude (metres)
49.057	100	22.9	Turn right on the tarmac road	The road initially runs parallel to the busy ring road and then bears left towards the road	S	59
49.058	500	23.4	Proceed under the ring road and continue straight ahead and parallel to the river	Road is closed to traffic	SE	63
49.059	600	24.0	Continue straight ahead on the unmade road	Parallel to the river	SE	59
49.060	400	24.4	Pass under the railway and continue on the riverside track		SE	55
49.061	200	24.6	Continue straight ahead on the riverside path	Ignore the turning to the right	SE	57
49.062	300	24.9	Continue straight ahead on the riverside path	Pass under road bridge	E	58
49.063	600	25.5	Pedestrians continue on the riverside path. Cyclists and riders should turn right and take the road to the entrance to the ponte coperto	Borgo Ticino to the right and the ponte coperto directly ahead	E	57
49.064	300	25.8	Climb the steps and cross the covered bridge	No Entry Sign on the bridge	N	64
49.065	170	25.9	At the traffic lights cross the piazzale Ponte Ticino and take the road ahead	Corso Strada Nuova	NE	67
49.066	200	26.1	Arrive in the centre of Pavia	Crossroads with Corso Garibaldi /via Giacomo Cardano		81

Note: the Alternate Route allows visitors to the sanctuary to recover the main route near Cascina Miradolo between Garlasco and Gropello Cairoli

Way Point N°	Way Point Distance (metres)	Total Distance (kilometres)	Directions	Verification Point	Compass	Altitude (metres)
1	0	0.0	With the Santuario Madonna della Bozzola behind, turn right to keep the sanctuary on your right	VF sign	NE	97
2	140	0.1	Turn right beside the canal immediately after crossing over the bridge	VF sign, canal on the right	S	98
3	1400	1.5	Continue straight ahead with a bridge on the right	VF sign, canal on the right	S	92
4	300	1.8	Emerge onto a road (SP185) cross the road and continue on the track beside the canal	Bridge on right	SE	94
5	500	2.3	Turn right, cross over bridge, then turn immediately left to skirt the large building on the right	Canal on the left	SE	92
6	300	2.6	Beside bridge, continue straight ahead with water on left	VF sign	SE	92
7	900	3.5	Cross over sluice gate bridge and cross bridge to the left to rejoin the main route at Way Point #11	VF sign		91

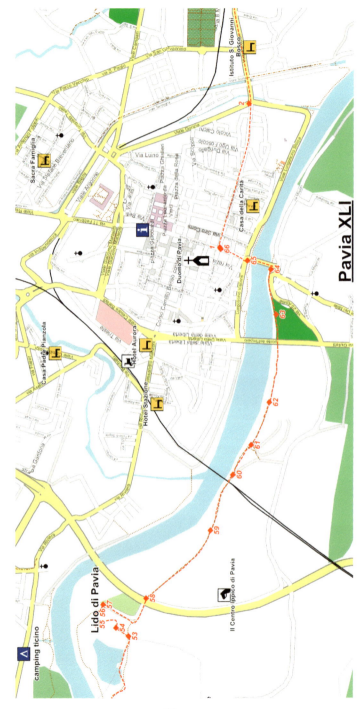

Pavia XLI

Hotel/B&B	Price
Flower Hotel, 14, v. Lecco - 27027 GROPELLO CAIROLI Tel: 0039 (0)382 815154	B3
Agriturismo Sant'andrea, 1, Cascina Delizia - 27027 GROPELLO CAIROLI Tel: 0039 (0) 348 4523005 raffaellamoroni@virgilio.it **Note:** Horses accepted	B2
Italia, 144/160, via della Libertà - 27027 GROPELLO CAIROLI Tel: 0039 (0)382815082	B2
Hotel Aurora, 25, viale Vittorio Emanuele II - 27100 PAVIA Tel: 0039 (0)382 23664	B3
Stazione, 8, Bernardino De Rossi - 27100 PAVIA Tel: 0039 (0)38235477	B2

Religious Hostel	Price
Parrocchia San Giorgio, 1, piazzale San Giorgio - 27027 GROPELLO CAIROLI Tel: 0039 (0)382 815049	Donation
Casa della Carità, 14, via Pedotti - 27100 PAVIA Tel: 0039 (0)382 23138 Mobile: 333 4477119	Donation
Sacra Famiglia, 1, viale Ludovico il Moro - 27100 PAVIA Tel: 0039 (0)382 575381 informazione@sacrafamigliapv.it www.sacrafamigliapv.it	Donation
Casa Padre Pianzola, 49, viale Golgi - 27100 PAVIA Tel: 0039 (0)382 525719	Donation
Parrocchia Del SS Crocifisso, 8, via Suardi - 27100 PAVIA Tel: 0039 (0)382 471040	Donation
Istituto S. Giovanni Bosco, 4, via San Giovanni Bosco - 27100 PAVIA Tel: 0039 (0)382 411011	Donation

Camping	Price
Camping Ticino, 16, via mascherpa - 27100 PAVIA Tel: 0039 (0)382 527 094 www.campingticino.it	B1

Equestrian

Il Centro Ippico di Pavia, Strada Per il Lido - 27100 PAVIA Tel: 0039 (0)382 6065179

Useful Contacts

Tourist/Information Offices

Piazza Italia, 5 - 27100 PAVIA Tel: 0039 (0) 382 597010 turismo@provincia.pv.it
www.turismo.provincia.pv.it

Internet Cafe Pavia

MuukaPaaza, 11, via Malpaga - MONTICELLI

Pala Biliardo, 10/a, via S.Giacomo - VIGEVANO

Polipiu'Amarican Bar, 20, corso Cavour - PAVIA

Porta dell'informatica, 2, via Valla - PAVIA

xfilespavia snc, 32, orso Manzoni - PAVIA

Alantide, 24, piazza V.Veneto - STRADELLA

Doctor

3/5, Piazza S.Bernardo - 27100 PAVIA   Tel: 0039 (0)382.472669

Veterinary

Amb. Veterinario, 61, Naviglio - 27100 viale Sicilia - 27100 PAVIA
Tel: 0039 (0)382 474393

Garlasco to Pavia 26.1km

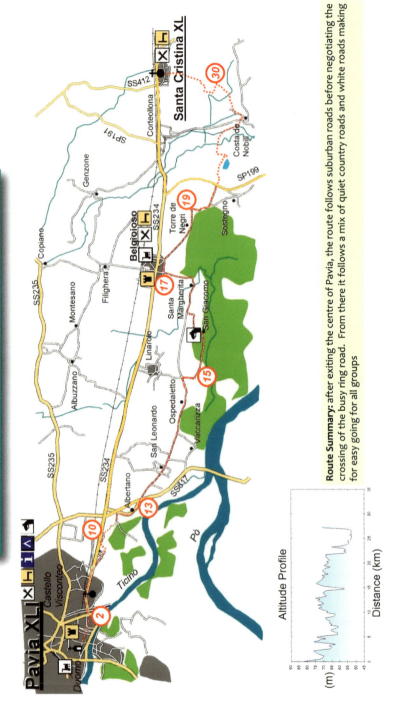

Pavia to Santa Cristina 27.4 km

Pavia XL

Santa Cristina XL

Route Summary: after exiting the centre of Pavia, the route follows suburban roads before negotiating the crossing of the busy ring road. From there it follows a mix of quiet country roads and white roads making for easy going for all groups

Altitude Profile

Distance (km)

42

Distance from Canterbury: 1331km   **Distance to Rome:** 752km

Ascent: 123m   **Descent:** 135m

Way Point N°	Way Point Distance (metres)	Total Distance (kilometres)	Directions	Verification Point	Compass	Altitude (metres)
50.001	0	0.0	From the crossroads turn right on corso Garibaldi		E	80
50.002	1000	1.0	At traffic lights go straight ahead direction Piacenza, San Lazaro	Cross waterway on viale dei Partigiani	E	71
50.003	1500	2.5	At San Pietro in Verzolo continue straight ahead	Pass church on the right	E	76
50.004	400	2.9	Turn right down via Francana	VF sign, kiosk on the corner	SE	67
50.005	600	3.5	Continue straight ahead	Ignore the turning to the left on via Scarenzio	SE	67
50.006	150	3.6	At the end of the road continue straight ahead on the tarmac which quickly becomes an unmade track and winds from left to right and then turns back towards the main toad		NE	67
50.007	400	4.0	At the crossroads at the end of the track take the tarmac road straight ahead	Uphill	NE	66
50.008	100	4.2	At the T-junction turn right on the broader road	Via Montebolone	SE	71
50.009	160	4.3	At roundabout continue straight ahead	Church on right	E	76

43

Way Point N°	Way Point Distance (metres)	Total Distance (kilometres)	Directions	Verification Point	Compass	Altitude (metres)
50.010	140	4.5	At T-junction turn right and follow the pedestrian and cycle path		SE	76
50.011	700	5.2	At T-junction turn left on strada Scagliona	Factory buildings directly in front at the junction	E	69
50.012	200	5.3	Turn right at junction with main road direction Broni	**Note:** major road works have been taking place, in the event of the described route being blocked proceed in the direction of San Leonardo and pass through the town on the SP13	SE	74
50.013	1300	6.7	At the roundabout, cross with great care and take the left turn direction San Leonardo, SP13	Industrial buildings on left	E	65
50.014	5000	11.7	After passing through Ospedaletto turn right	Where the tarmac road turns to the left	S	68
50.015	400	12.1	At the first crossroads turn left and pass through San Giacomo and Santa Margherita	VF sign	E	72
50.016	3900	15.9	Remain on the road into Belgioioso with factory to the right	via Molino	N	63
50.017	1100	17.1	In Belgioioso turn right down via P. Nenni	VF sign, direction carabinieri	E	72
50.018	500	17.6	At T-junction turn right on SP9 towards Torre de' Negri	Exit from Beligioioso sign	SE	66
50.019	2100	19.6	Pass through Torre de' Negri and on crown of the right hand bend continue on the road	Ignore the track to the left	S	71

44

Way Point N°	Way Point Distance (metres)	Total Distance (kilometres)	Directions	Verification Point	Compass	Altitude (metres)
50.020	700	20.4	On the crown of a further bend to the right continue straight ahead on the white road	Direction Cascina Campobello, pass farm buildings immediately on the right	SE	70
50.021	700	21.1	At the crossroads with the SP199 continue straight ahead		E	67
50.022	300	21.4	At the first crossroads turn left through the barrier to take the white road	Skirt the quarry on the right	E	68
50.023	800	22.1	At the T-junction turn left		N	69
50.024	400	22.6	At the next junction at the end of the field continue straight ahead	Slightly downhill	E	70
50.025	300	22.9	Cross the bridge and continue straight ahead on the broad track beside the canal	Woodland to the right and canal close on the left	SE	56
50.026	900	23.8	Turn left over the next bridge	Via Aldo Moro	E	59
50.027	200	23.9	At the T-junction turn right on the main road into the village of Costa de' Nobili	Via Roma	S	65
50.028	80	24.0	Turn left towards Cascina Padulino	Shortly after turning the tarmac gives way to an unmade road	NE	65
50.029	500	24.3	By the farm entrance continue straight ahead	Farm on the left	NE	55
50.030	900	25.1	At the T-junction turn left		N	53
50.031	1900	27.1	Continue straight ahead into Santa Cristina	The unmade road returns to the tarmac via Italia	N	64
50.032	120	27.2	At the T-junction turn left		NW	70
50.033	50	27.2	Take the next turning to the right	Via Gibelli	N	71
50.034	160	27.4	Arrive in centre of Santa Cristina	Beside the church		70

Hotel/B&B	Price
Cavaliere, 50/1, Felice Cavallotti - 27011 BELGIOIOSO Tel: 0039 (0)382 969666	B2
La Locanda DELLA Pesa, 111, via XX Settembre - 27011 BELGIOIOSO Tel: 0039 (0)382 969073	B2

Religious Hostel	Price
Oratorio of San Guiseppe, Via Vittorio Veneto, 118 - SANTA CRISTINA Tel: 0039 (0)382 70106 Mobile: 00 39 333 3429685 pedanto@libero.it	Donation

Equestrian

Centro di Equitazione La Castellana, Fraz. S.giacomo della Cerreta 27011 - BELGIOIOSO
Tel: 0039 (0)382/970207

Useful Contacts

Tourist/Information Offices

Ufficio Informazioni e di Accoglienza Turistica, 13, via XX Settembre - 27011
BELGIOIOSO Tel: 0039 (0)382 971120

Doctor

Ciuffarella Grugni Dr. Giuliana, via Gerolamo Criminall - 27011 BELGIOIOSO
Tel: 0039 (0)382 960686

Veterinary

Ambulatorio Veterinario Di Belgioioso, via Tre Martiri - 27011 BELGIOIOSO
Tel: 0039 (0)382 969219

Altitude Profile

Distance (km)

(m)

Santa Cristina to Piacenza 38.2 km

Route Summary: this is a long (total distance includes 4km by ferry) but unforgettable part of the journey. We again use farm tracks and minor roads over generally level ground with the opportunity to break the journey in Orio Litta or after the Pò crossing. The final entry into Piacenza will be difficult for all groups on the via Emilia Pavese. Unfortunately horse riders will need to bypass the ferry and take the Alternate Route.

Distance from Canterbury: 1358km

Distance to Rome: 725km

Ascent: 105m

Descent: 110m

Way Point N°	Way Point Distance (metres)	Total Distance (kilometres)	Directions	Verification Point	Compass	Altitude (metres)
51.001	0	0.0	Facing the church in Santa Cristina turn right and proceed along the main street	Via Vittorio Veneto	E	62
51.002	300	0.3	Turn left. **Note:** the main route leads from hereto the Pò ferry crossing which is unable to carry horses or large numbers of bikes. The Alternate Route bypasses the ferry	Viale Rimembranze	N	70
51.003	200	0.5	Cross the main road (SS234) and continue straight ahead	Pedestrian traffic lights	N	68
51.004	120	0.6	Cross the railway line and immediately turn right on the path beside the railway	Open fields to the left and railway to the right	E	67

Way Point N°	Way Point Distance (metres)	Total Distance (kilometres)	Directions	Verification Point	Compass	Altitude (metres)
51.005	600	1.2	Turn right and then immediately left	Small bridge on left, take the white road that initially follow the railway then quickly bears left through the fields	E	67
51.006	2700	3.9	Cross the main road and continue straight ahead	Towards Miradolo on via Nerone	NE	67
51.007	400	4.3	In piazza del Comune bear right	Via Garibaldi	SE	69
51.008	300	4.6	Bear right	Via Garibaldi	S	70
51.009	90	4.7	Turn left and follow the road through open country to Compo Rinaldo	Via San Marco	E	70
51.010	2200	6.9	In the centre of Campo Rinaldo turn right on via Cavour		S	70
51.011	200	7.1	At the T-junction with the main road turn left and then cross the road using the pedestrian crossing beside the traffic lights and continue along the main road	SS234	E	68
51.012	120	7.2	Turn right on the first track between fields	Towards the railway	S	68
51.013	150	7.4	Shortly after crossing the railway bear left		SE	67
51.014	500	7.9	Turn right	Towards the canal	S	65
51.015	150	8.0	Turn right	Cross small canal bridge	S	65

Way Point N°	Way Point Distance (metres)	Total Distance (kilometres)	Directions	Verification Point	Compass	Altitude (metres)
51.016	300	8.3	At the T-junction turn left	Initially parallel to canal	E	65
51.017	1000	9.3	Continue straight ahead	Towards Chignolo Po	E	58
51.018	110	9.4	Continue straight ahead	Towards the town centre	E	56
51.019	180	9.6	Beside the castle continue straight ahead	Castle to the left	SE	57
51.020	130	9.8	At the traffic lights bear left	Via Garibaldi, towards Lambrinia	E	56
51.021	600	10.4	At the crossroads with the Strada Provinciale continue straight ahead	Towards Lambrinia	E	57
51.022	1600	12.0	Continue straight ahead on the cycle track	Pass cemetery on the right	E	64
51.023	500	12.5	At the fork bear left	Via Mameli	NE	64
51.024	300	12.8	Bear right	Via Bellaria	E	62
51.025	400	13.2	At the end of the tarmac road turn left and immediately right on the footpath	Near pink house	E	61
51.026	150	13.3	Turn left beside the canal		NW	55
51.027	600	13.9	Keep left	Remain beside canal	N	53
51.028	200	14.1	Turn left and immediately right towards the main road		NW	54
51.029	80	13.4	Using the guard rail for protection turn right at the T-junction with the main road	SS234	E	56

50

Way Point N°	Way Point Distance (metres)	Total Distance (kilometres)	Directions	Verification Point	Compass	Altitude (metres)
51.030	400	13.8	Immediately after crossing the river bridge turn right onto the unmade road	Towards railway	SE	52
51.031	1500	15.3	Leave the embankment on the second track to the left	Towards Orio Litta and between fields	E	50
51.032	900	16.2	Beside the first houses in Orio Litta turn left on the tarmac road	Via Roma	NE	50
51.033	190	16.4	In the centre of Orio Litta bear right remaining on via Roma	Piazza dei Benedettini to the left	E	55
51.034	300	16.7	At the T-junction beside Villa Litta bear right	Via Montemalo	SE	62
51.035	200	16.9	At the bottom of the hill bear right on the unmade road	Beside the water course, Cascina Cantarana	S	52
51.036	600	17.5	Take the left fork beside the gas sub-station	Remain beside the water course	S	49
51.037	1700	19.2	At the T-junction turn left	Returning to the embankment above the river	SE	52
51.038	400	19.6	Turn right	Remain on the embankment	SW	49
51.039	300	19.9	Arrive at the Pò river ferry (Guado di Sigerico)	Beside Corte Sant'Andrea	SE	54
51.040	4300	24.2	After climbing from the ferry landing stage proceed on the gravel track with the Pò on the left		E	47
51.041	900	25.1	At fork in the track bear right on grassy track	VF sign	SE	50

51

Way Point Nº	Way Point Distance (metres)	Total Distance (kilometres)	Directions	Verification Point	Compass	Altitude (metres)
51.042	500	25.6	Turn right onto a minor road towards the village of Calendasco	VF sign	S	50
51.043	900	26.5	Turn left directly in front of large building - Commune di Calendasco	Via Mazzini	SE	53
51.044	2200	28.7	On the crown of the bend in the hamlet of Incrociata, turn left direction Cotrebbia Nuova	VF sign	SE	52
51.045	2100	30.8	At fork bear right and continue on road passing under Autostrada	VF sign	S	52
51.046	1600	32.4	After passing under the railway and the road bridges turn immediately right and climb the ramp		W	55
51.047	160	32.5	At junction with the main road turn right to cross the bridge and continue on the long straight via Emilia Pavese. **Note:** caution narrow pavement over the long bridge beside the very busy road	Direction Piacenza	E	57
51.048	3800	36.3	At roundabout in piazzale Torino turn left on via XXI Aprile	Fountain in roundabout	NE	56

Way Point N°	Way Point Distance (metres)	Total Distance (kilometres)	Directions	Verification Point	Compass	Altitude (metres)
51.049	300	36.6	At the next roundabout turn right	Via Campagna, pass park and citadel walls on the left	E	53
51.050	900	37.5	In piazza del Borgo go straight ahead	Via Garibaldi	SE	64
51.051	400	37.9	At the crossroads with corso Vitorio Emanuele II go straight ahead	Strada Sant'Antonino	SE	64
51.052	300	38.2	Arrive in the centre of Piacenza	Beside the church of Sant'Antonino		64

Note: the Pò ferry is unable to carry horses and only a small number of bikes. This route bypasses the ferry crossing

Way Point Nº	Way Point Distance (metres)	Total Distance (kilometres)	Directions	Verification Point	Compass	Altitude (metres)
1	0	0.0	Continue straight ahead on via Vitorrio Veneto	Do not take via Rimembranze	E	63
2	150	0.2	Take right fork on via Pò/via Giuseppe Mazzini	Soccer field on the right	SE	70
3	1000	1.2	At junction with main road turn right	SS412	SE	68
4	500	1.7	Leave main road and turn left towards Bissone		S	66
5	1300	2.9	On rejoining the main road turn left		SE	66
6	1600	4.5	Leave main road and turn right towards Piave Porto Morone		S	55
7	2300	6.8	At T-junction in piazzale San Vittore turn left	Via Felice Cavallotti	SE	55
8	400	7.3	At fork bear right on via Marconi		SE	52
9	900	8.2	At junction with main road turn right	SS412 towards the river bridge	S	52
10	1600	9.8	After crossing the Pò turn left	Towards power plant	E	53
11	4500	14.3	At T-junction turn right on the embankment		S	53
12	200	14.5	Cross the waterway and then turn sharp left onto the track	Via Pò	E	51
13	600	15.1	Turn right on the track, via Pò	Derelict building on the left	S	52
14	1800	16.9	Turn left and then right to take the bridge over the Autostrada	Via Pò	SE	55
15	600	17.5	Turn left remaining on the via Pò	Direction Rottofreno	E	55

Way Point N°	Way Point Distance (metres)	Total Distance (kilometres)	Directions	Verification Point	Compass	Altitude (metres)
16	800	18.3	At the T-junction turn right		S	64
17	500	18.8	Just before the level crossing turn left on the track	Railway close to the right	E	62
18	300	19.1	Cross the river bed and pass under the railway. **Note:** in the event that the river is impassable return to the last Way Point and turn left over the level crossing, turn left at the junction with the main road, pass one farm entrance and then take the next left rejoining this route at Way Point #19	Continue with railway on the left	E	55
19	300	19.4	Turn left over the level crossing	Farm buildings just ahead on the left, road passes through the farm and bears left and right before recrossing the motorway	N	61
20	1600	20.9	Turn left following the via Pò sign	Farm entrance to the right	NE	55
21	600	21.6	Turn left following the via Pò sign	Proceed with the river close on the left	NE	52
22	600	22.2	Turn right onto the tarmac road	Farm buildings close on the right	E	52
23	1800	23.9	In Sant'Imento continue straight ahead direction Calendasco		NE	58
24	120	24.1	Bear right towards Calendasco on via Anguissola		NE	59
25	2400	26.5	Arrive in Calendasco and rejoin main route at Way Point #43			52

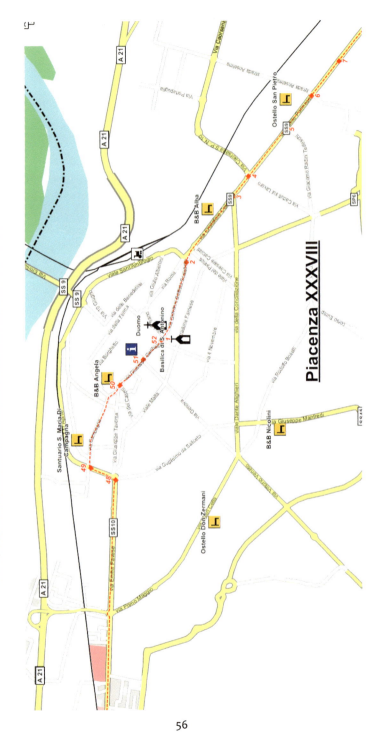

Piacenza Town Map

Piacenza XXXVIII

Hotel/B&B - wide choice - list selected from recommended options	Price
B&B Angela, via Giuseppe Mazzini - 29100 PIACENZA Tel: 0039 (0)523 499098 Mobile: 0039 339-6408589	B2
B&B Nicolini, 41, via Cipelli - 29100 PIACENZA Tel: 0039 (0)523 712420 info@viphotel.it	B2
B&B San Raimondo, 28/C, via Galileo Galilei - 29100 PIACENZA Tel: 0039 (0)523 380150 **Note:** accepts horses	B2
B&B Alba, 7, via C.Colombo - 29100 PIACENZA Tel: 0039 (0)523 592511	B2

Religious Hostel	Price
Cascina San Pietro, piazza dei Benedettini - 26863 ORIO LITTA Mobile: 0039 377 944436	Donation
Palestra Comunale, 2, piazza Aldo Moro - 26863 ORIO LITTA Mobile: 0039 335 6468587	Donation
Guado di Sigerico (Danilo Parisi - ferry master), Boscone Cusani - 26863 ORIO LITTA Tel: 0039 (0)523 771607 Also: Caupona Sigerico, via Soprarivo 21 - 29010 CALENDASCO ser.pe@libero.it semroby@alice.it	Donation
Ostello San Pietro, via Emilia Parmense - 29100 PIACENZA Tel: 0039 (0)523 614256 Mobile: 0039 333 1493595 sanlazzaro@libero.it	B1
PR Ostello don Zermani, 38/40, via Zoni - 29100 PIACENZA Tel: 0039 (0)523 712319 ostellodipiacenza@libero.it	Donation
PR Basilica SantuarioConvento s.ta Maria di Campagna, 5, Place Crociate - 29100 PIACENZA Tel: 0039 (0)523 490728 santuariocrociate@libero.it	Donation
Oratorio Parrocchiale, 1, via Verdi - 29010 CALENDASCO Tel: 0039 (0)523)771497	Donation
La Bellotta, Casa Diocesana Pastorale, 10, Strada Val Conasso - 29010 PONTENURE Tel: 0039 (0)523 517110 **Note:** groups only	B2

Youth Hostel	Price
Ostello don Zermani, 38/40, via Zoni - 29100 PIACENZA Tel: 0039 (0)523 614256 ostellodipiacenza@libero.it www.ostellodipiacenza.it	B1

Useful Contacts

Tourist/Information Offices

Ufficio Informazioni e di Accoglienza Turistica, piazza Cavalll, 7 - 29100 PIACENZA Tel: 0039 (0)523329324 www.provincia.piacenza.it/turismo iat@comune.piacenza.it

Piacenza Internet Cafe

Internet Train, via Cittadella 36   info@dmatechnology.it www.internettrain.it

Futurshop, via Malaspina info@futurshop.it www.futurshop.it

Doctor

Civardi Dott.ssa Roberta , 24, v. XXIV Maggio - 29100 PIACENZA
Mobile: 0039 340 2514908

Veterinary

Dottori Chiappelloni Lunati Vignola, 28/30, via Trebbia - 29100 PIACENZA
Tel: 0039 (0)523 490272

Santa Cristina to Piacenza 38.2 km

Altitude Profile

(m)

Distance (km)

Route Summary: another long section through farmland, finally leaving the rice fields behind. The exit from Piacenza is extremely dangerous on the busy via Emilia. Thereafter we enter the countryside where again there is the difficulty of navigation with few distinct landmarks but also with a number of small river crossings to be negotiated. There are no real opportunities for intermediate stops and so be sure that you have sufficient water for the day.

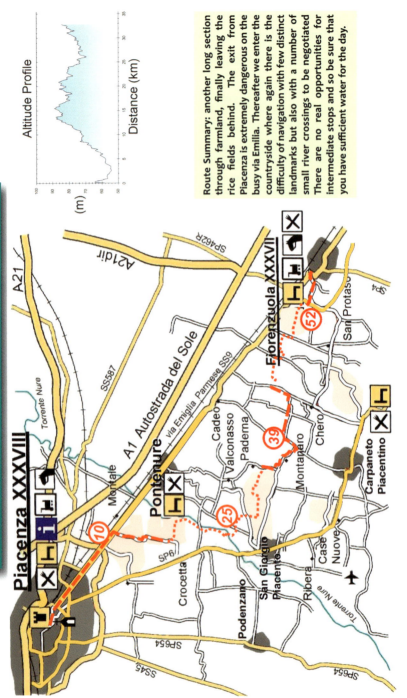

Distance from Canterbury: 1397km   **Distance to Rome:** 687km

Ascent: 110m   **Descent:** 82m

Way Point N°	Way Point Distance (metres)	Total Distance (kilometres)	Directions	Verification Point	Compass	Altitude (metres)
52.001	0	0.0	From the church of Sant'Antonino continue straight ahead on via Sant'Antonino and via Scalabrini	Church to the right	E	86
52.002	800	0.8	In piazzale Roma continue straight ahead on the right side of the long, straight, broad road	Via Emilia Parmense/via Cristoforo Colombo, SS9	SE	59
52.003	800	1.6	At the roundabout continue straight ahead	Via Emilia Parmense, SS9, Hotel ahead and cycle track on the right	SE	56
52.004	300	1.9	At the next roundabout continue straight ahead	Direction Parma, spire ahead	SE	56
52.005	600	2.5	Continue straight ahead at the traffic lights	Pass the Parrocchia San Lazzaro on the right	SE	54
52.006	400	2.9	Continue straight ahead at the traffic lights	Via Emilia Parmense, SS9	SE	54
52.007	500	3.4	Continue straight ahead on the pavement	Via Emilia Parmense, SS9	SE	55
52.008	600	4.0	At the junction continue straight ahead on the cycle path	Large commercial centre to the right	SE	58
52.009	200	4.2	With great care cross the major highway intersection and continue straight ahead	Via Emilia Parmense, SS9	SE	58
52.010	1500	5.7	Turn right to leave the via Emilia on Strada della Mussina	Towards the B&B	S	59

Piacenza to Fiorenzuola d'Arda 32.7 km

Way Point N°	Way Point Distance (metres)	Total Distance (kilometres)	Directions	Verification Point	Compass	Altitude (metres)
52.011	3100	8.8	At the first crossroads in the hamlet of I Vaccari turn left on the unmade road		SE	87
52.012	170	9.0	At the T-junction turn right	Via L.Rocci	S	74
52.013	170	9.1	Turn left on the tarmac road	Strada I Vaccari	E	72
52.014	600	9.7	Continue straight ahead on the white road	Farm buildings to the right	E	73
52.015	200	9.9	Continue straight ahead on the track	Ignore turnings to the left and then right	E	71
52.016	100	10.0	Quickly turn right onto a partially obscured path into the trees	Path leads beside the river – torrent Nure	S	71
52.017	600	10.6	Bear right on the path	Remain beside the river	SW	73
52.018	700	11.3	At the first intersection beside an old kiln turn left	Remain beside the river	S	77
52.019	600	11.9	At the T-junction with the white road turn left	Remain beside the river	S	79
52.020	300	12.2	Continue straight ahead	Between the fields and the river	S	80
52.021	200	12.4	Continue straight ahead on the white road	Remain beside the river	SW	82
52.022	500	12.9	At the crossroads turn left	Across the river ford	SE	86
52.023	200	13.1	On the far side of the river turn right and follow the path beside the river	River to the right at first and then the path left bears towards the cultivated fields	SW	85
52.024	300	13.4	At the junction at the end of the first field turn left on the track		SE	88
52.025	300	13.7	Cross the main road and continue straight ahead	Towards the farm	E	88

Way Point N°	Way Point Distance (metres)	Total Distance (kilometres)	Directions	Verification Point	Compass	Altitude (metres)
52.026	110	13.8	Pass through the farm buildings turning left and then immediately right on the track		E	88
52.027	500	14.3	At the T-junction turn right	Remaining on the track	SE	84
52.028	400	14.8	At the T-junction turn right on the tarmac road		S	84
52.029	300	14.2	At the next T-junction turn left and then immediately right onto a white road	Località Montanaro	S	86
52.030	600	14.8	Turn left	Cascina del Lupo to the right	E	89
52.031	130	14.9	At the junction, continue straight ahead on the tarmac		E	87
52.032	1400	16.3	At the junction next to a farm turn right on the white road	At the end of the tarmac section	E	82
52.033	300	16.6	Continue straight ahead on the tarmac	Farm buildings immediately to the left	E	79
52.034	110	16.7	At the T-junction turn right		SE	81
52.035	1000	17.7	At the crossroads turn right	Shortly after passing Castello di Paderna	S	81
52.036	800	18.5	At the T-junction turn left	Signpost for I Castilli	SE	83
52.037	300	18.8	In the hamlet of Montanaro turn left	Towards Carpaneto	SE	87
52.038	1600	20.4	At the junction beside the small chapel turn sharp left	Towards Cadeo	NE	86
52.039	900	21.3	Pass through Zena and at the exit from the hamlet turn right	Towards Chero	E	81
52.040	2300	23.6	At the T-junction turn left. **Note:** beware of the traffic	Strada dello Zappellazzo	NE	80

Way Point N°	Way Point Distance (metres)	Total Distance (kilometres)	Directions	Verification Point	Compass	Altitude (metres)
52.041	1000	24.6	After passing the concrete water-tower in Zappellazzo turn right on the tarmac road		E	74
52.042	400	25.0	At the end of the tarmac road ford the torrente Chero and turn left on the track	Keep trees to the left and cultivated field to the right	NE	75
52.043	200	25.2	Turn right passing a barrier	Track between fields	E	73
52.044	200	25.4	Continue straight ahead on the white road	Ignore the turning to the left	E	73
52.045	600	26.0	At the T-junction with the tarmac road turn right	Keep trees to the left	S	73
52.046	300	26.3	Take the next turning to the left	Towards the trees and fording torrente Chiavenna	SE	74
52.047	300	26.6	Shortly after the ford turn left	Between fields. The road quickly turns right and passes between two farms	E	75
52.048	1200	27.8	At the T-junction with the tarmac road turn right		S	72
52.049	500	28.3	Immediately after passing farm buildings, close on the left side of the road, turn left on the unmade road	Strada Vicinale della Felina	E	76
52.050	1800	30.1	Continue straight ahead		E	78

Way Point N°	Way Point Distance (metres)	Total Distance (kilometres)	Directions	Verification Point	Compass	Altitude (metres)
52.051	100	30.2	Shortly after a junction on the left, turn right and skirt the farm buildings to join a track between fields		S	77
52.052	300	30.5	Turn left beside the line of trees		SE	79
52.053	400	30.9	At the junction after the underpass continue straight ahead		E	82
52.054	900	31.8	Follow the main road to the left	Enter Fiorenzuola d'Arda	NE	81
52.055	300	32.1	Turn right on the cycle track	Cross the bridge over the river Arda and bear left towards the main road	E	81
52.056	200	32.3	Take the pedestrian crossing on the main road and turn right into the centre of the town	SS9	SE	81
52.057	100	32.4	Continue straight ahead on the main street	Corso Giuseppe Garibaldi	SE	82
52.058	300	32.7	Arrive in the centre of Fiorenzuola d'Arda (XXXVII)	Crossroads with via della Liberazione		84

Hotel/B&B	Price
Val Vezzeno, Cimafava - 29103 CARPANETO PIACENTINO Tel: 0039 (0)523 853219	B3
Veranda barabasca, Località Barabasca - 29017 FIORENZUOLA D'ARDA Tel: 0039 (0)523 982398	B1
Ruota, 46, via Scapuzzi - 29017 FIORENZUOLA D'ARDA Tel: 0039 (0)523 943072	B2

Religious Hostel	Price
Parroccia San Fiorenzo, piazza Molinari - 29017 FIORENZUOLA D'ARDA Tel: 0039 (0)523 982247	Donation

Equestrian

Scuderia Rossetti Arturo E Biselli Massimo S.N.C., 378, Cascina Felina - 29017
FIORENZUOLA D'ARDA Tel: 0039 (0)523 981042

Useful Contacts

Doctor

Villani Dr. Damiano Medico Chirurgo, 1, via tolla - 29017 FIORENZUOLA D'ARDA
Tel: 0039 (0)523 944083

Veterinary

Coperchini Dr. Maurizio Medico Veterinario, 7, via Cavalieri - 29017 FIORENZUOLA
D'ARDA   Tel: 0039 (0)523 942635

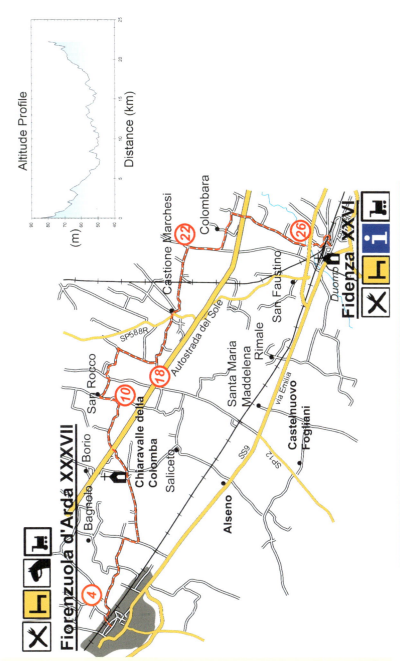

Route Summary: a gentle stage on level ground generally using country roads.

Distance from Canterbury: 1429km   **Distance to Rome:** 654km

Ascent: 110m   **Descent:** 82m

Way Point N°	Way Point Distance (metres)	Total Distance (kilometres)	Directions	Verification Point	Compass	Altitude (metres)
53.001	0	0.0	From the centre of Fiorenzuola, near N° 55 Corso Garibaldi, turn left onto the narrow street	Via della Liberazione	NE	84
53.002	110	0.1	Go straight ahead across the main road onto viale Corridoni	Tree lined road and then take underpass under the railway emerging on Viale dei Tigli	E	81
53.003	600	0.7	Bear left on the pavement on the left side of the road	Pass beside the cemetery	NE	76
53.004	200	0.9	Just after the cemetery cross the road and turn right	Towards agriturismo Battibue	E	71
53.005	2300	3.2	At the T-junction at the end of the road turn right		S	63
53.006	500	3.7	Turn left on Località Corti	Towards Chiaravalle	E	68
53.007	1700	5.4	Continue straight ahead on the pavement on the left side of the road	Stada del Termine	E	57
53.008	700	6.1	Continue straight ahead	Towards the Abbey courtyard	E	55
53.009	120	6.2	In front of the Abbey of Chiaravalle de Colomba bear left to follow the road	Towards Busseto and shortly crossing the bridge over the autostrada	E	56
53.010	2300	8.5	Bear left on the road and ignore the junction to the right	Beside Cascina Ongina	N	52
53.011	300	8.8	Continue straight ahead on Strada Borre	Beside the entrance to the village of San Rocco	N	54
53.012	200	9.0	Turn right	Before reaching a small church turn right	E	52

Way Point N°	Way Point Distance (metres)	Total Distance (kilometres)	Directions	Verification Point	Compass	Altitude (metres)
53.013	700	9.7	At the T-junction at the end of the road turn left	Strada Bianca, pass pond on the right	N	50
53.014	140	9.9	Take the next turn to the right	Strada Orsi , the road will turn to the right	SE	51
53.015	400	10.3	At the entrance to the farm bear left on the unmade road		E	51
53.016	600	10.9	At the T-junction turn right	Farm entrance ahead	SW	49
53.017	900	11.8	Continue straight ahead on Strada Fossa Superiore	Ignore the turning on the tarmac road to the left	S	53
53.018	400	12.2	At the T-junction with a tarmac road turn left	Strada Portone	E	54
53.019	1500	13.7	Take the first turning to the left and then immediately right at the traffic lights on the main road	Castione Marchesi	SE	56
53.020	300	14.0	After rounding the first bend turn left	Towards Bastelli	E	56
53.021	110	14.1	At the T-junction turn right	Towards Bastelli, shortly reach long straight road with railway crossing at mid-point	E	56
53.022	2200	16.3	At the T-junction turn right	Towards Bastelli	S	52
53.023	1000	17.3	In hamlet of Bastelli with silos on the right turn left	Towards Soragna	E	58
53.024	1300	18.6	At broad junction turn right	Follow bridge over autostrada and keep straight ahead	SW	56

Way Point N°	Way Point Distance (metres)	Total Distance (kilometres)	Directions	Verification Point	Compass	Altitude (metres)
53.025	2500	21.1	At the end of the long straight road continue straight ahead towards the farm	Ignore the bend to the right	S	67
53.026	200	21.3	Take the ford across the river	Torrente Stirone - follow the track under the ring road	S	69
53.027	300	21.6	Bear right	Ignore the turning to the left	S	70
53.028	200	21.8	Take the next turning to the left	Before reaching the railway, via Croce Rossa	SE	73
53.029	400	21.7	At the traffic lights turn right under the railway	Car park on the left at the junction	S	70
53.030	150	21.8	After emerging from under the railway turn right direction Duomo	Pass Hotel Astoria on the left	W	76
53.031	300	22.1	Continue straight ahead at the roundabout and then quickly bear left towards old city gate	Piazza Grandi, large VF sign on entry to piazza	SW	76
53.032	120	22.3	Arrive in the centre of Fidenza	Piazza Cremonini beside the Duomo		80

Fidenza Town Map

Fidenza XXXVI

Hotel/B&B	Price
Agriturismo, Zucchi Vittorio, Montà Dell'orto - 29010 CASTELNUOVO FOGLIANi Tel: 0039 (0)523 947146	B2
Pizzeria Ugolini Albergo Di Stigliano Mario, 90, via Malpeli - 43036 FIDENZA Tel: 0039 (0)524 522422	B2
Il Pinguino, 42, Località S. Faustino - 43036 FIDENZA Tel: 0039 (0)524 522609	B2
Due Spade, 42, piazza Pezzana - 43036 FIDENZA Tel: 0039 (0)524 523389 www.hotelduespade.it reception@hotelduespade.it	B2

Religious Hostel	Price
Cenacolo di Spiritualita Maria Mediatrice, 19, via G. Micheli - 43036 FIDENZA Tel: 0039 (0)524 528070	Donation
Convento di san Francesco, 1, via Berzieri - 43036 FIDENZA Tel: 0039 (0)524 522035/520118	Donation
Convento dei Padri Cappuccini, Parrocchia di San Francesco d'Assisi, Via San Francesco 7 - 43036 FIDENZA Tel: 0039 (0)524 522035	Donation

Useful Contacts

Tourist/Information Offices

Casa Cremonini, 16, P.zza Duomo - 43036 FIDENZA Tel: 0039 (0)524519159 infoturist@comunedifidenza.pr.it

Associazione dei Comuni Italiani sulla via Francigena, 16, sede nazionale P.zza Duomo - 43036 FIDENZA Tel: +39 (0) 524 833 77 segreteria.acivf@comune.fidenza.pr.it www.associazioneviafrancigena.com

Doctor

Dr. Anna Paola Gabriella, 18, via Bacchini Benedetto - 43036 FIDENZA Tel: 0039 (0)524 523476

Veterinary

Cattivelli Dr. Renato, 86, Frazione Fornio - 43036 FIDENZA Tel: 0039 (0)524 60171

Fiorenzuola d'Arda to Fidenza 22.3 km

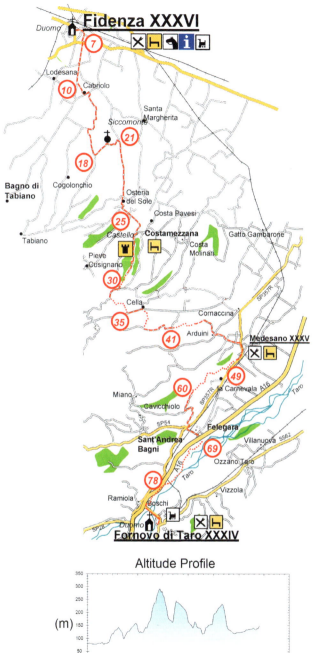

Fidenza XXXVI

Duomo

Lodesana

Cabriolo

Santa Margherita

Siccomonte

Bagno di Tabiano

Cogolonchio

Osteria del Sole

Costa Pavesi

Castello

Costamezzana

Costa Molinari

Gatto Gambarone

Tabiano

Pieve Cusignano

Cella

Cornaccina

Arduini

Miano

Cavicchiolo

Medesano XXXV

la Carnevala

Taro

Sant'Andrea Bagni

Felegara

Villanuova

Ozzano Taro

Ramiola

Boschi

Vizzola

Duomo

Fornovo di Taro XXXIV

Altitude Profile

(m)

Distance (km)

Route Summary: this is a long and strenuous section with limited opportunity for intermediate stops. After leaving Fidenza the well marked route begins to climb into the rolling foothills of the Apppenines. The route generally follow farms tracks and some small roads. Great care needs to be exercised on the final approach to Fornovo where the traffic can be heavy on the river bridge.

Distance from Canterbury: 1452km   **Distance to Rome:** 632km

Ascent: 577m   **Descent:** 504m

Way Point N°	Way Point Distance (metres)	Total Distance (kilometres)	Directions	Verification Point	Compass	Altitude (metres)
54.001	0	0.0	From piazza Cremonini beside the Duomo pass in front of the church turn left to skirt the church	Church on the left	SE	80
54.002	120	0.1	At the rear of the church turn right	In the pedestrian zone, via Micheli. VF sign	E	79
54.003	90	0.2	Continue straight ahead across the small square and take via Antini	VF sign	E	81
54.004	160	0.4	Continue straight ahead in piazza del Palazzo under the porch and turn right	Via Amendola	SW	82
54.005	60	0.4	Bear left across the small park		SE	81
54.006	100	0.5	At the roundabout turn right into the tree lined street	Via Gramsci	S	79
54.007	300	0.8	At the roundabout, cross the main road – via 24 Maggio – and bear a little to the left towards the trees	Via Caduti di Cef alonia	S	79
54.008	900	1.7	At the roundabout continue straight ahead on the cycle track	Sports ground to the right before the roundabout	S	77
54.009	300	2.0	Continue straight ahead keeping to the left side of the road		S	79
54.010	400	2.4	Shortly after passing farm on the left, bear left	Narrow tree lined road	SE	81
54.011	400	2.8	Bear right into the trees	Towards the Pieve di Cabriolo	S	82

Fidenza to Fornovo di Taro 34.4 km

72

Way Point N°	Way Point Distance (metres)	Total Distance (kilometres)	Directions	Verification Point	Compass	Altitude (metres)
54.012	100	2.9	Turn left on the tarmac driveway		SE	86
54.013	120	3.0	At the T-junction at the end of the road turn left	Main road	NE	82
54.014	180	3.2	Take the first turning to the right	Towards trees, via Cabriolo	S	78
54.015	300	3.5	Continue straight ahead on the unmade road	Ignore the turning to the right	S	79
54.016	1000	4.5	Turn right towards the hilltop	Via Cabriolo	SW	88
54.017	700	5.2	At the junction with a tarmac road – on a sharp bend – turn left	Uphill, towards the top of the ridge	S	116
54.018	1100	6.3	Turn left	Towards Siccomonte	NE	137
54.019	800	7.1	In front of the Chiesa di Siccomonte turn left on the grassy path and downhill	Keep church to the left	E	122
54.020	180	7.3	Leave the grass and turn left on the road		NE	99
54.021	400	7.7	At the T-junction at the top of the hill turn right on the tarmac road	Via Monfestone	S	112
54.022	2300	10.0	Take the left fork	Towards Pieve Cusignano	S	157
54.023	300	10.3	At the T-junction - beside the Osteria del Sole – turn right	Towards Costamezzana	SW	126
54.024	140	10.4	Turn left	Towards Costamezzana	SE	125
54.025	400	10.8	Continue straight ahead	Towards Costamezzana	S	123

73

Way Point N°	Way Point Distance (metres)	Total Distance (kilometres)	Directions	Verification Point	Compass	Altitude (metres)
54.026	800	11.7	Shortly after a left-hand bend in the road, at the entrance Costamezzana, turn right and slightly downhill		SW	146
54.027	200	11.8	At the crossroads, just before reaching the farm, turn left	Via Costa Canali	S	136
54.028	160	12.0	Take the narrow road to the left	Towards the Hostaria Castello	S	152
54.029	1000	13.0	Beside the Castello di Costamezzana bear left on the track alongside the vineyard	Castello di Costamezzana to the right	SW	217
54.030	1200	14.2	Turn left on the tarmac road		SW	286
54.031	120	14.3	At the T-junction turn right	Top of the hill, via Gabbiano	SW	288
54.032	700	15.0	On the crown of the bend to the right take the track downhill to the left	Between fields and then beside woods before the track bears left away from the woods	SE	278
54.033	700	15.7	Beside the first farm turn right onto the road	Towards the stables	S	226
54.034	200	15.9	Skirt another farm and bear right	Beside trees	S	204
54.035	200	16.1	At the T-junction turn left on the main road	Via Varano	E	176
54.036	300	16.4	Continue straight ahead on the pavement	Via Varano	E	172
54.037	300	16.7	Cross the road and continue straight ahead on the other side		E	169
54.038	190	16.9	Pass through the hamlet of Cella and turn right on the track	Just after slight bend to the right in the road	SE	165
54.039	200	17.1	Cross the river and continue straight ahead	Between fields	S	162

74

Way Point N°	Way Point Distance (metres)	Total Distance (kilometres)	Directions	Verification Point	Compass	Altitude (metres)
54.040	800	17.9	At the T-junction after a steep climb turn left on a tarmac road		E	242
54.041	1500	19.4	At a bend in the road to the left continue straight ahead on an unmade road	Immediately pass farm buildings on the left	E	220
54.042	1100	20.5	At the T-junction turn left on the track	Towards farm	E	161
54.043	1100	21.6	Continue straight ahead on the tarmac		SE	149
54.044	150	21.8	At the crossroads at the top of the hill in the hamlet of Arduini continue straight ahead	VF sign, via Giuseppe Verdi	SE	164
54.045	600	22.4	At the roundabout at the entry to Medesano continue straight ahead	Via Giuseppe Verdi, towards spire, VF sign	E	143
54.046	400	22.8	At the crossroads with via Dante Alighieri continue straight ahead	Via Giuseppe Verdi, No Entry sign, footpath and cycleway on the right of the road	E	140
54.047	180	22.9	Before reaching the main road turn right	Towards the church, VF sign	SE	137
54.048	90	23.0	Pass beside the church and turn right on the main road to leave the town	SP357R, pavement protected by crash barrier	S	134
54.049	700	23.7	Just before the gantry for the exit from Medesano, turn right onto a small road	VF sign, road quickly bears left after passing through trees	W	117
54.050	200	23.9	Continue straight ahead on the unmade road	Towards farm	SW	139
54.051	90	24.0	Continue straight ahead on the track	Track skirts field to the right	SW	142

Way Point N°	Way Point Distance (metres)	Total Distance (kilometres)	Directions	Verification Point	Compass	Altitude (metres)
54.052	500	24.5	Pass beside the farm fence and turn left in front of the woods		SW	150
54.053	200	24.7	Continue straight ahead on the tree lined road		SW	151
54.054	200	24.9	Take the right fork slightly downhill		NW	158
54.055	60	25.0	After a short descent take the faint pathway across the ditch to the left	Between fields	W	153
54.056	200	25.2	At the end of the field turn left on the track	Uphill	S	154
54.057	400	25.6	Turn right on the tarmac road		SW	191
54.058	150	25.7	Beside the farm bear right on the track		W	195
54.059	100	25.8	Bear left on the track		SW	196
54.060	600	26.4	Continue straight ahead	Driveway to a house on the right	S	216
54.061	700	27.1	At the T-junction turn left	Via Cesare Battisti	NE	233
54.062	300	27.4	Turn right on the tarmac road	Steep descent	S	224
54.063	600	28.0	On the crown of a bend to the left, on the entry Felegara, turn right	Via Damiano Chiesa	SW	147
54.064	150	28.2	At the T-junction turn left, downhill	Via Campioni	SE	142
54.065	140	28.3	At the T-junction with the main road turn right	Via Repubblica towards the pharmacy, VF sign	SW	134
54.066	130	28.5	At the roundabout with fountain turn left. **Note:** the riverside path ahead involves a number of water crossings. Cyclists may wish to continue straight ahead on the busy road to rejoin the main route on the bridge over the river Taro – Way Point #81	Via G. Picelli, VF sign	SE	133

Way Point Nº	Way Point Distance (metres)	Total Distance (kilometres)	Directions	Verification Point	Compass	Altitude (metres)
54.067	500	29.0	At the roundabout continue straight ahead	Via Pattigna	SE	126
54.068	160	29.1	Bear right on the track under the autostrada	Chain barrier across track and VF sign	SE	122
54.069	150	29.3	At the exit from the underpass turn right and immediately left	Initially with the river close on the left	SW	120
54.070	300	29.6	Ford the stream and continue straight ahead		SW	118
54.071	200	29.8	Take the right fork slightly downhill		W	121
54.072	200	30.0	Turn left on the footpath	Parallel to the autostrada	SW	124
54.073	80	30.1	At the T-junction turn left		SW	122
54.074	600	30.6	Continue straight ahead		S	124
54.075	130	30.8	Cross a small ditch and continue straight ahead	Close beside the river	SW	124
54.076	200	31.0	Continue straight ahead		SW	125
54.077	500	31.5	Cross the stream, pass under the railway bridge and bear right	Keeping the quarry on the left	SW	129
54.078	1100	32.6	Take the left fork away from the motorway and close beside the quarry	Beside Fornace Grigolin and further barrier	S	136
54.079	300	32.9	On reaching the football field turn right	Keep football field to the left	NW	135

Way Point N°	Way Point Distance (metres)	Total Distance (kilometres)	Directions	Verification Point	Compass	Altitude (metres)
54.080	110	33.0	Cross the car park and turn left		S	139
54.081	200	33.2	At the T-junction turn left and cross the bridge over the river Taro. **Note:** take great care as there is frequently heavy traffic on the bridge and only narrow pavement	Towards Fornovo di Taro, bar opposite the junction	SE	141
54.082	700	33.9	At the end of the bridge turn sharp left	VF sign	NW	139
54.083	100	34.0	At the bottom of the hill turn left, Piazzo Mercato	Under the bridge	SW	138
54.084	50	34.0	Immediately after passing under the bridge turn left	Via Pietro Zuffardi	SE	139
54.085	120	34.2	At the end of the road turn right and immediately left in the small piazza		SW	141
54.086	80	34.2	Bear right across piazza Giacomo Matteotti	Direction the Duomo , via 20 Settembre	S	143
54.087	150	34.4	Arrive in the centre of Fornovo di Taro	In piazza IV Novembre in front of Duomo		149

Hotel/B&B	Price
Casa di Preghiera S. Giovanni Battista, Loc. Siccomonte - 43036 FIDENZA Tel: 0039 (0)524 63408	Donation
Fraternità Francescana, Loc. Costamezzana - COSTAMEZZANA Tel: 0039 (0)521 624052	Donation
Locanda Cornaccina, 32/36, strada Cornaccina - 43014 MEDESANO Tel: 0039 (0)525420481	B2
Albergo Centrale da Silvia, 51, strada Valle - Varano de' Marchesi - 43014 MEDESANO Tel: 0039 (0)52559339	B2
Hotel Cavalieri, 8, via Prinzera - Salita - FORNOVO DI TARO Tel: 0039 (0)5253100	B3

Religious Hostel	Price
Don Bosco, 2, via Conciliazione - MEDESANO Tel: 0039 (0)525 420447 dontorri@libero.it www.parrocchiadimedesano.com	Donation
Casa di Spiritualità, Strada Magnana, 18 Riccò - 43045 FORNOVO DI TARO Tel: 0039 (0)525 400158 villa_santamaria@libero.it	Donation
Parrocchia di Maria Assunta, via 20 Settembre - 43045 FORNOVO DI TARO Tel: 0039 (0)525 2218	Donation
Parrocchia di Santa Margherita, Loc. Sivizzano - 43045 FORNOVO DI TARO Tel: 0039 (0)525 56258	Donation

Useful Contacts

Doctor

Riva Dr. Augusto, 2, piazza IV Novembre - 43045 FORNOVO DI TARO
Tel: 0039 (0)525 2378

Veterinary

Panarelli Chiara, la Nazionale - 43045 FORNOVO DI TARO Tel: 0039 (0)525 3849

Farrier

Ugolotti Luigi & Ugolotti Gian Piero Fabbri, strada la Torre - 43013 LANGHIRANO Tel: 0039 (0)521 852940

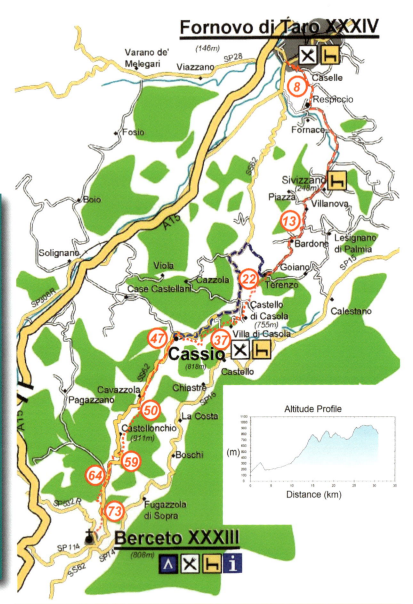

Altitude Profile

Distance (km)

(m)

Fornovo di Taro to Berceto 30.9 km

Route Summary: another long and strenuous section that is undertaken largely on forest and mountain tracks. Some of these are narrow, steep and over broken ground. There is the opportunity to break the climb at Cassio.

80

Distance from Canterbury: 1486km   **Distance to Rome:** 597km

Ascent: 1353m   **Descent:** 693m

Way Point N°	Way Point Distance (metres)	Total Distance (kilometres)	Directions	Verification Point	Compass	Altitude (metres)
55.001	0	0.0	From the Duomo in Fornovo take via XXIV Maggio	VF sign, pass Duomo on the left	SE	149
55.002	130	0.1	Cross Piazza Tarasconi and continue straight ahead	Kiosk on the right, No Entry sign ahead	SE	156
55.003	50	0.2	Cross the main road – SS62 – and continue straight ahead	Via Guglielmo Marconi, VF sign, pass bank on the right	SE	158
55.004	180	0.4	At the end of the pavement bear left on the road uphill	Via Guglielmo Marconi	E	170
55.005	150	0.5	Follow the road as it turns right and winds up the hill	Via Guglielmo Marconi	SE	182
55.006	500	1.0	Continue to follow the road to the left as it climbs the hill	Avoid track to right	NE	225
55.007	400	1.4	Continue straight ahead	Strada Caselle, VF sign	SE	250
55.008	1000	2.4	At the fork in Caselle bear right and downhill	Narrow road	S	317
55.009	600	3.0	Beside house, turn right on the tarmac road	Downhill	S	267
55.010	500	3.5	Take the next right turn		SW	196
55.011	80	3.6	At the T-junction at the bottom of the hill turn left on the main road	SP39	S	189
55.012	4100	7.7	Continue straight ahead on the SP39	Village of Sivizzano to the right	SW	248
55.013	2000	9.7	1 kilometre after Villanova, fork right on the road direction Terenzo	VF sign, località Braglia di Bardone	SW	301
55.014	1200	10.9	After passing through Bardone bear left	Towards Terenzo	S	408

Way Point N°	Way Point Distance (metres)	Total Distance (kilometres)	Directions	Verification Point	Compass	Altitude (metres)
55.015	600	11.5	Bear right up the hill	Towards Terenzo	SW	422
55.016	1200	12.7	Fork left into Terenzo	VF sign	SW	534
55.017	180	12.9	In front of the Piave di Terenzo take the right fork	VF sign	W	546
55.018	90	13.0	Fork left up a small tiled passageway	VF sign	W	555
55.019	150	13.1	At T-junction turn left uphill	VF sign, via Capoluogo	SW	567
55.020	150	13.3	Turn left at the top of the hill. **Note:** the route ahead is off-road and strenuous with steep climbs over broken ground. Cyclists are advised to turn right on the Alternate Route rejoining the SS62	VF sign	E	585
55.021	60	13.3	Turn right on to an unmade road	VF sign	SW	582
55.022	800	14.1	Continue straight ahead on the track		SW	706
55.023	1000	15.1	Bear right on the widening track	VF sign	SW	794
55.024	80	15.2	At T-junction turn right onto a minor road	VF sign, località Casola Castello	W	795
55.025	120	15.3	Just after passing the house on the left turn left on the grassy path	VF sign	S	784
55.026	500	15.8	At the end of the footpath turn right on the track		S	742
55.027	190	16.0	In Castello di Casola cross the tarmac road and continue straight ahead downhill		SW	741
55.028	200	16.2	Cross the track and continue straight ahead on the faint path		W	710

Way Point N°	Way Point Distance (metres)	Total Distance (kilometres)	Directions	Verification Point	Compass	Altitude (metres)
55.029	300	16.5	Continue on the track	Towards the houses	S	669
55.030	150	16.7	Turn right between the houses	Villa di Casola	SW	657
55.031	50	16.7	Continue straight ahead on the tarmac		SW	659
55.032	40	16.8	Continue straight ahead at the next junction		NW	659
55.033	100	16.9	Continue straight ahead at crossroads	VF sign	NW	672
55.034	90	16.9	Proceed straight ahead onto a small track	Uphill	N	690
55.035	100	17.0	At the T-junction turn left	VF sign	SW	709
55.036	50	17.1	Turn left onto the grassy track	VF sign	SW	709
55.037	700	17.8	Cross the unmade road and continue straight ahead on the footpath	VF sign	W	785
55.038	700	18.5	Immediately after a bend in the track turn left on the footpath	Ignore the signpost to Cassio	SW	859
55.039	300	18.8	Continue straight ahead on the footpath following the sign		SW	848
55.040	300	19.1	Join a broader track and bear left		S	815
55.041	200	19.3	Turn right on the footpath		W	765
55.042	800	20.1	Join a track and continue straight ahead uphill		W	786
55.043	40	20.1	Continue straight ahead	Ignore turnings on both sides	W	789
55.044	70	20.2	Join a broadening track and turn to the right		NW	788

Way Point Nº	Way Point Distance (metres)	Total Distance (kilometres)	Directions	Verification Point	Compass	Altitude (metres)
55.045	300	20.5	Take the right fork	Enter Cassio	NW	814
55.046	100	20.6	Turn left along the main street through Cassio	In front of Pieve di Cassio	SW	821
55.047	200	20.8	At the end of the street turn right and then left on the main road – SS62	Towards the old hostel	SW	801
55.048	600	21.4	On a bend in the road to the left take the footpath to the right		SW	768
55.049	500	21.9	Rejoin the main road and continue straight ahead on the right side of the road		SW	740
55.050	2400	24.3	On the crown of the bend to the right take the tarmac road to the left	Uphill and into the forest	S	748
55.051	400	24.7	After a long stretch on a level track turn right	Steep forest track uphill	SW	767
55.052	400	25.1	Turn left on the track		SW	866
55.053	300	25.4	Take the left fork		SW	894
55.054	170	25.6	Join a track and bear left		SW	912
55.055	120	25.7	Turn right into the main street	Castellonchio	SW	912
55.056	500	26.2	Before the exit from the town take the left fork	Right fork leads back to the main road	S	901
55.057	300	26.5	Continue straight ahead on the unmade road		S	913
55.058	110	26.6	Take the right fork on the footpath		SW	923
55.059	110	26.7	At the junction with the main road turn right and cross the road to continue on the left side	SS62	SW	930

Way Point N°	Way Point Distance (metres)	Total Distance (kilometres)	Directions	Verification Point	Compass	Altitude (metres)
55.060	160	26.9	On the crown of the next bend turn left on the track		W	937
55.061	150	27.0	At the junction in the middle of the woods turn left		S	937
55.062	170	27.2	Bear right	Ignore the turning to the left	SW	956
55.063	180	27.4	Rejoin the main road and turn right remaining on the right side of the road	SS62	S	950
55.064	900	28.3	Bear right to leave main road on the track into the woods. **Note:** the pathway through the woods includes crossing a stile. To avoid this cyclists and riders should remain on the road to Way Point #72	Beside the turning for Pagazzano	SW	941
55.065	170	28.4	Continue straight ahead over the stile on the path through the woods	Main road close on the left	S	942
55.066	120	28.6	Continue straight ahead as the path joins a track		SW	939
55.067	80	28.6	Continue straight ahead as the track broadens into a road		SW	942
55.068	300	28.9	Bear left towards the radio mast	Across stile	S	953
55.069	200	29.1	After a short paved section turn right on the footpath		S	958
55.070	200	29.3	Bear right on the track		SE	944
55.071	200	29.5	Pass through the cattle gate and continue on the path	Towards the main road	S	908

Way Point N°	Way Point Distance (metres)	Total Distance (kilometres)	Directions	Verification Point	Compass	Altitude (metres)
55.072	90	29.6	Bear right on the main road remaining on the right side	SS62	S	896
55.073	300	29.8	As the road bears left, bear right on the footpath	Towards Berceto below	S	884
55.074	500	30.3	Bear right towards the centre of the town	Ignore the turning to the left	SW	867
55.075	190	30.5	Continue straight ahead on the tarmac	Via Ripasanta	SW	838
55.076	150	30.7	Continue straight ahead, towards the centre of Berceto	Castle to the left	SW	819
55.077	60	30.7	In Largo Castello continue towards the centre of the town on the paved road	Via Rossi	SW	813
55.078	110	30.9	Arrive in the centre Berceto	Piazza San Moderanno in front of the Duomo		808

Alternate Route from Terenzo to Cassio 9.6km

Note: the Alternate Route allows cyclists and those not wishing to deal with the steepest climbs over broken ground to rejoin the main road over the pass.

1	0	0.0	Turn right away from the main route		NW	583
2	2200	2.2	At T-junction turn left on the main road	SS62 direction Cassio and Berceto	SW	657
3	4600	6.8	Continue straight ahead on the main road		SW	876
4	2800	9.6	Arrive in Cassio at the end of the main street and close beside the old hostel	Way Point #47 on the main route		801

Hotel/B&B	Price
Gioli, 5, via Ripasanta - 43042 BERCETO Tel: 39 (0)52564251	B2
Vittoria, 5, via Marconi - 43042 BERCETO Tel: 0039 (0)52564306 www.darino.it info@darino.it	B2
Ostello Cisa, Tugo di Berceto - TUGO Tel: 0039 (0)525-64521	B1

Religious Hostel	Price
Parrocchia Di Santa Margherita, Loc. Sivizzano - SIVIZZANO Tel: 0039 (0)525 56258	Donation
Ostello Di Cassio, via Nazionale, loc. Cassio - CASSIO Tel: 0039 (0)525 64521	B1
Ostello del Seminario, C/o ex seminario, Via E. Colli 8 - 43042 BERCETO Tel: 0039 (0)521 960628 Mobile: 0039 380 7014886	Donation

Youth Hostel/Camping	Price
Pianelli, 146, via Nazionale - 43042 BERCETO Tel: 0039 (0)525 64521 www.campingipianelli.com camping.ipianelli@libero.it	B1
Casa della gioventù parrocchiale, Via Martino Iasoni - 43042 BERCETO Tel: 0039 (0)525 60087	B1
Ostello della Casa Grossa, Casa Cantoniera km 58 - 43042 BERCETO Tel: 0039 (0)525 60271	B1

Useful Contacts

Tourist/Information Offices

Centro Di Documentazione della Via Francigena, via Romea - 43042 BERCETO
Tel: 0039 (0)525629027 www.puntotappa.com   info@puntotappa.com

Veterinary

Molinari Dr. Roberto, localita' Passo della Cisa - 43042 BERCETO
Tel: 0039 (0)525 60326

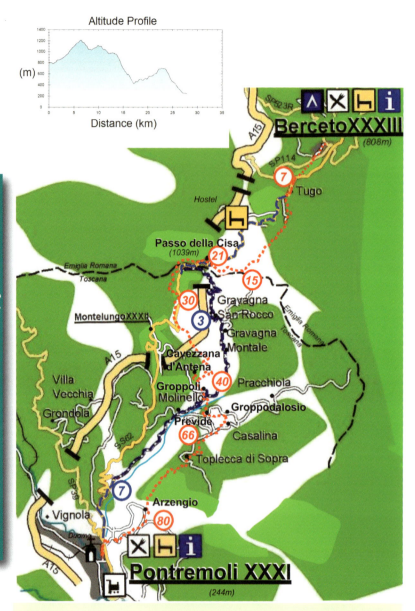

Altitude Profile

(m)

Distance (km)

Berceto to Pontremoli 27.9 km

Route Summary: although shorter this is a challenging section including many water crossings, cresting the summit of the Cisa and Crocetta passes. Much of the track follows the Club Alpino Italiano route and is most suited to fit hikers with light packs. **Note:** the Aternate Routes offer better underfoot conditions and are recommended for Cyclists and horse-riders

Distance from Canterbury: 1517km   Distance to Rome: 566km

Ascent: 888m   **Descent:** 1451m

Way Point Nº	Way Point Distance (metres)	Total Distance (kilometres)	Directions	Verification Point	Compass	Altitude (metres)
56.001	0	0.0	From the Duomo in the piazza at the junction of via Martiri Libertà and via P.M. Rossi take via Romea		S	808
56.002	40	0.0	Continue on via Romea	Information Office to the left	SW	807
56.003	90	0.1	At the end of the small cobbled street in piazzale le Baruti turn right and then immediately left	Via al Seminario, VF sign	SW	806
56.004	130	0.3	Proceed straight ahead onto via E. Colli	VF sign	SW	808
56.005	700	1.0	At T-junction with main road turn right and almost immediately left onto a gravel track	VF sign	SW	784
56.006	500	1.5	At fork bear right	VF sign	SW	820
56.007	300	1.8	Fork right at the top of the rise	VF sign	SW	850
56.008	600	2.4	Track emerges onto a small tarmac area continue straight ahead	VF sign, old factory on right	SW	878
56.009	150	2.5	Cross the main road and continue straight ahead towards Monte Valoria. **Note:** to avoid climbing on further forest tracks which include stiles and to pass directly beside the hostel follow Alternate Route #1 by turning right on the SS62	VF sign	S	874
56.010	200	2.7	Continue straight ahead		S	884
56.011	300	3.0	Continue straight ahead		S	910
56.012	400	3.4	Take the right fork	Farm Felgara to the left	SW	939
56.013	300	3.7	On the crown of a bend to the left bear right on the track	Uphill	SW	957
56.014	1600	5.31	Take the left fork uphill towards il Valoria	Sign for the hostel to the right	SW	1125

Berceto to Pontremoli 27.9 km

Way Point N°	Way Point Distance (metres)	Total Distance (kilometres)	Directions	Verification Point	Compass	Altitude (metres)
56.015	1200	6.5	Near the summit of Valoria take the right fork	Towards the summit	SW	1201
56.016	80	6.6	At the summit take the path to the right	Along the ridge	W	1204
56.017	150	6.7	Continue straight ahead	Ignore the turning to the right	W	1177
56.018	600	7.3	Continue straight ahead	Cross the stile	W	1132
56.019	500	7.8	After a steep descent continue straight ahead	Cross a second stile	NW	1076
56.020	40	7.9	Join a track and bear right		W	1070
56.021	700	8.6	Arrive at the summit of the Cisa Pass, cross the main road and bear right on the footpath. Alternate Route #2 offers a pleasant descent to Pontremoli on generally quiet roads and is recommended for cyclists and horse riders. The main route includes further and sometimes difficult water crossings as well as steep descents and steps	Parallel to the steps to the church **Note:** from this point the signs become the red and white signs of the Club Alpino Italiano. The VF variants of the signs also show a small pilgrim painted in black. There are many intersecting CAI routes and so be sure to check for the pilgrim on the signs.	W	1032
56.022	800	9.4	Take the left fork		SW	1073
56.023	800	10.2	Continue straight ahead across the stream		S	1120
56.024	150	10.3	Continue straight ahead on the path	Ignore the turning to the right	SW	1100
56.025	200	10.5	Make a more difficult crossing of a stream and continue straight ahead		SW	1098
56.026	50	10.6	Cross a further but easier stream		S	1098

Way Point Nº	Way Point Distance (metres)	Total Distance (kilometres)	Directions	Verification Point	Compass	Altitude (metres)
56.027	110	10.7	Turn right on the forest road		SW	1095
56.028	30	10.7	Turn left on another forest road and cross another stream		SE	1100
56.029	400	11.0	In the middle of the forest bear right		SE	1064
56.030	120	11.1	Ignore a turning to the right and continue to descend. After a further 30m turn right on the path	Gentle descent, parallel to the main road below	S	1045
56.031	1000	12.1	The path enters a track and continues straight ahead	Parallel and closer to the main road	SE	980
56.032	200	12.3	At the junction with the main road bear right on the road	SS62	SE	969
56.033	200	12.5	On the apex of the next bend, bear left to leave the main road and join a track. **Note:** to visit Montelungo (Sigeric site XXXII) follow the main road with care. The main road continues to Pontremoli		SE	966
56.034	700	13.2	Pass a radio mast and continue straight ahead	Descend in open space between woods	SE	980
56.035	1000	14.2	Continue straight ahead	Ignore the turning to the right	E	913
56.036	40	14.2	Bear right on the track		SW	904
56.037	200	14.4	Continue straight ahead	Ignore the turning to the left	SW	878
56.038	120	14.6	Continue straight ahead	Ignore the turning to the right	SE	855

Way Point N°	Way Point Distance (metres)	Total Distance (kilometres)	Directions	Verification Point	Compass	Altitude (metres)
56.039	300	14.9	Continue straight ahead	Ignore turning to left and to the right	S	795
56.040	200	15.1	At a turn in the track continue straight ahead on the path	Into the woods	W	736
56.041	300	15.4	Continue straight ahead	Ignore the turning to the right	W	697
56.042	600	16.0	On just reaching the first houses in the village of Cavezzana D'Antena turn left	VF sign	SE	607
56.043	300	16.3	Turn right on the track		S	590
56.044	400	16.7	Continue straight ahead	Enter Groppoli	SE	512
56.045	60	16.7	At the intersection with the tarmac road continue straight ahead	Pass through the village	S	500
56.046	150	16.9	Continue straight ahead	Paved track	S	486
56.047	100	17.0	At the exit from Gropolli take the left fork		E	466
56.048	40	17.0	At the junction with the main road turn right and immediately left on the track	Towards the woods and then downhill	SE	462
56.049	300	17.3	Continue straight ahead	Difficult ford of the Civasola torrente and back uphill	SW	421
56.050	400	17.7	At the intersection with the tarmac road turn right and immediately left onto a footpath	Steep descent into Previdè	SW	464
56.051	120	17.8	On reaching Previdè turn left onto the tarmac and then immediately left again	Towards the village centre	E	454
56.052	110	17.9	At the exit from the village take the left fork	Uphill	E	448
56.053	200	18.1	Take care to locate an indistinct junction and bear right over a dry wall	Between the olive trees	E	474
56.054	200	18.3	After an uphill section take a footpath to the right	Across the hillside	E	497
56.055	300	18.6	Continue straight ahead	Enter Groppodalosio	E	506

Way Point N°	Way Point Distance (metres)	Total Distance (kilometres)	Directions	Verification Point	Compass	Altitude (metres)
56.056	120	18.8	In the centre of the village turn right down a flight of steps	Over the old river Magra bridge	SW	509
56.057	150	18.9	Continue straight ahead	Over the old river Magra bridge	SW	479
56.058	300	19.2	Join a tarmac road and turn right	Towards the village	SW	502
56.059	80	19.3	Bear left away from the road on a footpath		SW	500
56.060	80	19.4	Continue straight ahead	Ignore the turning to the left	S	502
56.061	100	19.5	At the first junction in Casalina continue straight ahead	On the paved road	S	509
56.062	150	19.6	Continue straight ahead	Pass an old mill	W	528
56.063	300	19.9	Join a tarmac road and continue straight ahead		SW	506
56.064	150	20.1	Bear left on the well signed path	Into the woods	SW	513
56.065	300	20.4	Join the track and bear left		SW	557
56.066	100	20.5	At a bend to the left in the track continue straight ahead on the path		S	555
56.067	300	20.8	Cross a ditch and turn sharply to the right		W	561
56.068	400	21.2	After a steep climb turn right on the track	Towards the village	W	582
56.069	100	21.3	At the junction with the tarmac road turn left on the road	Uphill	SW	588
56.070	50	21.3	Bear left away from the road on a footpath	Skirt the village of Toplecca di Sopra	SW	594
56.071	60	21.4	At the T-junction turn left		SW	600
56.072	110	21.5	Cross the tarmac road and continue straight ahead		S	607

Way Point N°	Way Point Distance (metres)	Total Distance (kilometres)	Directions	Verification Point	Compass	Altitude (metres)
56.073	200	21.7	Continue straight ahead	Over the bridge	SW	610
56.074	1700	23.4	Arrive at the summit of the Crocetta pass after a long climb and continue straight ahead on the track	Pass beside the chapel	SW	694
56.075	50	23.4	Take the grass track to the left and downhill	Towards the village of Arzengio	S	692
56.076	1400	24.8	Arrive at the first houses in Arzengio and take the tarmac road to the left		SW	486
56.077	200	25.0	Take the first turning to the left	Skirt the village, with the village centre on the hilltop to the right	SE	460
56.078	150	25.2	On the far side of the village take the small path to the left	Between the olive trees	SW	452
56.079	70	25.3	At the next junction turn right on the path	Across the hillside	W	444
56.080	70	25.3	Cross the tarmac road and take right fork on the small road beside the house	Initially parallel to the tarmac road on the left	SW	447
56.081	120	25.4	Continue straight ahead	The road becomes a track	SW	439
56.082	600	26.1	Continue straight ahead	Ignore the turning to the right	SW	367
56.083	180	26.2	Continue straight ahead	Tarmac road	W	342
56.084	800	27.0	At the T-junction turn right		N	255

Way Point N°	Way Point Distance (metres)	Total Distance (kilometres)	Directions	Verification Point	Compass	Altitude (metres)
56.085	60	27.1	Continue straight ahead over the old bridge over the Magra	Towards the hospital	W	250
56.086	90	27.2	At the junction with the main road turn left	SS62	S	257
56.087	60	27.2	Take the pedestrian crossing and enter Pontremoli on the pavement		SW	254
56.088	170	27.4	Just before the main road crosses the river, bear right and continue straight ahead through the underpass		S	254
56.089	80	27.5	Turn right after coming up from the underpass and go around the mini roundabout	VF sign, shrine directly in front	NW	252
56.090	40	27.5	Go under the archway – Porta Parma – and into the narrow street ahead	Via Garibaldi	S	262
56.091	400	27.9	Arrive in Pontremoli centre	Piazza della Republica		244

Fonte San Moderanno to the Cisa Pass Summit - allowing cyclists and those not wishing to deal with further forest tracks to proceed on the main road.   5.7km

Way Point N°	Way Point Distance (metres)	Total Distance (km)	Directions	Verification Point	Compass	Altitude (metres)
1	0	0.0	Turn right onto on the SS62	VF sign points ahead, but route is difficult and bypasses hostel and historic route	SW	874
2	3200	3.2	Continue straight ahead on the SS62	Ostello della via Francigena to the right	SW	982
3	2500	5.7	Continue straight ahead on the SS62 and rejoin the main route	Summit of Passo della Cisa		1031

Alternate Route from the summit of the Cisa Pass to Pontremoli - after a short stretch on the main road, the route follows quiet country roads for much of its length before rejoining the SS62 2km before the entry to Pontremoli. The route is recommended for cyclists. 19.6km

Way Point N°	Way Point Distance (metres)	Total Distance (km)	Directions	Verification Point	Compass	Altitude (metres)
1	0	0.0	Continue straight ahead on the main road	Church on the right	SW	1030
2	1200	1.2	Turn left away from the SS62. **Note:** to visit Montelungo (Sigeric site XXXII) follow the main road with care. The main road continues to Pontremoli.	Direction Gravagna	SE	1022
3	5400	6.6	At the bottom of the hill continue straight into the village of Gravagna San Rocco	VF sign	E	708
4	250	6.8	At the bottom of the hill continue straight ahead	VF sign	SE	697
5	400	7.3	Fork right before entering Gravagna Montale	Large house directly in front and on left as you turn	SW	693
6	6000	13.3	A T-junction turn right	Towards Pontremoli	SW	398
7	3900	17.2	Rejoin the main road and turn left. Proceed with caution on the potentially busy road.	Towards Pontremoli	S	363
8	2400	19.6	Rejoin the main route at Way Point #86 and continue straight ahead	Towards the centre of Pontremoli		257

Hotel B&B	Price
Falco Delle Apuane, via Castello - Arzelato - 54027 PONTREMOLI Tel: 0039 (0)187 835003/8335140	B2
Ai Chiosi, 15, Chiosi - 54027 PONTREMOLI Mobile: 0039 340 2357383 aichiosi@libero.it	B2
Appennino, via Montelungo, Montelungo - 54027 PONTREMOLI Tel: 0039 (0)187436131 hotelristoranteappen@libero.it	B2
Ostello castello del Piagnaro, Porta di Parma- 54027 PONTREMOLI Tel: 0039 (0)187 4601243 istruzione@comune.pontremoli.ms.it (Closed on Monday)	B2

Religious Hostel	Price
PR Casa Padre Pio da Pietrelcina , 2, via Cappuccini - 54027 PONTREMOLI Tel: 0039 (0)187 830395	B1
Ostello Castello Del Piagnaro, Porta di Parma - 54027 PONTREMOLI Tel: 0039 (0)187 831439 cooperativapuntremal@libero.it www.comune.pontremoli.ms.it	B1
Seminario di Pontremoli, Piazza San Francesco - 54027 PONTREMOLI Mobile: 0039 334 5446198	Donation

Useful Contacts

Tourist/Information Offices

Ufficio Informazioni, C/O COMUNALE - 54027 PONTREMOLI
Tel: 0039 (0)187833278

Doctor

Arrighi Dr. Paolo, 46, VIA PIRANDELLO   Tel: 0039 (0)187 831252

Veterinary

Molinari Dr. Roberto, 94, localita' Passo della Cisa - 43042 Berceto   Tel: 0525 60326

Berceto to Pontremoli 27.9km

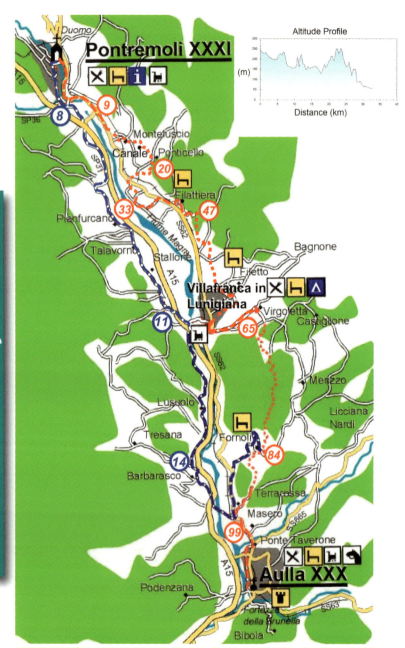

Pontremoli XXXI

Altitude Profile

Pontremoli to Aulla 32.8 km

Route Summary: the main route is another strenuous section with mixed conditions varying from busy and dangerous roads near Pontremoli to challenging tracks through hilly woodland

98

Distance from Canterbury: 1545km   **Distance to Rome:** 538km

Ascent: 431m   **Descent:** 625m

Way Point N°	Way Point Distance (metres)	Total Distance (kilometres)	Directions	Verification Point	Compass	Altitude (metres)
57.001	0	0.0	Continue across the piazza della Reppublica and into the narrow street ahead	Via Armani	SE	241
57.002	160	0.2	At the crossroads continue straight ahead. **Note:** to use the cycle route turn right and continue over the bridge on Alternate Route #1. The official route leaves Pontremoli following the main road with few pavements and little protection for walkers and horse-riders. The cycle route may be preferred.	Via Cavour	S	243
57.003	110	0.3	Turn left	Cross the river bridge, Ponte Cesare Battisti	E	236
57.004	90	0.4	Pass through the archway and turn right	Via Mazzini	S	238
57.005	600	1.0	At the crossroads continue straight ahead to join the main road, remaining on the right-hand side	VF sign	S	228
57.006	600	1.6	Continue straight ahead	Pass beside the church of San Lazzaro	SE	232
57.007	130	1.7	Cross the road and bear left on the narrow paved street	Via Santissima Annunziata	E	225
57.008	180	1.9	Return to the main road and turn left	Direction Massa on the SS62	SE	219
57.009	1200	3.1	Continue straight ahead direction Villafranca	VF sign	SE	205
57.010	800	3.9	Turn left off the main road	VF sign	E	197
57.011	150	4.0	Take the right fork onto the gravel track	VF sign	SE	197

Way Point N°	Way Point Distance (metres)	Total Distance (kilometres)	Directions	Verification Point	Compass	Altitude (metres)
57.012	400	4.4	At the junction with a minor road turn sharp left on the road	VF sign, towards railway	NE	194
57.013	120	4.5	Take the right fork	Direction Ponticello	E	200
57.014	300	4.8	Continue straight ahead	Up the hill	E	200
57.015	300	5.1	Bear left on the road	Direction Canale, VF sign	E	214
57.016	200	5.3	Continue to the right on the road	VF sign	SE	221
57.017	150	5.5	At the crossroads continue straight ahead on the gravel track	VF sign	SE	222
57.018	140	5.6	At the T-junction with a minor road turn left	VF sign	E	224
57.019	110	5.7	At the road junction, cross over and pass on the left side of the church	Borgo de Ponticello, red and white CAI sign	SE	229
57.020	80	5.8	Pass under an archway turn right and pass under a second arch	Volta a Crociera	S	229
57.021	200	6.0	At the crossroads take the second turning on the left	VF sign, track crosses river and climbs ridge	S	223
57.022	800	6.8	Turn sharp right	VF sign	SW	238
57.023	200	7.0	Take the right fork	VF sign	W	232
57.024	300	7.3	Take the left fork, downhill towards railway	Line of trees on the left, VF sign	SW	204
57.025	300	7.6	Pass under the railway		SW	179
57.026	30	7.7	Bear left and then turn right in a narrow passageway	Red and white signs	SW	178
57.027	40	7.7	Cross straight over the main road and continue straight ahead	VF sign	SW	174
57.028	50	7.7	Turn left between houses	Red and white CAI signs	S	173

Way Point N°	Way Point Distance (metres)	Total Distance (kilometres)	Directions	Verification Point	Compass	Altitude (metres)
57.029	160	7.8	At the fork in the track bear left	Yellow VF sign	SE	167
57.030	300	8.1	At the T-junction turn right	Towards farm buildings	SW	162
57.031	100	8.2	Turn left	Keep farm buildings to the right	SE	162
57.032	90	8.3	At the T-junction with the tarmac road turn right		S	161
57.033	300	8.6	Facing a house turn left, road quickly turn right then left	Yellow VF sign	SE	161
57.034	300	8.9	Take the left fork		E	159
57.035	300	9.2	At the T-junction turn left	After passing through farm	NE	154
57.036	500	9.7	At the T-junction with the main road turn right	Towards the church – Pieve di Sorano	E	158
57.037	90	9.8	Take the left fork and leave the SS62	Direction Biglio	SE	159
57.038	400	10.2	Turn left under the railway bridge	Brown VF sign	E	159
57.039	200	10.4	Turn right up a flight of steps. **Note:** riders should remain on the road and bear right to Way Point #41		N	181
57.040	110	10.5	Continue straight ahead	Beside the square	N	201
57.041	30	10.5	At the road junction turn right	Towards the square in the centre of Filattiera	SE	205
57.042	110	10.6	Turn right to leave the square	Via Borgo di Mezzo	S	212

Way Point Nº	Way Point Distance (metres)	Total Distance (kilometres)	Directions	Verification Point	Compass	Altitude (metres)
57.043	110	10.8	At the end of the road take the left fork	Through archway, brown VF sign	SE	205
57.044	400	11.2	At the T-junction turn left and then right over a bridge and up the hill on a grass track	Railway bridge on the right at the junction	SE	157
57.045	140	11.3	Bear left towards the chapel on the brow of the hill	Yellow VF sign	NE	183
57.046	140	11.4	Take the right fork	Yellow VF sign and red and white signs	E	204
57.047	500	11.9	Turn right towards the pylon	Yellow VF sign	S	212
57.048	400	12.3	Continue straight ahead		S	176
57.049	700	13.0	Turn right beside the river	Red and white CAI signs	S	151
57.050	200	13.2	At the road junction turn left	Brown VF sign	NE	147
57.051	150	13.4	Turn right off the road	Brown VF sign	S	150
57.052	700	14.1	At the junction with the road turn left and then immediately right	Brown VF sign	S	154
57.053	500	14.6	Continue straight ahead on the narrow track	Trees on the right field on the left	S	157
57.054	140	14.7	Continue straight ahead	Red and white sign painted on stones on the ground	S	157

Way Point N°	Way Point Distance (metres)	Total Distance (kilometres)	Directions	Verification Point	Compass	Altitude (metres)
57.055	120	14.8	Bear left onto the road	Golf course on the right	S	156
57.056	300	15.1	At the crossroads in Filetto continue straight ahead	Via San Genesio	SE	158
57.057	600	15.7	At the end of the road turn left into the old town of Filetto		NE	164
57.058	130	15.9	Immediately after leaving the old town, turn right	Via del Canale	SE	166
57.059	300	16.2	At the T-junction turn right	Parallel to the river and wooded ridge	SW	160
57.060	900	17.1	Turn left	Via Chiusura	SW	142
57.061	300	17.4	Bear left across piazza della Resistenza	Towards the main road	SW	132
57.062	110	17.5	Cross the main road and bear left across the piazza Aeronautica to take the old bridge over the river	Into the old town of Villafranca	SW	128
57.063	200	17.7	Turn left and leave the old town	After passing the church	S	131
57.064	60	17.7	Cross the main road and turn left onto via della Libertà	SP26	E	134
57.065	600	18.3	Fork left direction Virgoletta		NE	173
57.066	1100	19.4	Fork right direction Virgoletta Centre		SE	176
57.067	50	19.5	Turn left up the narrow alleyway in the direction of the Church	Shrine on left	NE	179

Way Point N°	Way Point Distance (metres)	Total Distance (kilometres)	Directions	Verification Point	Compass	Altitude (metres)
57.068	110	19.6	Walkers continue straight ahead. To avoid a flight of steps, riders turn right and proceed behind the houses and take the next right at Way Point #71		NE	186
57.069	160	19.8	Turn right to proceed under an archway and down the flight of steps	Red-and-white painted sign	SE	191
57.070	40	19.8	Turn right at the bottom of the steps, turn right again towards an archway, then turn left before passing underneath		SW	190
57.071	40	19.8	Take the first turning to the left leaving the village behind you	Shortly passing natural water source on the left	S	189
57.072	200	20.0	Bear left continuing up the hill	Via delle Fontane	SE	196
57.073	500	20.5	At crossroads continue straight ahead towards the cemetery	Red-and-white painted sign	S	213
57.074	150	20.7	Road becomes a track continue straight ahead with the football pitch on left	Red-and-white painted sign	S	214
57.075	200	20.9	Fork left downhill	Red-and-white painted sign	SW	207
57.076	300	21.2	Fork left	Red-and-white painted sign	SE	192
57.077	200	21.4	Take right fork up the hill	Red-and-white painted sign	S	203
57.078	400	21.8	Turn left at the top of the hill	Wooden balustrade on left	SE	251
57.079	40	21.8	Fork left continuing downhill		SE	251

Way Point N°	Way Point Distance (metres)	Total Distance (kilometres)	Directions	Verification Point	Compass	Altitude (metres)
57.080	300	22.1	Turn sharp right at T-junction		S	247
57.081	1300	23.4	At fork bear right	Red-and-white painted sign	S	241
57.082	1000	24.4	Continue straight ahead		SW	174
57.083	500	24.9	Bear left		S	165
57.084	1200	26.1	Track leads onto minor road, bear left direction La Valle del Sole . Horse riders should take Alternate Route #2 to the right to avoid treacherous pathway and steps	House directly in front	S	141
57.085	20	26.1	Skirt house and turn right up a gravel track	Red-and-white painted sign	SW	140
57.086	30	26.2	Turn right to go between two buildings and then immediately left	Red-and-white painted sign	W	141
57.087	300	26.5	After coming up a steep ascent and a rough flight of steps, bear left with an old building immediately on left and a wall on right	Red-and-white painted sign	W	132
57.088	60	26.5	Turn left onto the road and proceed up the hill		W	136
57.089	20	26.6	Turn left almost immediately up the steep narrow track	VF sign	S	138
57.090	200	26.8	Bear right on track	Red and-white painted sign	SW	143
57.091	100	26.9	Continue straight ahead		SW	152
57.092	120	27.0	Turn left at T-junction	Private property sign on right	S	149

Way Point N°	Way Point Distance (metres)	Total Distance (kilometres)	Directions	Verification Point	Compass	Altitude (metres)
57.093	130	27.1	Take the right fork		S	143
57.094	400	27.5	Take the left fork		S	151
57.095	400	27.9	Bear right	In the clearing	SE	94
57.096	40	27.9	Bear right on the broader track	White house directly on left behind trees	SW	92
57.097	800	28.8	Take right fork	Red-and-white painted sign	SW	87
57.098	200	28.9	Track emerges onto a minor tarmac road – via dei Pini, continue straight ahead	Cemetery on right	S	88
57.099	500	29.4	At crossroads turn left onto via Nazionale Cisa, SS62 - Alternate Route #2 joins from the right		SE	73
57.100	200	29.6	Continue straight ahead on SS62 - Alternate Route #1 joins from the right		S	73
57.101	1400	31.1	Turn right to proceed into small tunnel under the railway	VF sign	W	64
57.102	30	31.1	After emerging from the tunnel turn left onto viale Lunigiana	VF sign	SW	64
57.103	200	31.3	Bear left away from the motorway entrance	Viale Lunigiana	S	62
57.104	600	31.9	At crossroads turn right and bear left still on viale Lunigiana	VF sign, parallel to river and autostrada	S	58
57.105	900	32.8	Arrive in Aulla centre at the bridge over the river Magra			59

Note: the route follows the cycle path on the western side of the river Magra. It also avoids a dangerous section of the SS62.

Way Point N°	Way Point Distance (metres)	Total Distance (kilometres)	Directions	Verification Point	Compass	Altitude (metres)
1	0	0.0	At crossroads turn right and cross the river bridge	Via Pietro Bologna	W	240
2	160	0.2	At crossroads on the far side of the bridge continue straight ahead on the via Roma		W	243
3	170	0.3	At crossroads turn left onto via Pirandello		S	247
4	400	0.7	At the T-junction turn right	Strada di Maggio Galante	SW	238
5	170	0.9	At crossroads turn left onto via Europa and via Groppomontone	Factory building straight ahead	SE	240
6	100	1.0	Bear right on via Groppomontone	Keep river and bridge to the left	S	237
7	700	1.7	Straight ahead crossing the bridge over the tributary	Via Antonino Siligato	SE	232
8	400	2.1	At fork bear left remaining beside the river	Direction La Spezia	E	220
9	300	2.4	Bear right on SP31 between autostrada and the river		S	230
10	1300	3.7	Continue straight ahead direction Villafranca	Entrance to the motorway for La Spezia, Parma and Genova on left	SE	233
11	8500	12.2	In Ponte Magra, turn right onto via Pontemagra	Do not cross the bridge, proceed with river Magra on the left	S	123
12	1800	14.0	Take the left fork	Towards autostrada	S	189

Alternate cycle route from Pontremoli to Aulla 21.6 km

Way Point Nº	Way Point Distance (metres)	Total Distance (kilometres)	Directions	Verification Point	Compass	Altitude (metres)
13	1800	15.8	At junction with main road turn left towards Lusuolo	SP61	S	181
14	2100	17.9	Bear left remaining on road	Continue beside autostrada on via Osca	SE	100
15	1000	18.9	Bear right into Barbarasco	Via Chiesa	SW	109
16	100	19.0	At T-junction in Barbarasco turn left	SP23 via Roma	SE	112
17	1800	20.8	After crossing the river continue straight ahead	via Barbarasco	SE	74
18	300	21.1	At T-junction turn right on the via Nazionale	Terrarossa	SE	75
19	500	21.6	At T-junction with the SS62 turn right direction Aulla and rejoin main route at Way Point #100			73

Alternate riders route Fornoli to Terrarossa, which also allows cyclists and those not wishing to deal with further forest tracks to proceed on the road. 4.9km

1	0	0.0	At Way Point #84 on the main route take the road to the right	Direction Finoli	NW	141
2	1400	1.4	At the T-junction in Fornoli, turn right	Via dell'Ardito	W	156
3	80	1.5	At fork bear left	Via dell'Ara	SW	158
4	1600	3.1	At T-junction with main road turn left	SS62, via Cisa	S	88
5	1800	4.9	At crossroads with via dei Pini go straight ahead and rejoin main route at Way Point #99			73

Hotel/B&B	Price
B&B Casa di Tata, via Cantiere 14, frazione Scorcetoli - 54023 FILATTIERA Tel: 0039 (0)187 458199 info@casaditata.it	B2
La Casa Del Lilla, 48, Regione San Grato - 14018 VILLAFRANCA D'ASTI Tel: 0039 (0)141942408	B2
Agriturismo La Torre, localita' La Torre - 55026 FORNOLI Tel: 0039 (0)583 808542	B2
Agriturismo La Valle del Sole - 14018 VILLAFRANCA Tel: 0039 (0)187 493023	B2
Locanda di Pratomedici, via Pratomedici 13, Bigliolo - 54011 AULLA Tel: 0039 (0)187 412005	B2

Religious Hostel	Price
Chiesa Di San Carpasio, piazza Abbazia - 54011 AULLA Tel: 0039 (0)187 420148 Mobile: 0039 339 6380331 cultura@comune.aulla.ms.it perignon@alice.it www.sancaprasio.it	Donation
Fortezza La Brunella, Parco della Brunella - 54011 AULLA Tel: 0039 (0)187 409077 coopnatur@libero.it **Note:** Closed on Mondays	B1
Convento Cappucini, 5, via Barcara - 54011 AULLA Tel: 0039 (0)187.40.90.13	B1

Camping	Price
Il Castagneto, Ponte Donico, 2, Filetto Nazionale - 54028 VILLAFRANCA Tel: 0039 (0)187 493492	B1

Equestrian

Associazione Sportiva Cavalli, via Stadano - 54011 AULLA Tel: 0039 (0)187415149

Useful Contacts

Tourist/Information Offices

Ufficio Informazioni, 6, via A.Salucci - 54011 AULLA   Tel: 0039 (0)187 421439

Internet Cafes

Spazio Computers, 12, piazza Mazzini - 54011 AULLA Tel: 0039 (0)187 423058

Doctor

Caponi Dr. Sandro Studio Medico, 29, piazza Mazzini Giuseppe - 54011 AULLA
Tel: 0039 (0)187 420045

Veterinary

Studio Veterinario Dott. Crespo H. L. 24, via Nazionale - 54011 Aulla
Tel: 0187 421967

Altitude Profile

(m)

Distance (km)

Aulla to Sarzana 16.3 km

Route Summary: this is another rugged segment on CAI signed pathways over the final ridge before the coastal plain. The Alternate Route offers options for all groups to bypass the most difficult sections and also to visit Santo Stefano di Magra XXIX.

Distance from Canterbury: 1577km   **Distance to Rome:** 506km

Ascent: 579m   **Descent:** 625m

Way Point N°	Way Point Distance (metres)	Total Distance (kilometres)	Directions	Verification Point	Compass	Altitude (metres)
58.001	0	0.0	With the bridge over the river Magra behind, bear right on piazza Abazzia		SE	58
58.002	100	0.1	At the T-junction turn right and then left	Pass under the arch	SE	59
58.003	70	0.2	At the riverside turn left direction Massa and La Spezia	Piazza L. Corbani, keep river to the right	NE	57
58.004	130	0.3	At T-junction, turn right and cross river bridge	SS62	S	58
58.005	180	0.5	At the end of the bridge, turn left across a disused railway line and then bear left direction Bibola	VF sign	E	61
58.006	200	0.7	Bear right away from the larger road. **Note:** the Alternate Route to the left offers an easier option for all groups and is recommended for cyclists and horse-riders as far as Ponzano Superiore	Via Prascara	S	82
58.007	60	0.7	Bear left on the footpath beside the wall		S	90
58.008	400	1.1	Cross the track and continue ahead up the hill	Beside the vineyard	S	155
58.009	90	1.2	At the junction with the road turn right and immediately left on the steep footpath	Into the woods	SE	172
58.010	500	1.7	At the T-junction with the track turn right		S	267

Aulla to Sarzana 16.3 km

111

Way Point Nº	Way Point Distance (metres)	Total Distance (kilometres)	Directions	Verification Point	Compass	Altitude (metres)
58.011	500	2.2	In the clearing continue straight ahead on the broad track over the crossroads - the Alternate Route crosses the main route and continues to the right	Uphill towards Bibola	SE	299
58.012	500	2.7	Approaching the top of the hill take the footpath to the right		E	344
58.013	200	2.9	Rejoin the broad track and turn right downhill	The village of Bibola is on the hilltop to the left	E	335
58.014	120	3.0	Take the next turning to the right and then immediately right again on the unmade road	Across the hillside towards Vecchietto	S	333
58.015	500	3.5	Bear right on the tarmac	Towards Vecchietto	S	294
58.016	800	4.3	Take the right fork into the village	Road bears right in the centre of the village	S	272
58.017	200	4.5	Turn right under the archway	Red and White Stripe sign, via Fontana	W	262
58.018	150	4.7	On the edge of the village bear right on the track	Initially beside the olive grove and then climbing into the forest	W	274
58.019	800	5.5	Take the steep footpath to the right	In the clearing	SW	387
58.020	1500	7.0	At the crossroads continue straight ahead on the forest track – the Alternate Route merges from the right	At the top of the hill	SW	536

Way Point N°	Way Point Distance (metres)	Total Distance (kilometres)	Directions	Verification Point	Compass	Altitude (metres)
58.021	800	7.8	Go straight ahead onto narrow track - the descent on the main route is over broken ground and is unsuitable for bikes and difficult for horses. The Alternate Route leaves to the right and descends on a broader easier track		SW	495
58.022	500	8.3	Continue straight ahead down a narrow track	VF sign direction Sarzana	W	486
58.023	130	8.4	Fork left		SW	456
58.024	700	9.1	Continue straight ahead - the Alternate Route rejoins from the right	Between Olive groves towards Ponzano Superiore	S	356
58.025	200	9.3	Turn right onto a small tarmac road and proceed downhill		SW	317
58.026	100	9.4	Turn left into the village of Ponzano Superiore		S	304
58.027	200	9.6	Turn left in the piazza Aia di Croce direction Sarzana - the pathway ahead has narrow sections over broken ground with steep descents and bypasses Santo Stefano di Magra (XXIX). Cyclists and those wishing to visit Santo Stafano should bear right on the Alternate Route	Via Cesare Orsini	NE	285
58.028	80	9.7	Road becomes a grassy track following the line of the ridge	Red and White Stripe sign	E	283
58.029	200	9.9	Turn right onto a minor road and proceed downhill on via Cattarello	Red and White Stripe sign	S	268
58.030	1400	11.3	Fork right up the hill		S	196

Way Point N°	Way Point Distance (metres)	Total Distance (kilometres)	Directions	Verification Point	Compass	Altitude (metres)
58.031	300	11.6	Bear right at the top of the hill	Archaeological dig site	S	187
58.032	70	11.7	After passing the dig, bear right down the hill		S	183
58.033	700	12.4	Take the lower track to the left	Red and White Stripe sign	S	108
58.034	200	12.6	Turn left onto the small tarmac road		S	69
58.035	80	12.7	Turn left at T-junction	Via Lago	E	63
58.036	130	12.8	In the valley turn right at T-junction direction Sarzana	Red and White Stripe sign, via Falcinello	S	57
58.037	1700	14.5	After crossing a small bridge turn left at the crossroads - the Alternate Route rejoins from the right	Via Falcinello	SE	28
58.038	170	14.7	Turn right	Via Turi	SW	28
58.039	700	15.2	At crossroads turn left	Via Cisa	SE	21
58.040	700	15.9	Go straight ahead to enter Sarzana through the Porta Parma		SE	24
58.041	400	16.3	Arrive Sarzana centre beside the church of Santa Maria			29

Aulla to Sarzana 16.3 km

Useful Contacts

Tourist/Information Offices

Servizi Turistici Alberghieri R. & M. Srl, 392. V. Cisa Sud - 19035 PONZANO MAGRA

Ufficio Informazioni e di Accoglienza Turistica, Piazza Matteotti - 19038 SARZANA
Tel: 0039 (0)187 6141

Doctor

Centro Medico Lunense Srl, 0039, via Variante Aurelia - 19038 SARZANA
Tel: 0039 (0)187 624965

Veterinary

Dott.Ri Bortolamiol E Roffo, via Variante Aurelia - 19038 SARZANA
Tel: 0039 (0)187 624288

Farrier

Morelli Davide Fabbro, 5, via Vincinella - 19037 SANTO STEFANO DI MAGRA
Tel: 0039 (0)187 630507

The Alternate Route takes a quiet road and broad gravel tracks over the ridge and recrosses the main route with the possibility of rejoining the main route in Ponzano Superiore to avoid a long diversion and busy road approaching Sarzana

Way Point N°	Way Point Distance (metres)	Total Distance (kilometres)	Directions	Verification Point	Compass	Altitude (metres)
1	0	0.0	Bear left on the road over a small bridge	Direction Bibola	SE	82
2	1000	1.0	Fork right up the hill	Strada Comunale Bibola-Vecchietto	S	172
3	900	1.9	Remain on the road to Bibola	Pass VF sign off-road, direction Monticello	SE	237
4	1000	2.9	Fork right direction Bibola		W	287
5	400	3.3	Turn right at the top of the hill in the direction of Bibola centre	VF sign	N	330
6	30	3.3	At T-junction turn left away from the hill-top centre of Bibola		W	333
7	100	3.4	Bear right onto the track	VF sign	NW	335
8	800	4.2	At fork in track bear left		SW	298
9	1100	5.3	Turn left onto a minor road and proceed uphill	Towards quarry	S	343
10	700	6.0	Bear right with the quarry directly on your left		SE	415
11	200	6.2	At fork bear right	Away from quarry	W	455
12	100	6.3	At T-junction turn right		S	454
13	3100	9.4	Fork right down the hill - the main route joins from the left		SW	536
14	800	10.2	The main route goes straight ahead onto a narrow track, to remain on the Alternate Route turn right		W	495

Way Point N°	Way Point Distance (metres)	Total Distance (kilometres)	Directions	Verification Point	Compass	Altitude (metres)
15	2000	12.2	Take the left fork	Pass la Volpara restaurant - provides excellent regional food	S	324
16	1000	13.2	Bear right to merge with the main route		S	356
17	200	13.4	Turn right onto a small tarmac road and proceed downhill		SW	317
18	90	13.5	Turn left into the village of Ponzano Superiore		S	304
19	190	13.7	In piazza Aia di Croce bear right on the road	Proceed down the hill on via Antonio Gramsci	W	285
20	2100	15.8	400 metres after third right-hand hairpin turn sharp right leaving the road - this is a difficult turning to spot	Via Brigate Alpine	NW	145
21	1700	17.5	At T-junction at the entry to Santo Stefano di Magra (XXIX) turn left	Via Roma	SW	55
22	300	17.8	At T-junction turn left	SP62 via Cisa Sud	S	53
23	1300	19.1	At roundabout continue straight ahead	SP62 via Cisa Sud	S	27
24	1500	20.6	At broad junction in Ponzano Magra bear right on the smaller via Cisa Vecchio		S	25
25	300	20.9	After passing under railway join via Seconda Piano Vezzano and proceed straight ahead	Keep railway to the left	SE	23

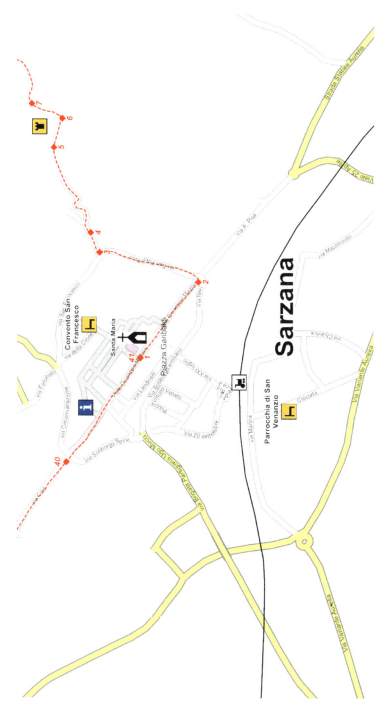

Sarzana

117

Way Point N°	Way Point Distance (metres)	Total Distance (kilometres)	Directions	Verification Point	Compass	Altitude (metres)
26	1800	22.7	At T-junction turn left and immediately right at the roundabout	Rejoining SS62	SE	18
27	150	22.9	Bear left to leave the main road on via Gabella		S	22
28	400	23.3	At the T-junction with SS62 turn left		S	21
29	300	23.6	At fork bear left to leave SS62	via San Gottardo	SE	16
30	800	24.4	At crossroads continue straight ahead and rejoin main route at Way Point #37			28

Hotel/B&B	Price
La Costa, 11, via Baria Mario - 19037 PONZANO SUPERIORE Tel: 0039 (0)187 630037 Mobile: 0039 333 9999870	B3
Santo Stefano di Magra, 18, via Crociata - 19037 PONZANO SUPERIORE Tel: 0039 (0)187 695035 Mobile: 0039 347 8317619 susannafedolfi@libero.it	B2
Agriturismo, Le Quattro Stagioni, 128, via Cisa Vecchia - 19035 PONZANO MAGRA Tel: 0039 (0)187 631508 Mobile: 0039 339 4450913 www.agriturismole4stagioni.com/home.html le.quattrostagioni@libero.it Note: takes horses	B2
Ai Cerreti, 109, via Cerreti - 19035 PONZANO MAGRA Tel: 0039 (0)187 630996 aicerreti@email.it	B2
Roma, 25, via Lungomare - MARINELLA DI SARZANA Tel: 0039 (0)187 64092	B2
Marinella, 4, via Parma - 19038 MARINELLA DI SARZANA Tel: 0039 (0)187 64690	B2

Religious Hostel	Price
Convento San Francesco, 8, via Paci - 19038 SARZANA Tel: 0039 (0)187 620356	Donation
Parrocchia di San Venanzio, Via Crociata 33 - 19038 SARZANA Tel: 0039 (0)187 621036	Donation

Sarzana to Pietrasanta 42.8 km

Route Summary: this is a long segment but with an option to reduce the length and avoid further climbing. There is also the possibility to break the segment at Avenza and Massa. At the time of writing there are unfinished discussions over the possibility of modifications to the route between Way Points #15 and #20

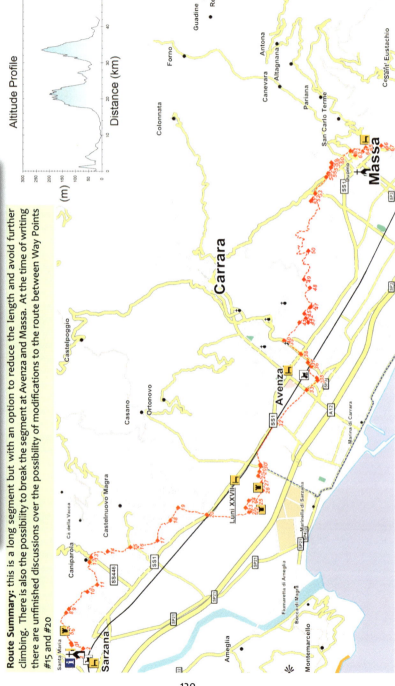

Altitude Profile

Azzano

Fabbiano

Riomagno

Seravezza

Cerreta San Nicola

Ripa

Duomo

Pietrasanta

SS439

SP68

SS1

SP81

A12

Marina di Pietrasanta

C.Sant'Eustachio

Montignoso

SP45

SP71

Vittoria Apuana

Forte dei Marmi

Massa

SP1

SP3

SP5

A12

SP3

Marina di Massa

Marina dei Ronchi

Distance from Canterbury: 1594km   **Distance to Rome:** 489km

Ascent: 715m   **Descent:** 720m

Sarzana to Pietrasanta 42.8 km

Way Point Nº	Way Point Distance (metres)	Total Distance (kilometres)	Directions	Verification Point	Compass	Altitude (metres)
59.001	0	0.0	Continue along via Giuseppe Mazzini	Church of Santa Maria on the left	SE	29
59.002	300	0.3	At roundabout turn left	Via San Francesco	N	21
59.003	300	0.6	Shortly after the road bends to the left turn right on the small road	Via Montata Sarzanello	NE	24
59.004	80	0.7	Bear right on the track	Towards the fortress on the hilltop	NE	29
59.005	300	1.0	Bear right	Keep the fortress of Sarzanello immediately on the left	E	84
59.006	100	1.1	Turn left on the cobbled road	Continue to skirt the fortress	NE	87
59.007	120	1.2	Take the right fork downhill	Via Montata Sarzanello	E	83
59.008	500	1.7	Continue straight ahead	Over the bridge	SE	25
59.009	140	1.8	At the road junction bear slightly left	Via Canalburo	SE	24
59.010	700	2.5	Bear left	Remaining on via Canalburo	SE	22
59.011	400	2.9	At the T-junction turn left	Via Paterno	E	44
59.012	800	3.7	At the complex junction continue straight ahead	Via Montevecchia towards the centre of Caniparola	E	63
59.013	150	3.9	On the apex of a bend to the left continue straight ahead on the small road	Pass beside an archway	S	61
59.014	600	4.5	At the T-junction turn right and then immediately left on via Montecchio	Olive grove on the left at the junction	S	47

Way Point N°	Way Point Distance (metres)	Total Distance (kilometres)	Directions	Verification Point	Compass	Altitude (metres)
59.015	700	5.2	Continue straight ahead	Via Provinciale in Colombiera	S	31
59.016	200	5.4	Take the left fork	Via Canale	S	28
59.017	600	6.0	Take the left fork into Molinicciara	Via della Pace	SE	16
59.018	800	6.8	At a crossroads continue straight ahead	Via Resistenza	SE	23
59.019	400	7.2	Turn right over the canal	Via Palvotrisia	S	23
59.020	900	8.1	At the junction with the main road – via Aurelia, SP1 – cross straight over and continue straight ahead	Under the railway bridge, via Provasco	S	9
59.021	1500	9.6	At the junction with the main road continue straight ahead	Towards the archaeological site of Luni	SE	2
59.022	70	9.7	At the entrance to the site turn left and follow the path around the site	Keep the site on the right	NE	2
59.023	190	9.8	At the end of the fence turn right	Keep the site on the right	SE	5
59.024	200	10.1	Cross via Luni and take the footpath ahead and slightly to the right	Footpath quickly turns right	S	7
59.025	200	10.3	Turn left on the road	Via Appia	SE	4
59.026	400	10.7	Continue straight ahead	Luni ampitheatre on the left, red and white CAI sign	E	4
59.027	200	10.8	Take the right fork	Via Appia	NE	6

Way Point N°	Way Point Distance (metres)	Total Distance (kilometres)	Directions	Verification Point	Compass	Altitude (metres)
59.028	200	11.1	Turn right on via Marina	Red and White Stripe sign	E	10
59.029	130	11.2	Continue straight ahead	No Entry sign	E	11
59.030	160	11.3	At the T-junction, cross the road and take the footbridge over the waterway.	**Note:** turning right and joining the Alternate Route along the coast road, will give the opportunity to put your toes in the sea, shorten the distance to Pietrasanta by 5km and provide relief from further climbing	E	9
59.031	60	11.4	Bear left on the road	Via del Parmignola, beside the waterway and then the railway track	SE	9
59.032	1600	13.0	At the junction with the main road continue straight ahead	Via Provinciale Avenza-Sarzana	SE	5
59.033	1400	14.4	At the crossroads with viale 20 Settembre continue straight ahead	Via Giovan-Pietro	SE	10
59.034	400	14.8	After crossing the bridge bear left on via Luigi Farini	Fortress to the right – Torre di Castruccio	E	10
59.035	90	14.9	Bear left	Via Colombera	NE	13
59.036	400	15.3	At the T-junction turn left	Over level crossing	NE	15
59.037	160	15.4	Turn right	Via Provinciale Carrara-Avenza	NE	17
59.038	300	15.6	At the crossroads with the via Aurelia continue straight ahead	Traffic lights	NE	22
59.039	600	16.2	Cross the via provinciale Nazzano and continue straight ahead		NE	29

Way Point N°	Way Point Distance (metres)	Total Distance (kilometres)	Directions	Verification Point	Compass	Altitude (metres)
59.040	130	16.3	Turn right uphill	Via Forma Bassa	SE	32
59.041	700	17.0	Continue straight ahead on the track		SE	53
59.042	200	17.2	Turn right	Into the woods	W	101
59.043	130	17.4	Turn left	Towards the farm	SW	94
59.044	40	17.4	Turn left beside the farm and then left again uphill	Towards the electricity pylon and between the vines	NE	91
59.045	400	17.8	At the top of the ridge turn right on the road, via Forma Alta	Vines on the right	SE	122
59.046	300	18.1	At the road junction continue straight ahead		SE	145
59.047	60	18.1	At top of the hill turn left on the road	Along the ridge towards the quarry	E	143
59.048	700	18.9	Bear left on the track	Quarry on the right	NE	149
59.049	500	19.4	Bear right on the white road	Via dell'Uva	E	175
59.050	1300	20.6	Turn sharp left uphill	Beside farm, via dell'Uva	E	172
59.051	3000	23.6	At the end of the road turn sharp right	Beside restaurant	SE	70
59.052	100	23.8	Cross the main road and take the smaller road opposite	Via Ponte del Vescovo	E	66
59.053	170	23.9	At the T-junction turn left into piazza della Libertà and then immediately right	Via San Vitale	SE	65
59.054	600	24.5	At the T-junction with the main road, turn right on the main road	Via Foce, Mirteto sign on the left	SE	64

Way Point N°	Way Point Distance (metres)	Total Distance (kilometres)	Directions	Verification Point	Compass	Altitude (metres)
59.055	150	24.7	Turn left opposite the pharmacy	Direction Lavacchio , via Frangola	NE	63
59.056	70	24.7	Take the first turning to the right	Via Ortola	SE	67
59.057	200	24.9	Turn left and then right	Take the bridge over the stream	SE	61
59.058	160	25.1	At the T-junction turn left	River on the right	NE	53
59.059	90	25.2	Turn right over the bridge	Continue on via Ponte Vecchio	S	57
59.060	250	25.4	Bear right and immediately take the left fork	Via Palestro towards the centre of Massa	SE	61
59.061	500	25.9	At the end of the road turn right on via Cavour and immediately left	Piazza Gora	S	71
59.062	130	26.1	Beside the Duomo turn right on via Dante Alighieri	Towards piazza Aranci	SW	74
59.063	120	26.2	Immediately on entry to the piazza turn left	Trees and fountain on the right	SE	70
59.064	200	26.4	Keep to the left side of piazza Mercurio and turn left and immediately right on the steps - to avoid the steps continue straight ahead on via Mario Bigini and via Prado to Way Point #67	Via Piastronata	SE	71
59.065	180	26.6	Bear right on via Santa Chiara	Beside Chiesa della Modonna del Carmine, keep castle to the left	S	91

Way Point N°	Way Point Distance (metres)	Total Distance (kilometres)	Directions	Verification Point	Compass	Altitude (metres)
59.066	500	27.1	At the T-junction turn left and immediately right	Via del Bargello	SW	77
59.067	200	27.3	At the T-junction turn left and proceed with caution on the main road	Via Aurelia, SS1, pizzeria on the left	SE	61
59.068	2000	29.3	After passing the hospital on the left, bear left away from the via Aurelia	Via Carlo Sforza, No Entry	SE	50
59.069	700	30.0	At the end of the road turn left between buildings	Via Roma	NE	45
59.070	500	30.5	Turn right across the road and then left	Towards Prato	NE	69
59.071	160	30.6	Cross the footbridge and turn left	Via Bottaccio	E	75
59.072	170	30.8	At the end of the road turn right up the hill	Via Palatina, pass Fortezza Aghinolfi on the hilltop	SE	89
59.073	7000	37.8	At the crossroads with the SP9 in Ripa continue straight ahead	Via Foccola	SE	29
59.074	300	38.1	At the traffic lights take the second turning to the right	Via Pescarella across river	E	32
59.075	600	38.7	At the junction with the SP8, in Vallecchia, turn right and immediately left	Via Solaio	E	26
59.076	200	38.9	At the crossroads turn right	Via Valecchia Vecchia	S	34
59.077	200	39.1	Turn right	Via Pozzone	S	37
59.078	600	39.7	Cross the SP8 and bear left on the grass track beside the river	River on the right	S	23

Way Point N°	Way Point Distance (metres)	Total Distance (kilometres)	Directions	Verification Point	Compass	Altitude (metres)
59.079	800	40.5	Bear left and descend from the river-side track	Pass beside a Marble depot	SE	16
59.080	170	40.7	At the T-junction turn right	Via San Bartolomeo, towards the river	SW	15
59.081	200	40.9	Turn left	Via Torraccia , towards railway	SE	13
59.082	1000	41.9	Bear left	Via Marconi	E	10
59.083	200	42.1	Continue straight ahead. The Alternate Route joins from the right	Via Marconi	E	11
59.084	200	42.3	In piazza Matteotti bear slightly right into the centre of Pietrasanta	Pass the gladiator sculpture and continue straight ahead into the pedestrian zone on via Giuseppe Mazzini	SE	15
59.085	500	42.8	Arrive in the centre of Pietrasanta	Piazza Duomo		24

Church of Saint Augustine (15th century), Pietrasanta

The main route returns to the foothills, climbing above the vineyards. The Alternate Route, shorter by 5km, provides relief from the climbs and descents following the broad promenade beside the beach before turning inland to find the centre of Pietrasanta. The Alternate Route is easy going for cyclists and riders with the exception of the final entry to Pietrasanta when the traffic can be heavy.

Way Point N°	Way Point Distance (metres)	Total Distance (kilometres)	Directions	Verification Point	Compass	Altitude (metres)
1	0	0.0	At T-junction turn right on via del Parmignola	Towards Autostrada	SW	9
2	2000	2.0	At crossroads turn left towards the sea	Via della Repubblica	S	3
3	120	2.1	At junction with main road cross onto the seaward side and turn left on the road	Cross the waterways on the SP432, viale Cristoforo Colombo	SE	3
4	3200	5.3	After passing through Marina di Carrara, bear left to turn inland and remain on the main road	Vialle delle Pinete, coast road dead ends at a boat marina	SE	3
5	4000	9.3	At traffic lights turn right towards the sea	Via Casola	SW	2
6	200	9.5	Turn left, continue with sea on right	Pass through Marina di Massa and Forte dei Marmi	SE	0
7	11400	20.9	In Fiumetto/Marina di Pietrasanta after crossing bridge over waterway turn left towards Pietrasanta	via Appua	NE	6
8	1700	22.6	Straight ahead at the roundabout		NE	3
9	2000	24.6	At the T-junction turn left	SS1, via Aurelia Nord, direction Seravezza	NW	8
10	300	24.9	At the roundabout take the first exit under the railway	Via Vincenzo Santini, direction Pietrasant centre	N	7
11	300	25.2	At the T-junction turn right to join the main route at Way Point #83	Via Marconi		11

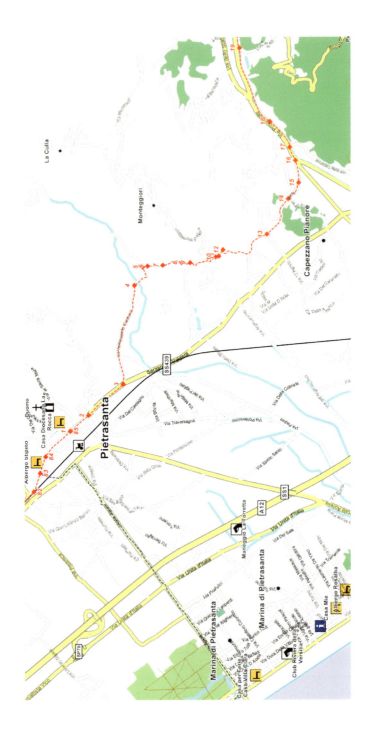

B&B/Hotel	Price
Riferimenti , 112, via Aurelia - 19034 ORTONOVO Tel: 0039 (0)187/66851	B2
Maurin Hotel, via Fiorino2, - 54033 AVENZA Tel: 0039 (0)585 859385	B2
PR Casa Villa Clara, via G. Carducci, 74, loc. Fiumetto - 55044 PIETRASANTA Tel: 0039 (0)584 20142 mdimieco@pcn.net	B2
PR Casa per Ferie la Versiliana, via G. Carducci, 1, Loc. Fiumetto - 55044 MARINA DE PIETRASANTA Tel: 0039 (0)584 20020 curiapo@scotty.masternet.it	B2
Stipino, 50, via Provinciale - 55044 PIETRASANTA Tel: 0039 (0)584 71448 stipino@tiscalinet.it	B3
Rosalba, via Tagliamento, 58 - Loc. Tonfano - 55044 MARINA DI PIETRASANTA Tel: 0039 (0)584 20117	B3
Casa Mia, via Manzoni, 23 - Loc. Tonfano - 55044 MARINA DI PIETRASANTA Tel: 0039 (0)584 20247 www.casamia.net info@hotelcasamia.net	B3
Religious Hostel	Price
Casa Di Accoglienza Caritas, v. Godola - 54100 MASSA Tel: 0039 (0)585792909 Mobile: 0039 339-5829566 buragino@tin.it	Donation
Convento Cappucini, 3, piazza San Francesco - 54100 MASSA Tel: 0039 (0)585 42181	Donation
Ostello Internazionale Turimar, 4, via Bondano Mare - MARINA DI MASSA Tel: 0039 (0)585 243282 info@ostelloturimar.com	B1
Casa Diocesana La Rocca, 10, via della Rocca - 55044 PIETRASANTA Tel: 0039 (0)584 793093/94 casarocca@tiscali.it	B1
Equestrian	
Azienda Agricola Le Mandrie Di Mazzei Walter Enrico, 11, via Del Lago - 55045 PIETRASANTA Tel: 0039 (0)584 752181	
Maneggio La Torretta, via Torretta - 55044 MARINA DI PIETRASANTA Tel: 0039 (0)584 23337	
Ass. Ippica " Club Riviera della Versilia" c/o Luciano Borzonasca, via Carducci - 55044 MARINA DI PIETRASANTA Tel: 0039 (0)584 745733	

Useful Contacts

Tourist/Information Offices

Ufficio Informazioni e di Accoglienza Turistica, via Donizetti, 14 - 55044 PIETRASANTA Tel: 0039 (0)58420331 marina@versilia.turismo.toscan

Internet Cafe

Caffè Al Teatro, piazza del Duomo - 55045 PIETRASANTA Tel· 0039 (0)584 793739

Doctor

Landi Dr. Paolo, 81, via Casone - 55045 PIETRASANTA Tel: 0039 (0)584 799288

Veterinary

Pelliccia Dr. Anacleto Michele. 102, via Provinciale Vallecchia - 55045 PIETRASANTA Tel: 0039 (0)584 71884

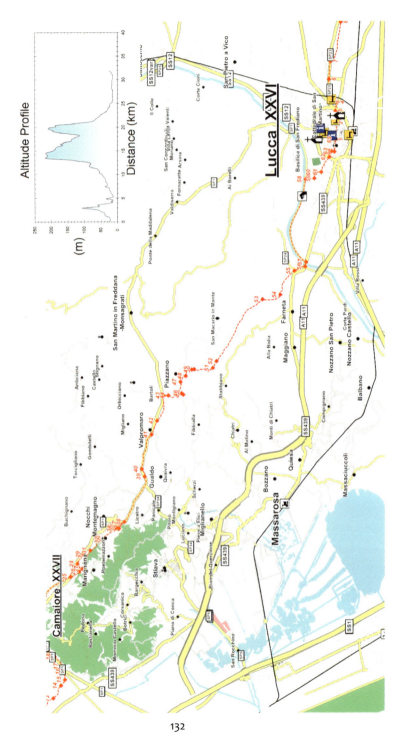

Pietrasanta to Lucca 32.0 km

Altitude Profile

Route Summary: the exit from Pietrasanta needs great care on the busy main road. The route then climbs and descends the ridge separating Valdicastello from Camaiore. After passing through Camaiore the route climbs on farm tracks parallel to the main road to Montemagno. The route then returns to the potentially busy road before returning to farm and forest tracks at Valpromaro. The route approaches Lucca along a riverside track before entering the walled city.

Distance from Canterbury: 1637km   **Distance to Rome:** 447km

Ascent: 485m   **Descent:** 485m

Way Point N°	Way Point Distance (metres)	Total Distance (kilometres)	Directions	Verification Point	Compass	Altitude (metres)
60.001	0	0.0	From piazza Duomo in Pietrasanta take via Giuseppe Garibaldi	Beside Duomo	SE	36
60.002	300	0.3	At the junction with the main road proceed straight ahead	SP439, via Garibaldi direction Lucca	SE	22
60.003	600	0.9	Opposite the cemetery turn left, to leave the main road on via Valdicastello Carducci	Sign post chiesa and VF map	E	22
60.004	1500	2.4	Turn right	Via Regnalla, road bends to the left	SE	54
60.005	400	2.8	Take the second right after the bend	Uphill	S	64
60.006	70	2.9	Take the right fork	Towards factory	S	70
60.007	200	3.1	Pass beside the factory and a quarry and take the footpath to the right through the woods	Towards the brow of the hill	S	93
60.008	300	3.4	Bear right on the footpath at the end of the woods and proceed directly downhill		S	81
60.009	150	3.5	Turn right and immediately left	Follow via Cannoreto between the houses	S	65
60.010	400	3.9	At the junction with the main road turn left and immediately right	Strada di Monteggiori	S	58
60.011	50	4.0	Bear left off the tarmac onto a small footpath		SE	54

Way Point N°	Way Point Distance (metres)	Total Distance (kilometres)	Directions	Verification Point	Compass	Altitude (metres)
60.012	100	4.1	Close beside farm buildings turn right on the track and quickly left	Through the trees	S	44
60.013	800	4.9	At the crossroads with via Aquarella continue straight ahead	Tarmac road	SE	15
60.014	600	5.5	Bear left	Via Dietro Monte	SE	19
60.015	200	5.7	At the junction turn left	Towards the main road	E	13
60.016	300	6.0	At the traffic lights continue straight ahead beside the main road SP1	Towards Camaiore	NE	15
60.017	190	6.2	Cross the main road and take the bridge over the canal and then turn left to follow the path on the canal-side	Via della Capanne	NE	16
60.018	400	6.6	Continue straight ahead beside the canal	Pass canal bridge on the left	E	20
60.019	1200	7.8	Continue straight ahead on the road beside the canal	Via Virgilio Boschi, pass football ground on the far side of the canal	E	35
60.020	600	8.4	Take the bridge to the left	Towards the centre of Camaiore (XXVII) on via Carignoni	NE	31
60.021	130	8.5	At the T-junction turn left	Via Guglielmo Oberdan	NW	32
60.022	80	8.6	Before reaching the petrol station turn right	Piazza 29 Maggio	NE	32
60.023	80	8.7	Take the second turning on the right	Via Vittorio Emanuele	SE	32
60.024	600	9.3	At the end of the road continue straight ahead across piazza Carlo Romboni	Via Roma, long tree lined road	SE	36

Way Point N°	Way Point Distance (metres)	Total Distance (kilometres)	Directions	Verification Point	Compass	Altitude (metres)
60.025	1300	10.6	At the junction with the SP1, cross over the main road and take the minor road over the bridge	Towards the sports ground "Tori"	SE	47
60.026	400	10.9	After passing the sports ground continue straight ahead on the footpath	Sports ground to the left	SE	56
60.027	180	11.1	At the T-junction with the tarmac road turn left	Frazione Marignana	NE	56
60.028	200	11.3	Just before reaching the canal turn right on the road	Keep canal to the left	SE	55
60.029	400	11.7	As the road enters a farm turn right on a track	Towards the woods	SW	60
60.030	110	11.8	Turn left on the footpath	Between the woods and a field	SE	65
60.031	200	12.0	Beside the farm buildings cross the tarmac driveway and bear right on the track	Beside the woods	SE	74
60.032	700	12.7	Turn left on the track	Towards the church	SE	82
60.033	80	12.8	At the T-junction with the road turn left and immediately right	Pass the church on the right	SE	82
60.034	500	13.3	Bear left onto track after passing large country house	Keep house on right	SE	120
60.035	60	13.4	Turn right onto the SP1 and proceed up the hill		SW	124
60.036	120	13.5	On the apex of the bend to the left, turn right up the stony track. **Note:** the track ahead may be overgrown, to avoid this remain on the main road until rejoining the main route on the entry Montemagno at Way Point #38	VF sign	E	136

Way Point N°	Way Point Distance (metres)	Total Distance (kilometres)	Directions	Verification Point	Compass	Altitude (metres)
60.037	200	13.7	Beside electricity substation continue straight up the narrow pathway		SE	168
60.038	200	13.9	Turn right onto the main road – SP1 and enter Montemagno	Bar and restaurant on left and right	SE	209
60.039	2000	15.9	Bear right off the main road onto the unmade road	Pass the restaurant "Purgatorio"	E	195
60.040	400	16.3	Return to the main road and bear right		E	189
60.041	1400	17.7	Bear right on a minor road into Valpromaro	VF sign	SE	161
60.042	500	18.2	After passing through the village turn right onto track running between houses	VF sign	E	139
60.043	1000	19.2	AT T-junction, turn right onto the minor road	VF sign, direction Piazzano	S	118
60.044	170	19.4	Turn right off the road onto a gravel track. **Note:** the off-road section is steep over broken ground. Cyclists should remain on the road to Way Point #46	VF sign	S	134
60.045	600	20.0	Turn left onto a minor road		NE	189
60.046	80	20.1	Right fork into Piazzano	VF sign	E	195
60.047	600	20.6	At the crossroads in centre of Piazzano turn right to proceed downhill	VF sign	SE	206
60.048	300	20.9	On leaving the village continue on the road		SE	190
60.049	300	21.3	Bear right on the track . **Note:** cyclists continue straight ahead on the road to the T-junction at Way Point #52		S	186
60.050	80	21.3	At the junction in the tracks continue straight ahead	Downhill	S	179

Way Point N°	Way Point Distance (metres)	Total Distance (kilometres)	Directions	Verification Point	Compass	Altitude (metres)
60.051	800	22.1	At the junction with the road turn left	At the bottom of the hill	SE	80
60.052	300	21.6	Continue straight ahead on via delle Gavine. Cyclists rejoin from the road on the left	VF sign	SE	69
60.053	2900	24.4	In Alla Bidia go straight ahead on via delle Gavine		S	32
60.054	800	25.3	On entering San Macario Piano turn left in the direction of the Church	VF sign, via della chiesa Ventitreesima	SE	21
60.055	1000	26.3	At crossroads continue straight over onto small road skirting the village (ignore No Entry sign)	VF sign, towards church	S	14
60.056	400	26.6	Turn left over the river bridge	VF sign, Ponte San Pietro	E	14
60.057	170	26.8	Turn left onto a small tarmac riverside road immediately after crossing the bridge	VF sign	E	15
60.058	3200	30.0	Fork right away from the riverside path	VF sign, No Entry ahead	S	16
60.059	300	30.3	At the crossroads turn left	VF sign, keep football ground on the right	E	14
60.060	200	30.5	At the end of the football pitch turn right onto a small tarmac road	VF sign	S	15
60.061	200	30.7	At T-junction with via dei Cavalletti turn left	VF sign, keep park on the right	SE	16
60.062	600	31.3	Continue straight ahead under the arch into walled centre of Lucca	VF sign	SE	17
60.063	200	31.5	At T-junction turn right on piazza Giuseppe Verdi	Grassed area to the right	S	18
60.064	110	31.6	Take the first left turn on via San Paolino		E	18
60.065	400	32.0	Arrive in piazza San Michele	Church to the left		25

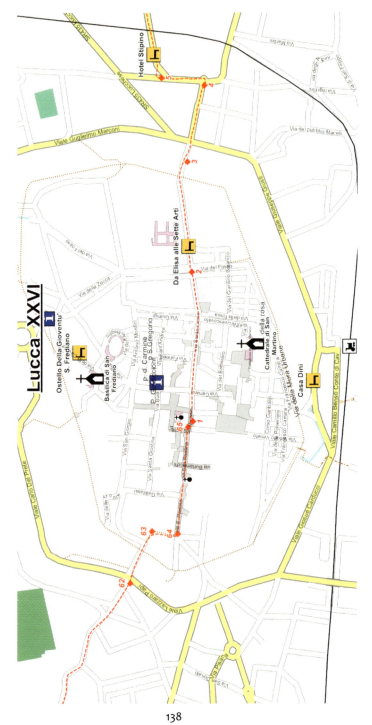

Lucca Town Map

Lucca XXVI

Hotel Stipino

Da Elisa alle Sette Arti

Ostello Della Gioventu
S. Frediano

Basilica di San
Frediano

p. d. Carmine
P. G. Anconi S.Gregorio

Cattedrale di San
Martino

Casa Dini

Hotel/B&B	Price
Frantoio Di Cannoreto, 120, via Cannoreto - 55040 CAPEZZANO PIANORE Tel: 0039 (0)584 914171 info@frantoiodicannoreto.it	B3
Il Monferrato, 3, str. Sottoripa - 14030 MONTEMAGNO Tel: 0039 (0)141 63162 manuela@monferratoturismo.it	B2
Da Elisa alle Sette Arti, 25, via Elisa - 55100 LUCCA Tel: 0039 (0)583 494539 info2@daelisa.com	B1
Hotel Stipino, 95, via romana - 55100 LUCCA Tel: 0039 (0)583 495077 info@hotelstipino.com	B3
Ostello della Gioventu' S. Frediano, via della Cavallerizza - 55100 LUCCA Tel: 0039 (0)583 469957	B2
Casa Dini, 195, viale Regina Margherita - 55100 LUCCA Tel: 0039 (0)583 467331 post@casadini.com	B2

Religious Hostel	Price
PR Da Elisa alle Sette Arti,25 via Elisa - 55100 LUCCA Tel: 0039 0583 494 539 info2@daelisa.com	B1

Camping	Price
Camping Versilia Mare, 175, Loc. Lido di Camaiore via Trieste - 55041 CAMAIORE Tel: 0039 (0)584 619862	B1

Equestrian

MANEGGIO LA VERSILIANA, Parco della Versiliana - 55041 LIDO DI CAMAIORE
Tel: 0039 (0)584 24280

Club Ippico Lucchese, via della Scogliera - 55100 LUCCA   Tel: 0039 (0)583 467302

Useful Contacts

Tourist Office

Ufficio Informazioni e di Accoglienza Turistica, 343, via Le Colombo - 55043 CAMAIORE
Tel: 0039 (0)584617397   lido@versilia.turismo.toscana.it
Azienda di Promozione Turistica, 2, piazza Guidiccioni - 55100 LUCCA
Tel: 0039 (0)5839199   1aptlucca@lucca.turismo.toscana.it
Ufficio Informazioni, V, piazza Santa Maria - 55100 LUCCA Tel: 0039 (0)583919931
influcca@lucca.turismo.it

Internet Cafe

The Netgate, 27/a, via dell'Anfiteatro - 55100 LUCCA

Doctor

Borelli Dr. Alberto, 74, via Pisana - 55100 LUCCA   Tel: 0039 (0)583 582656

Veterinary

Biagioni Gagliani Del Bono, via Luporini Gaetano - 55100 LUCCA
Tel: 0039 (0)583 580333

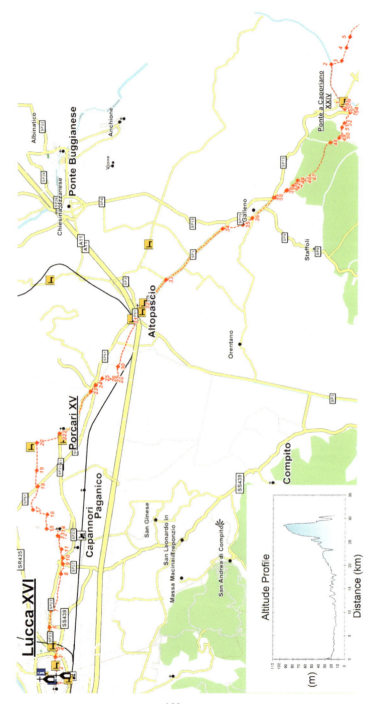

Albinatico

Anchione

Ponte Buggianese

Chiesina Uzzanese

Vione

Ponte a Cappiano
XXIV

Staffoli

Galleno

Altopascio

Orentano

Porcari XV

Capannori
Paganico

San Ginese

San Leonardo in
Treponzio

Massa Macinaia

Compito

San Andrea di Compito

Lucca XVI

Altitude Profile

Distance (km)

(m)

Route Summary: the route to Altopascio is substantially undertaken on tarmac, with sections on major roads. After Altopascio the route enters the low hills and woods of le Cerbaie on quiet pathways before descending to the valley of the Arno.

Distance from Canterbury: 1669km   **Distance to Rome:** 415km

Ascent: 210m   **Descent:** 211m

Way Point N°	Way Point Distance (metres)	Total Distance (kilometres)	Directions	Verification Point	Compass	Altitude (metres)
61.001	0	0.0	From Piazza San Michele take via Roma and then via San Croce	Keep church to the left	E	26
61.002	600	0.6	Proceed through gateway (Porta San Gervasio) and across the canal onto via Elisa	VF sign	E	20
61.003	400	1.0	After going through the last arch continue straight ahead across the main road onto viale Luigi Cadoma	VF sign, direction Pontedera	E	20
61.004	300	1.3	At T-junction turn left onto via di Tiglio	Towards the domed Santuario di S.Gemma	N	19
61.005	180	1.5	Turn right onto via Romana	Towards Hotel Stipino, pass Hotel Bernadino on the left	E	18
61.006	800	2.3	Continue straight ahead at roundabout	Petrol station on right	E	17
61.007	600	2.9	Turn right off the main road on via dei Paladini	VF sign, pass doorway with crucifix above on your left	E	17
61.008	1600	4.5	At junction bear right onto minor road via Vecchia Romana	VF sign, pass church of San Michele on the left	E	18
61.009	500	5.0	Continue straight ahead at crossroads with SP27	VF sign	E	17
61.010	300	5.3	At crossroads with SP23 continue straight over into small road	VF sign, enter Capannori	E	16

Lucca to Ponte a Cappiano 30.6 km

141

Way Point N°	Way Point Distance (metres)	Total Distance (kilometres)	Directions	Verification Point	Compass	Altitude (metres)
61.011	300	5.6	After passing cemetery on the right, turn left in front of a shrine	VF sign	E	15
61.012	500	6.1	Beside the church of San Rocco turn left		N	17
61.013	90	6.2	At the end of the road turn right	Via Romana	E	17
61.014	200	6.4	At the crossroads turn left. **Note:** the route can be reduced by approximately 2km by proceeding carefully straight ahead on the SP23 to Way Point #21 in Pocari (XXV)	Via del Popolo, church od San Quirico ahead at the junction	N	16
61.015	400	6.8	At the T-junction turn right	Via dei Colombini	E	16
61.016	500	7.3	Turn left and remain on the road as it turns right and then left	Via del Fontana, pass sports ground on the left	N	13
61.017	600	7.9	At the T-junction turn right	Via G. Pieraccini	E	15
61.018	1000	8.9	At the junction with the main road, SP61, turn left and immediately right	Over bridge, towards industrial buildings	E	16
61.019	600	9.5	Turn right and then left on the road	Via Ciarpi	E	14
61.020	1100	10.6	Just after crossing the stream turn right	Via Pacconi	S	16
61.021	900	11.5	At the T-junction turn left	Via Capannori, towards post office	E	16
61.022	120	11.6	In Porcari (XXV) turn right at the traffic lights	VF sign, via Roma, church on the left immediately following turn	SE	18
61.023	2300	13.9	Turn right off the main road onto a small gravel track, towards industrial area	VF sign	SE	14
61.024	300	14.2	At junction with a major road cross straight over onto another smaller road via Pistoresi-Tappo-Turchetto	VF sign, pass beside and behind large supermarket	SE	16

Way Point N°	Way Point Distance (metres)	Total Distance (kilometres)	Directions	Verification Point	Compass	Altitude (metres)
61.025	300	14.5	Turn right onto the track towards trees	Turn away from a large factory building on left	S	22
61.026	300	14.8	Continue straight ahead onto a gravel track	VF sign	S	21
61.027	180	15.0	Continue straight ahead towards church and wall of cemetery on left	VF sign	S	22
61.028	110	15.1	Turn left at the end of the wall	VF sign	SE	22
61.029	40	15.1	After turning left into a quadrangle in front of the church follow road keeping the church to your left	Via Chiesa	E	22
61.030	500	15.6	At crossroads proceed straight ahead into Badia Pozzeveri on via Catalani	VF sign, small shrine to the right	E	24
61.031	1900	17.5	At T-junction with the SP3 turn right to go under the road bridge	VF sign, towards the bell-tower in Altopascio	SE	20
61.032	700	18.2	Bear right on via cavour, direction Fucecchio	VF sign, keep small building with arched portico to the left	SE	20
61.033	1400	19.6	At roundabout continue straight ahead on via Romana, SP3, direction Fucecchio	VF signs, large commercial buildings on left	SE	23
61.034	3000	22.6	Fork right onto the unmade road	The ancient via Franchigena	S	34
61.035	800	23.4	Cross the small bridge and continue straight ahead		SE	20
61.036	400	23.8	Arrive in Galleno and continue straight ahead on the main road	Via Romana Lucchese, direction Fucecchio	SE	35

Lucca to Ponte a Cappiano 30.6 km

143

Way Point N°	Way Point Distance (metres)	Total Distance (kilometres)	Directions	Verification Point	Compass	Altitude (metres)
61.037	1200	25.0	Bear right at the major road junction and shortly after crossing a bridge turn right on the unmade road	Direction Fucecchio at the junction	S	38
61.038	80	25.1	Take the left fork		SE	38
61.039	500	25.6	Cross over the driveway and continue straight ahead	Equestrian centre on the right	S	52
61.040	50	25.6	Keep left on the track into the woods	Downhill	SE	51
61.041	190	25.8	At the junction with the road turn right		SE	41
61.042	90	25.9	Shortly after passing the buildings on the left join a white road and continue straight ahead		SE	39
61.043	120	26.1	Turn left at the next junction	In the woods	SE	42
61.044	170	26.2	Continue straight ahead	Pond on the left	S	50
61.045	200	26.4	At the first junction after a short climb continue straight ahead		S	65
61.046	50	26.5	At the next junction bear left		SE	67
61.047	200	26.7	Join a broader track and bear slightly left	Pass horse track below on the left	SE	71
61.048	1600	28.3	At T-junction with a busy tarmac road and bear right	Via Poggiadorno, SP 61	SE	89

Way Point N°	Way Point Distance (metres)	Total Distance (kilometres)	Directions	Verification Point	Compass	Altitude (metres)
61.049	400	28.7	Turn left off the main road at the start of a right hand bend. **Note:** caution a narrow busy road, keep to the right side	Via di Poggio Adorno, direction Santa Croce	SE	92
61.050	170	28.8	After curve to the left, turn sharp left on the track downhill into the woods	VF sign	E	83
61.051	300	29.1	Take the right fork on the track	Pond on the right	SE	48
61.052	190	29.3	Bear right on the road	via De Medici	SE	42
61.053	500	29.8	Cross the busy SP11 and continue straight ahead		SE	21
61.054	90	29.9	Turn sharp left up the hill	Unmade road	N	23
61.055	300	30.2	Cross the open space beside the vineyard and continue down the hill on the track	Towards the river	NE	38
61.056	180	30.4	Bear right on the road	Enter Ponte a Cappiano (XXIV)	SE	31
61.057	110	30.5	Cross piazza A. Donnini and continue straight ahead	Towards the covered bridge	SE	20
61.058	70	30.6	Arrive in the centre of Ponte a Cappiano	Beside the hostel on the old covered bridge		16

B&B/Hotel	Price
Da Rino, via Pacini, 23/a 55016 PORCARI Tel: 0039 (0)583 299377	B2
Corallo, Via Romana Ovest, 189, Fraz. Rughi 55016 PORCARI Tel: 0039 (0)583 29160	B2
Da Paola, via F. Romea, 24 55010 ALTOPASCIO Tel: 0039 (0)584 276453	B2
PR Barbieri Amelia, 55, via Firenze 55010 ALTOPASCIO Tel: 0039 (0)583 25265	B2
PR Farm Sibolla info@agriturismosibolla.it Loc. Ferranti, 20 Spianate 55010 ALTOPASCIO Tel: 0039 (0) 583 269181 info@agriturismosibolla.it	B2
La Vecchiaccia, 2, v. Mammianese - 55010 ALTOPASCIO Tel: 0039 (0)583 286648	B2
Albergo da Paola, 24, v. Romea - 55011 ALTOPASCIO Tel: 0039 (0)583 276453	B2

Hostel	Price
Foresteria degli Ospitalieri, Via Casali - 55011 ALTOPASCIO Tel: 0039 (0)583 216280/0583 216525 turismo@comune.altopascio.lu.it	Donation

Religious Hostel	Price
PR Ostello Ponte de' Medici, viale Colombo, 237 - 50054 PONTE A CAPPIANO Tel: 0039 (0)571 297831 pontemedici@ponteverde.it	B1
PR Santa Maria a Monte (nr Ponte a Cappiano)5, Il Casolare di Bonci via Bonci, Loc. Cerretti 56020 S. MARIA A MONTE Tel: 0039 (0)5 87473131 info@casolaredibonci.it	B2

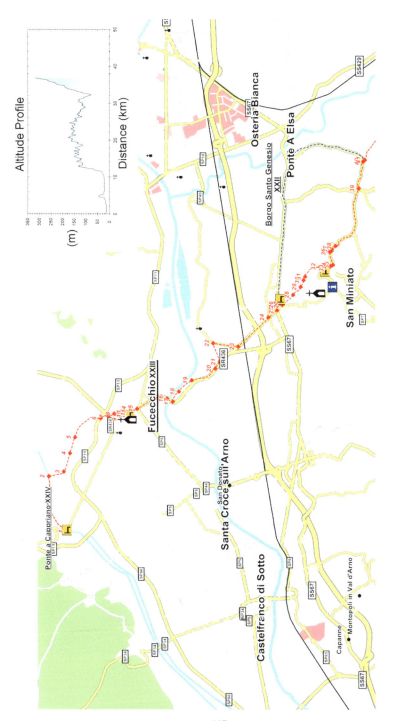

Altitude Profile

Ponte a Cappriano to Gambassi Terme 36.9 km

Ponte a Cappriano XXIV

Fucecchio XXII

San Donato

Santa Croce sull'Arno

Castelfranco di Sotto

Capanne

Montopoli in Val d'Arno

San Miniato

Borgo Santo Genesio XXII

Ponte A Elsa

Osteria Bianca

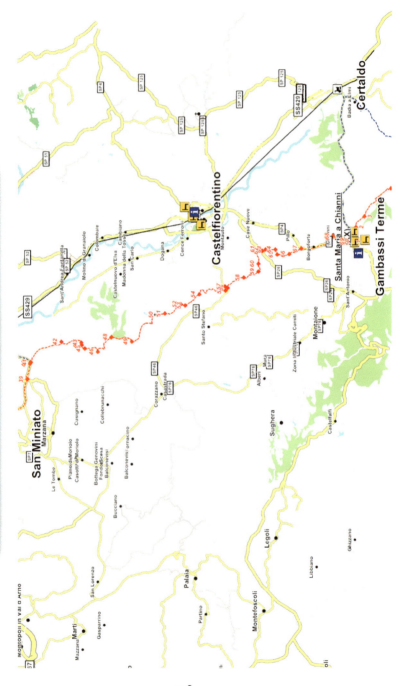

Route Summary: the route initially alternates between canal-side tracks and highways before reaching the historic hilltop town of San Miniato. From there the route follows a mix of country roads and broad tracks over the rolling Tuscan hills

Distance from Canterbury: 1699km   **Distance to Rome:** 384km

Ascent: 748m   **Descent:** 449m

Way Point N°	Way Point Distance (metres)	Total Distance (kilometres)	Directions	Verification Point	Compass	Altitude (metres)
62.001	0	0.0	Cross the bridge and turn left down the steps into the car park and continue along the banks of the canal. **Note:** riders should continue to the end of the bridge and then turn sharp left	Canal immediately to the left	E	17
62.002	2000	2.0	Shortly after the canal begins to bend to the left, turn right from the canal-side onto another embankment	Right angle to canal	S	13
62.003	400	2.4	Cross the waterway and turn left - riders can continue on the left bank to the next Way Point where they can cross on a more substantial bridge	Waterway on the left	E	12
62.004	500	2.9	Cross the road and continue straight ahead on the embankment		E	15
62.005	400	3.3	Cross a second road and continue straight ahead on the embankment	Pass industrial complex on the right	SE	16
62.006	1100	4.4	Cross the SP11 and continue on the small road opposite	No Entry, via Ponte del Rio, pass roundabout on the left	S	19
62.007	200	4.6	Cross viale Napoleone Buonaparte and continue straight ahead	Via Sotto la Valle	S	21

149

Way Point N°	Way Point Distance (metres)	Total Distance (kilometres)	Directions	Verification Point	Compass	Altitude (metres)
62.008	180	4.8	Take the next turning to the right	Via Sant'Antonio	SW	22
62.009	200	5.0	At the T-junction turn left into the centre of Fucecchio	Via Castruccio	SE	45
62.010	180	5.2	Take the next turning to the right	After passing piazza S Lavagnini on the left	S	46
62.011	50	5.2	Continue straight ahead across piazza Garibaldi		S	45
62.012	90	5.3	Turn left	Pass church on the left	E	39
62.013	70	5.4	Cross piazza Vittorio Veneto and bear right down the hill	Via del Cassero	E	44
62.014	100	5.5	In the next square turn right	Via Donateschi	S	41
62.015	200	5.7	Continue straight ahead across piazza G. Montanelli	Take via Nazario Sauro, via Roma and viale Antonio Gramasci in the direction of San Miniato, SR436	S	27
62.016	1000	6.7	Take the road bridge over the river Arno	**Note:** caution narrow pavements on the bridge	SW	18
62.017	170	6.8	At the end of the bridge, turn sharp left and then right through the industrial area	Trees and river on the left	SE	21
62.018	300	7.1	Continue straight ahead on the footpath	On the embankment	SE	20
62.019	400	7.5	Bear right on the track	Away from the river	SE	21
62.020	800	8.3	Continue straight ahead between the embankment and the busy road		SE	21
62.021	200	8.5	Turn left on the track	Into the fields, pass garden allotments on the right	E	20

Way Point N°	Way Point Distance (metres)	Total Distance (kilometres)	Directions	Verification Point	Compass	Altitude (metres)
62.022	500	9.0	At the T-junction with a road turn right back towards the main road	Between houses, via Asmara	S	21
62.023	700	9.7	At crossroads turn left	Via Guglielmo Marconi, under the railway bridge	SE	22
62.024	1200	10.9	At the roundabout continue straight ahead	Tree lined, via Guglielmo Marconi, pass pharmacy on the right	SE	25
62.025	300	11.2	At the crossroads with the SS67 turn left	Pass Tabacchi on the left	E	28
62.026	140	11.4	Turn right on the small road - to visit the Sigeric location – Borgo Santo Genesio (XXII) - continue straight ahead on the Alternate Route on the main road	Pass the church on your left	S	28
62.027	140	11.5	Bear left on the embankment		SE	30
62.028	400	11.9	Bear right on the road	Via Pozzo	SE	33
62.029	300	12.2	At the end of via Pozzo continue straight ahead on the footpath		SE	56
62.030	200	12.4	Bear right on the road	Downhill	E	68
62.031	120	12.5	At the junction with the main road turn right uphill	Via Fontevivo, towards the centre of the high town	SE	66
62.032	600	13.1	Bear left onto viale Giacomo Matteotti	Enter the historic centre	S	109
62.033	200	13.3	Bear left onto via San Francesco	Beside the convent	SE	138
62.034	100	13.4	Bear left in Piazza Buonparte	Statue of Leopold II	SE	120

Way Point N°	Way Point Distance (metres)	Total Distance (kilometres)	Directions	Verification Point	Compass	Altitude (metres)
62.035	80	13.5	Continue straight ahead after leaving piazza Buonparte	via Paolo Maioli	E	110
62.036	300	13.8	Turn right on via Vicolo Borghizzi and almost immediately turn left through an archway. **Note:** the pathway ahead involves a flight of steps - horse and bike riders are advised to remain on the road (direction Calenzano) for the descent to Way Point #38	VF sign	SE	119
62.037	150	14.0	Turn right down a small brick passage separated by metal balustrades	VF sign	SE	122
62.038	130	14.1	At T junction turn right - riders rejoin from the left	Direction Calenzano	SE	113
62.039	2100	16.2	Fork left, via Castelfiorentino	VF sign, church on right	E	150
62.040	700	16.9	Fork right downhill direction Castelfiorentino	VF sign	SE	148
62.041	70	17.0	At junction turn right - Alternate Route rejoins from the left	VF sign	SE	145
62.042	2100	19.1	Following a bend to the left, turn sharp right onto a gravel track	VF sign	S	120
62.043	1100	20.2	Fork right	VF sign	W	132
62.044	100	20.3	Fork left up the hill towards trees	VF sign	SW	137
62.045	300	20.6	At T-junction turn left	VF sign	S	162
62.046	800	21.4	Turn sharp left up the hill	VF sign	SE	155
62.047	1300	22.7	Turn left with house directly on right	VF sign	SE	157
62.048	40	22.7	Fork right onto on via di Meleto, with the farmhouse on right	VF sign	S	159
62.049	1200	23.9	Turn onto the furthest left of the tracks via della Poggiarella	VF sign	SE	152

Way Point N°	Way Point Distance (metres)	Total Distance (kilometres)	Directions	Verification Point	Compass	Altitude (metres)
62.050	1900	25.8	At crossroads in Coiano (XXI) continue straight ahead, via Coianese	VF sign	S	172
62.051	300	26.1	Continue straight ahead on a slightly wider gravel track	VF sign	SE	148
62.052	800	26.9	Fork right down the hill	VF sign	S	146
62.053	200	27.1	Fork left up the hill	VF sign	SE	132
62.054	800	27.9	Continue straight ahead	VF sign	S	138
62.055	1500	29.4	At T-junction turn left between two houses	VF sign	SE	110
62.056	200	29.6	Turn left onto the road	VF sign	NE	103
62.057	140	29.8	Turn sharp right onto track	VF sign	SE	104
62.058	900	30.6	After passing a house continue straight ahead onto the grass track	VF sign	S	115
62.059	700	31.4	At T-junction turn left	VF sign	E	125
62.060	300	31.6	Fork right	VF sign	E	117
62.061	600	32.3	Turn right at elevated T-junction with road, SP26, descend ramp and join the main road	VF sign	SW	86
62.062	200	32.5	Turn left onto unmade road	VF sign	SE	83
62.063	150	32.6	Bear right after passing house on right	VF sign	S	78

Way Point N°	Way Point Distance (metres)	Total Distance (kilometres)	Directions	Verification Point	Compass	Altitude (metres)
62.064	400	33.0	At T-junction turn right with house on left	VF sign	SW	115
62.065	200	33.2	Fork left up the hill	Red and white sign	S	119
62.066	500	33.7	A track bears off to right but continue straight ahead	VF sign	S	152
62.067	600	34.3	At T-junction, turn right onto the SP4	VF sign, shrine just before the junction on the left	S	183
62.068	1600	35.9	Santa Maria a Chianni (XX) is to the left. To follow the route to Gambassi Terme continue uphill on the main road bearing right	VF sign	S	253
62.069	800	36.7	At traffic lights, fork left direction Gambassi	VF sign	S	295
62.070	200	36.9	Arrive in Gambassi Terme	Beside the church at the junction of via Volterrana Nord and via Icilio Franchi		315

(Side tab: Ponte a Cappriano to Gambassi Terme 36.9 km)

Useful Contacts

Tourist/Information Offices

Ufficio Informazioni, P.zza del Popolo - 56027 CASTELFIORENTINO
Tel: 0039 (0)571 42745

Ufficio Informazioni Turistiche, 8, piazza Roma - 50050 GAMBASSI TERME
Tel: 0039 (0)571 639192 www.firenzeturismo.it info@comune.gambassi-terme.fi.it

The Alternate Route bypasses the historic centre of San Miniato to allow a visit to the location of Borgo Santo Genesio (Sigeric location XXII). The route initially follows the busy road from San Miniato Basso towards Ponte a Elsa before climbing back to rejoin the main route near Calenzano

Way Point N°	Way Point Distance (metres)	Total Distance (kilometres)	Directions	Verification Point	Compass	Altitude (metres)
1	0	0.0	Continue straight ahead on SP40	Direction Ponte a Elsa	E	28
2	3800	3.8	At the entry to Ponte a Elsa bear right on via Nazionale - the chapel of San Genesio and an archaelogical dig is to the left		E	32
3	170	4.0	Turn right on via Poggio a Pino		S	34
4	2300	6.3	Turn left to rejoin main route at Way Point #41			145

B&B/Hotel	Price
La Pieve, 2, via O. Bacci - 50051 CASTELFIORENTINO Tel: 0039 (0)571 629203 www.lapievedipucci.it albergo@lapievedipucci.it	B3
Lami, 82, p.zza Gramsci - 50051 CASTELFIORENTINO Tel: 0039 (0)57164076 www.albergolami.it info@albergolami.it	B3
PR Hotel Le Torri, 3, via Volterrana - 50050 GAMBASSI TERME Tel: 0039 (0)571 638188 valentina.comparini@inwind.it	B2
Albergo Osteria L'Acquolina, Via Volterrana 3 - 50050 GAMBASSI TERME Tel: 0039 (0)571 638188 12	B3

Youth Hostel	Price
Ostello Castelfiorentino, 26, viale Roosevelt - 50051 CASTELFIORENTINO Tel: 0039 (0)571 64002 hostelcast@interfree.it	B2

Religious Hostel	Price
Abbazia di San Salvatore, 1, piazza Garibaldi - 50054 FUCECCHIO Tel: 0039 (0)571 20025	Donation
Misericordia Di San Miniato Basso, 9, piazza Vincenzo Cuoco 56028 SAN MINIATO Tel: 0039 (0)571 419455 Mobile: 0039 339 8723682 mario.giugni@libero.it www.misericordiasanminiatobasso.org	Donation
PR Seminary S Francesco, 1, piazza San Francesco - 56028 SAN MINIATO Tel: 0039 (0)571 401013 info@aolmaia.net	B1
Sala parrochiale 50050 - GAMBASSI TERME Tel: 0039 (0)571 638 208 Contact: don Evaristo Masini	Donation

Altitude Profile

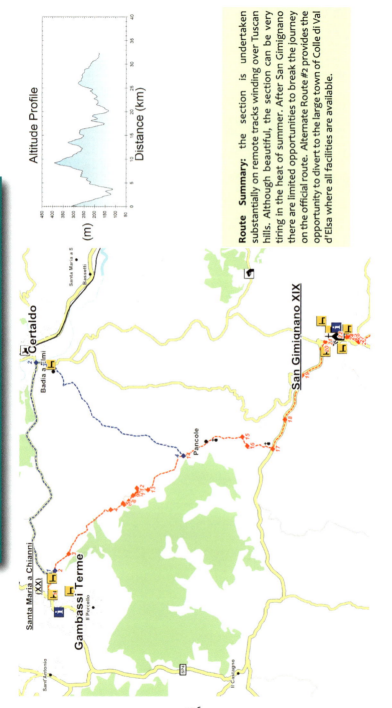

Route Summary: the section is undertaken substantially on remote tracks winding over Tuscan hills. Although beautiful, the section can be very tiring in the heat of summer. After San Gimignano there are limited opportunities to break the journey on the official route. Alternate Route #2 provides the opportunity to divert to the large town of Colle di Val d'Elsa where all facilities are available.

San Gimignano XIX

Poggibonsi

Colle di Val d'Elsa

Gracciano d'Elsa XVII

Moli d'Aiano XVIII

Gambassi Terme to Gracciano d'Elsa 32.5 km

157

Gambassi Terme to Gracciano d'Elsa 32.5 km

Way Point N°	Way Point Distance (metres)	Total Distance (kilometres)	Directions	Verification Point	Compass	Altitude (metres)
63.001	0	0.0	From the church in Gambassi Terme at the junction of via Volterrana Nord and via Icilio Franchi, take via Icilio Franchi	VF sign	E	317
63.002	800	0.8	Take right fork onto a smaller road. **Note:** the route ahead is passable and generally pleasant for all groups, however there are sections where cyclists will be challenged by steep off-road climbs. Cyclists may want to remain on the road and bear left to follow the Alternate Route to Pancole via the Elsa valley	VF sign	SE	267
63.003	700	1.5	Take left fork	VF sign	SE	209
63.004	2000	3.5	Continue ahead on the left track down the hill	VF sign	SE	149
63.005	400	3.9	Fork right up the hill	VF sign	SW	113
63.006	50	4.0	Bear left through a gap in the fence, continue keeping fence on left	VF sign	SE	112
63.007	120	4.1	Bear left uphill away from the field and into the trees	VF sign	SE	119
63.008	70	4.1	Turn right at the top of the track	VF sign, trees on the right	SE	126
63.009	200	4.3	Track comes out into another field, turn right keeping fence to left	Turn up the hill	SE	151

Way Point N°	Way Point Distance (metres)	Total Distance (kilometres)	Directions	Verification Point	Compass	Altitude (metres)
63.010	110	4.5	Bear left up the hill	VF sign (large white arrow on the tree)	SE	166
63.011	70	4.5	Directly in front of a farmhouse turn left onto a gravel track	Proceeding up the hill	E	178
63.012	150	4.7	T-junction in track turn right up the hill	VF sign	S	187
63.013	300	5.0	Fork left	VF sign, via San Piero	SE	225
63.014	1800	6.8	At T-junction with a tarmac road (SP1) turn right up the hill - Alternate Route rejoins from the left	VF sign, pass through Pancole	S	267
63.015	2100	8.9	Turn right onto the track. **Note:** to reduce overall distance by 1km and distance on the main road, continue on the minor road and rejoin the official route at the T-junction Way Point #18	VF sign to the right	SW	308
63.016	300	9.2	Take the left fork	Beside the woods	S	346
63.017	900	10.1	At the junction with the main road turn left	Pass Pieve di Cellole on the left	SE	364
63.018	900	11.0	Continue straight ahead down the hill	Direction San Gimignano	SE	323
63.019	1400	12.4	At roundabout bear right direction San Gimignano centre	Via Martiri di Citerna	SE	262

Way Point N°	Way Point Distance (metres)	Total Distance (kilometres)	Directions	Verification Point	Compass	Altitude (metres)
63.020	1100	13.5	At fork bear right up the hill	Via Nord Cannicci	SE	278
63.021	200	13.7	At intersection with main road go ahead via the underpass to enter San Gimignano (XIX) through Port San Matteo		SE	305
63.022	300	14.0	Continue straight across piazza Duomo	Long flight of steps and the tourist offices to the right	S	329
63.023	30	14.0	In piazza Cisterna, continue straight ahead down a narrow passage way, via San Giovanni	VF sign and passage way marked no entry for cars	S	329
63.024	300	14.3	After passing underneath the last archway bear left . **Note:** cyclists and riders should follow the road ahead - viale Romana - to avoid a flight of steps and rejoin at Way Point #27	Porto San Giovanni	S	305
63.025	90	14.4	Turn left and take the steps	Towards the stopping place for buses	S	299
63.026	90	14.5	Turn right	Via Vaccanella	SW	294
63.027	150	14.6	At a mini roundabout take the exit direction Montauto	Red-and-white VF sign painted on the signpost	SW	281

Way Point N°	Way Point Distance (metres)	Total Distance (kilometres)	Directions	Verification Point	Compass	Altitude (metres)
63.028	90	14.7	Turn left direction Santa Lucia	VF sign	SE	273
63.029	2100	16.8	Shortly after passing the sports field on the left, turn right on an unmade road	**Note:** for the Alternate Route via Colle di Val d'Elsa continue straight ahead on the road. Cyclists are advised to take this route to avoid a number of water crossings	SW	268
63.030	60	16.9	Turn right	Near to shed	S	269
63.031	200	17.1	Bear right on the white road	Downhill	S	249
63.032	1000	18.1	Beside the house in the valley bottom turn left and ford the stream		SW	153
63.033	100	18.2	Continue straight ahead across the field towards the house		SW	158
63.034	130	18.3	Turn right and skirt the house		SW	173
63.035	110	18.4	Turn right on the access road to the house	Leave the house directly behind	S	180
63.036	400	18.8	At the junction at the top of the ridge turn left		SE	218
63.037	60	18.9	Take the track to the right	Downhill	S	209
63.038	300	19.2	At the bottom of the hill cross the stream and continue straight ahead		SE	183

Way Point Nº	Way Point Distance (metres)	Total Distance (kilometres)	Directions	Verification Point	Compass	Altitude (metres)
63.039	400	19.6	Beside the house turn right and then left to skirt the house	Villa della Torraccia di Chiusi	SE	212
63.040	200	19.8	At the intersection with the entrance to the house turn right on the road	Downhill	SE	210
63.041	500	20.3	In the hamlet of Aiano turn right	Near to farm building	SW	146
63.042	200	20.5	Take the left fork	Lake below on the right	S	145
63.043	300	20.8	Continue straight ahead across the ford		SW	133
63.044	100	20.9	Take the left fork		SE	134
63.045	300	21.2	Take the right fork	Proceed along the ridge top	S	151
63.046	1600	22.8	At the road junction continue straight ahead		SE	185
63.047	600	23.4	At the junction with the main road turn left and then turn right to leave the road on the apex of the next bend – direction Bagnoli	SS68	SE	202
63.048	200	23.6	Take the next turning to the right		S	200
63.049	900	24.5	After a section of an old paved road bear right		S	206
63.050	100	24.6	Turn right		SW	213
63.051	150	24.7	At the T-junction turn left	Uphill	S	208
63.052	70	24.8	Cross the road and bear right	Direction Badia a Coneo	S	214

Way Point N°	Way Point Distance (metres)	Total Distance (kilometres)	Directions	Verification Point	Compass	Altitude (metres)
63.053	190	25.0	Pass to the right of the abbey and continue straight ahead on the unmade road		S	223
63.054	50	25.0	Take the old paved road to the right	Downhill	SW	224
63.055	700	25.7	Emerge from the woods and skirt the house before turning left	Keep the house on the left	SE	247
63.056	300	26.0	At the T-junction at the end of the field turn left and then right	Into the woods	SE	266
63.057	150	26.2	Take the right fork		SE	273
63.058	140	26.3	At the crossroads continue straight ahead		SE	278
63.059	300	26.6	At the T-junction turn left on the unmade road		E	276
63.060	180	26.8	At the crossroads continue straight ahead		SE	276
63.061	500	27.3	At the T-junction turn left towards the village	San Donato	E	265
63.062	300	27.6	Take the left fork		NE	260
63.063	150	27.8	At the T-junction with the main road (SP27) turn sharp right	Take crossing to pavement on the left side of the road	S	257
63.064	180	27.9	Turn left into Quartaia	Via degli Aragonesi , VF sign	E	259
63.065	150	28.1	Turn right	Via della Concordia	S	261

Way Point N°	Way Point Distance (metres)	Total Distance (kilometres)	Directions	Verification Point	Compass	Altitude (metres)
63.066	130	28.2	At the T-junction turn left on the unmade road	Exit village	NE	260
63.067	1000	29.2	Pass through the farm and continue on the unmade road	Road bears right shortly after leaving the farm and passes beside water source	SE	251
63.068	400	29.6	At the T-junction at the foot of the hill turn left and continue straight ahead	Beside the woods	E	226
63.069	400	30.0	Turn left on the track	Just before reaching the bridge	E	219
63.070	80	30.1	Take the right fork		NE	219
63.071	500	30.6	Take the right fork		NE	213
63.072	200	30.8	Bear right on the white road	Towards Molino le Vene	NE	210
63.073	900	31.7	Join a tarmac road and bear right	Village of Onci to the left	E	180
63.074	70	31.8	Turn left on the road	Beside the canal	NE	178
63.075	500	32.3	After crossing the waterway bear right and immediately left	Via Nino Bixio	E	177
63.076	190	32.5	Arrive in the centre of Gracciano d'Elsa	At the crossroads between via Fratelli Bandiera and via Nino Bixio		180

Useful Contacts

Tourist/Information Offices

Ufficio Informazioni, 1, piazza Duomo - 53037 SAN GIMIGNANO
Tel: 0039 (0)577940008   www.sangimignano.com prolocsg@tin.it

Ufficio Informazioni, 43, via Campana - 53034 COLLE DI VAL D'ELSA
Tel: 0039 (0)577922791 www.siena.turismo.toscana.it

Doctor

Bocci Dr. Stefania Studio Medico, 12, via dei Fossi - 53034 COLLE DI VAL D'ELSA
Tel: 0039 (0)577 922560

Veterinary

Clinica Veterinaria, 13, viale dei Mille - 53034 COLLE DI VAL D'ELSA
Tel: 0039 (0)577 929919

Alternate Route #1 via Badia a Cerrato allows cyclists to bypass some strenuous off-road climbs by descending into the Val d'Elsa and then returning to Pancole on provincial roads. 6.3km

Way Point N°	Way Point Distance (metres)	Total Distance (kilometres)	Directions	Verification Point	Compass	Altitude (metres)
1	00	0.0	Remain on the SP64	Direction Certaldo	E	267
2	5800	6.8	In Badia a Cerreto shortly before reaching the Elsa river bridge turn right on the SP1	Direction Pancole	S	66
3	400	7.2	In Badia a Elmi take the right fork on the SP1		SW	6934
4	5200	12.4	At the top of the hill bear left to join the main route at Way Point #14	Entry to Pancole		268

Alternate Route #2 via Colle Val d'Elsa provides the opportunity to find accommodation in Colle di Val d'Elsa. It progresses to the town on minor roads and tracks, but returns to the official route on more major roads that can be be extremely busy. 12.4km

Way Point N°	Way Point Distance (metres)	Total Distance (kilometres)	Directions	Verification Point	Compass	Altitude (metres)
1	0	0.0	Continue straight ahead		E	268
2	190	0.2	At a fork in the road take right fork	VF sign	E	267
3	300	0.5	Bear left on a small unmade road	VF sign and shrine on the corner	E	262
4	400	0.9	After passing two houses, on the left and right, continue straight ahead down the hill		E	237
5	600	1.5	At the T-junction in track, turn left	VF arrow on tree and houses directly on left	E	178
6	600	2.1	At crossroads with a small tarmac road turn left on the road	VF Sign	N	115
7	300	2.4	At T-junction with a major road (SP1) turn right	VF sign	E	120
8	40	2.4	Take the right fork direction Volterra	SP36, pass bar on the left	E	119
9	500	2.9	Shortly after first right hand bend turn left onto a track	VF Sign	SE	107

Way Point N°	Way Point Distance (metres)	Total Distance (kilometres)	Directions	Verification Point	Compass	Altitude (metres)
10	140	3.1	At a junction with a number of tracks continue straight ahead on the narrowest - the third track from the left		E	113
11	500	3.6	The small track joins a larger track, bear right towards the crest of the hill between vines		SE	150
12	500	4.1	Take right fork up the hill		SE	185
13	200	4.3	At T-junction in Bibbiano turn right	VF Sign	SW	205
14	200	4.5	Turn left onto the small gravel track	VF Sign	E	214
15	1400	5.9	At the top of the hill, T-junction, turn left downhill and away from the house		SE	209
16	2100	8.0	Track comes out onto a tarmac road, bear right	Main road directly in front	SE	148
17	60	8.0	At the T-junction with main road turn right, SS68	VF sign, also large crash barrier directly in front	SW	134
18	900	8.9	At roundabout continue straight ahead towards the centre of Colle di Val d'Elsa		S	142
19	120	9.1	Turn left direction Siena	VF Sign	SE	143
20	110	9.2	Continue straight ahead towards the centre		S	142
21	90	9.3	Arrive in the centre of Colle di Val d'Elsa, continue straight ahead	Piazza Arnolfo di Cambio	S	143
22	300	9.6	At the end of the road bear left	Via Armando Diaz	SE	152
23	400	9.9	At roundabout go straight ahead	SS541	SE	169
24	200	10.2	At roundabout go straight ahead	SS541, viale dei Mille	S	165
25	1500	11.7	After crossing the river Elsa on the entry to Gracciano d'Elsa bear right at the large roundabout	Via Fratelli Bandiera, SS541	S	174
26	700	12.3	Arrive in Gracciano d'Elsa at Way Point #76 on the official route			180

Hotel/B&B	Price
Hotel Latini, via Dei Platani 1 - La Steccaia - 53037 SAN GIMIGNANO Tel: 0039 (0)577 945019 www.ristorantelatini.com latini@dada.it	B3
Hotel Vecchio Asilo, via Delle Torri 4 - Ulignano - 53037 SAN GIMIGNANO Tel: 0039 (0)577 950032 www.vecchioasilo.it info@vecchioasilo.it	B3
Casa Giovanna, 58, via S. Giovanni - 53037 SAN GIMIGNANO Tel: 0039(0)577 940419 info@casagiovanna.com	B2
Appartamenti di Montagnani Sara, Vicolo dell'Oro, n°2, angolo piazza del Duomo - 53037 SAN GIMIGNANO Tel: 0039 (0)577 938838 info@appartamentifabio.com **Note:** minimum booking 3 days - internet access available	B2
Agriturismo Podere Campinovi, Localita, Campinovi - 53034 COLLE DI VAL D'ELSA Tel: 0039 (0)577 909097 info@poderecampinovi.com	B2
Albergo il Nazionale, 20, via Garibaldi - 53034 COLLE VAL D'ELSA Tel: 0039 (0)577 920039	B3

Religious Hostel	Price
Convento san Agostino, piazza Sant'Agostino - 53037 SAN GIMIGNANO Tel: 0039 (0)577 940383/907012 **Note:** ensure you confirm accommodation before arriving sangimignanoconvento@yahoo.it	Donation
Foresteria del Monastero san Girolamo, Presso Porta San Giacomo - 53037 SAN GIMIGNANO Tel: 0039 (0)577 940573 vallombrosane@virgillo.it	B2
Monache Benedettine Vallombrosane, 30 via Folgore - 53037 SAN GIMIGNANO Tel: 0039 (0)577 940573 nasterosangimignano@gmail.com	Donation
Comunità Salesiana s. Agostino, piazza S.Agostino - 53034 COLLE VAL D'ELSA Tel: 0039 (0)577 920195 sdbcolle@tin.it	Donation
Casa Parrocchiale le Grazie, 55, via Volterrana - 53034 COLLE VAL D'ELSA Tel: 0039 (0)577 959068	Donation

Camping	Price
Il Boschetto di Piemma, loc. SantaLucia - 53037 SAN GIMIGNANO Tel: 0039 (0)577 940352 bpiemma@tiscalinet.it	B1

Equestrian

Azienda Agricola Biologica Il Vecchio Maneggio, 22 località Sant'Andrea - 53037 SAN GIMIGNANO Tel: 0039 (0)577 950232 Just outside San Gimignano

Gracciano d'Elsa XVII

Abbadia Isola XVI

Monteriggioni

Strove

San Salvatore e Cirino

Turchiano Valmaggiore

Casa Certino

Certino di Sopra

Castel Petraia

Casa al Bosco

Montauto

Poggiarello

San Monti

Campo ai Meli

Casa Giubileo

Comune

Ebbio

Mandorlo

Casella

Bracciano

Fioreta

Ston

Colonna di Monteriggioni

Via

Strada Colligiana

Carpignoni

Argignano

SS541

SS2

SP5

RA03

Siena Tracks

Altitude Profile

(m)

400
350
300
250
200
150

0 5 10 15 20 25 30 35

Distance (km)

168

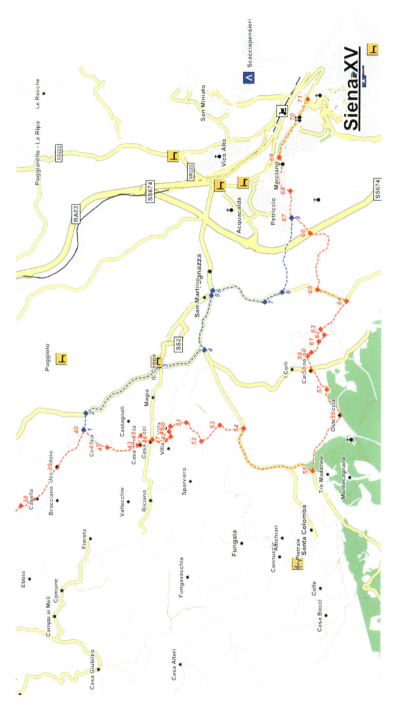

Gracciano d'Elsa to Siena 30.5 km

169

Route Summary: this substantially off-road section follows farm, woodland and horse tracks returning to the roads on the final entry to the centre of Siena. There is the possibility to break the journey in the medieval walled town of Monteriggioni and also the option to avoid some of the rougher tracks and reduce the overall distance by 5.5km by using additional tarmac roads.

Distance from Canterbury: 1769km　　　　**Distance to Rome:** 315km

Ascent: 568m　　　　**Descent:** 413m

Way Point N°	Way Point Distance (metres)	Total Distance (kilometres)	Directions	Verification Point	Compass	Altitude (metres)
64.001	0	0.0	At the crossroads between via Fratelli Bandiera (SP541) and via Nino Bixio, continue straight ahead	Via Pastrengo	E	180
64.002	140	0.1	Turn right	Via Goito	S	183
64.003	90	0.2	At the T-junction turn left	Via Grifo	E	183
64.004	160	0.4	At the roundabout continue straight ahead	Pass industrial buildings on the left	E	185
64.005	300	0.7	Take the right fork and keep straight ahead into open country		SE	186
64.006	800	1.5	Bear left	Pass line of trees on the right of the track	E	190
64.007	400	1.9	Continue straight ahead on the path beside the fence		E	194
64.008	400	2.3	Take the right fork	Woods on the left	SE	201
64.009	110	2.4	Bear left and continue straight ahead up the hill	Into the woods	NE	209
64.010	400	2.8	Continue straight ahead on the road	Strada della Cerreta	E	222
64.011	130	2.9	Turn right direction Acquaviva/Strove	Strada di Acquaviva	S	223
64.012	700	3.6	Bear right	Towards Acquaviva	SE	244

Gracciano d'Elsa to Siena 30.5 km

Way Point N°	Way Point Distance (metres)	Total Distance (kilometres)	Directions	Verification Point	Compass	Altitude (metres)
64.013	800	4.4	In Strove turn left on strada di Strove towards Abbadia a Isola	SP74	E	267
64.014	300	4.7	Turn right and leave the main road	Towards Castel Pietraia	E	256
64.015	180	4.9	On the apex of the bend to right turn left on the track		NE	266
64.016	200	5.1	Turn right towards woods	After passing between houses	E	270
64.017	300	5.4	Turn right on the path into the woods and then quickly fork to the left	Ignore road on the left – leads into an industrial site	SE	282
64.018	200	5.6	Take the left fork		E	280
64.019	300	5.9	Turn left	Remain in the woods	NE	280
64.020	100	6.0	Continue straight ahead	Exit woods and cross the olive grove	NE	279
64.021	180	6.2	At T-junction turn left on the white road	Strada di Certino	N	275
64.022	600	6.8	At the T-junction turn right		NE	226
64.023	100	6.9	Take the left fork	Towards the main road	NE	222
64.024	200	7.1	Rejoin the main road and turn right	Abbadia a Isola(XVI)	NE	204
64.025	30	7 1	Continue straight ahead on the main road	Pass the ancient church on the right	NE	203
64.026	200	7.3	At crossroads turn right in the direction of the hill-top fortified town of Monteriggioni	VF sign, strada di Valmaggiore	SE	199

171

Way Point N°	Way Point Distance (metres)	Total Distance (kilometres)	Directions	Verification Point	Compass	Altitude (metres)
64.027	1700	9.0	At the end of the road turn left along the edge of the woods	**Note:** the turning to the right bypasses Monteriggioni and involves a steep climb	NE	204
64.028	1500	10.5	At the T-junction with the SP5 turn right and right again – keep to the grass verge on the right	SR2 towards Monteriggioni, café on the left at the junction	SE	206
64.029	200	10.7	Carefully cross the main road and turn left onto the unmade road	Uphill towards the entrance to the walled town, VF sign on the right and vines to the left	E	215
64.030	300	11.0	Pass through the arched Porta Fiorentina and continue straight ahead	Via Primo Maggio	SE	251
64.031	200	11.2	On leaving the town take the tarmac road downhill towards the main road	Porta Senese	S	262
64.032	600	11.8	At the junction with the main road, cross over turn left and then right on the unmade road	Strada del Gallinaio, VF sign	S	242
64.033	160	12.0	Take the right fork		SW	243
64.034	300	12.3	Take the next turning to the left	White road between trees	S	278
64.035	110	12.4	At the crossroads turn left on the track		SE	282
64.036	700	13.1	Take second fork from the left	Red and white VF sign	SE	261
64.037	200	13.3	Bear right	VF sign	SE	275
64.038	300	13.6	Track T-junction turn right	VF sign	SE	287

Way Point N°	Way Point Distance (metres)	Total Distance (kilometres)	Directions	Verification Point	Compass	Altitude (metres)
64.039	800	14.4	At T-junction, turn left	VF sign and large farmhouse on left	SE	330
64.040	800	15.2	Turn right on the track. **Note:** to avoid broken ground and reduce distance by 5.5km continue ahead on the Alternate Route	Across the fields	SW	303
64.041	400	15.6	On the apex of the bend to the right take the pathway into the woods on the left	Beside old buildings	S	320
64.042	170	15.8	Take the left fork		S	330
64.043	700	16.5	After leaving the woods take the track to the right	Towards the farm buildings	S	322
64.044	60	16.5	Turn left on the access road to the farm		E	322
64.045	200	16.7	At the T-junction turn right		S	310
64.046	200	16.9	Cross the Strada di Ricciano and take the road straight ahead	Pass the castello on the right	S	318
64.047	300	17.2	Bear left on the track		SE	319
64.048	150	17.4	Turn left on the road	Towards Villa	E	318
64.049	100	17.5	Take the right fork	Towards the Villa castello	E	318
64.050	100	17.6	Turn right onto the track	Uphill	S	316
64.051	400	18.0	Take the right fork	Downhill and with fields on the left	SW	284
64.052	500	18.5	Turn left on the track between fields	Line of trees on the left of the track	SE	275
64.053	500	19.0	At the end of the track turn right on the footpath		S	258
64.054	600	19.6	At the T-junction with the tarmac road turn right	Strada del Plan del Lago	SW	256

Way Point Nº	Way Point Distance (metres)	Total Distance (kilometres)	Directions	Verification Point	Compass	Altitude (metres)
64.055	2100	21.7	At T-junction in woods, turn left	Via dell'Osteriaccia	SE	287
64.056	1300	23.0	Bear left on the road and quickly take the pathway to the left	Beside house on the edge of the woods	NE	268
64.057	500	23.5	Bear right and then left on the track	Beside monument	NE	262
64.058	500	24.0	Beside the house turn right and cross the main road to continue straight ahead on the track	Strada del Plan del Lago	E	279
64.059	300	24.3	Take the track to the right uphill	Into the woods	SE	275
64.060	130	24.4	At the crossroads turn left and then right		SE	282
64.061	200	24.6	Turn right on the track		SE	294
64.062	170	24.8	Turn left on the track		NE	305
64.063	140	24.9	At the T-junction turn right		SE	298
64.064	700	25.6	At the junction with the tarmac road turn left	Beside cemetery, Strada di Casciano	N	291
64.065	600	26.2	At the top of the hill turn right	Via delle Coste	E	303
64.066	1400	27.6	Continue straight ahead	Under the highway and then up the hill	NE	264
64.067	500	28.1	At the crossroads turn right. Alternate Route rejoins from the left	Via Gaetano Milanesi	E	299
64.068	500	28.6	At the T-junction turn left on strada di Marciano		E	355
64.069	700	29.3	At roundabout turn right direction Centro	Viale Camillo Benso Conte di Cavour	SE	342
64.070	800	30.1	Go straight ahead under the archway avoiding the worst of the traffic and look ahead for the sign for Centro		SE	343
64.071	400	30.5	At junction go straight ahead and arrive in Siena at Porta Camollia			345

Note: the Alternate Route allows cyclists to bypass some very broken ground on the woodland and horse tracks. Initially the route follows the via Cassia (SR2) before continuing on quieter country roads and reduces the length of the section by 5.5km

Way Point N°	Way Point Distance (metres)	Total Distance (kilometres)	Directions	Verification Point	Compass	Altitude (metres)
1	0	0.0	Continue straight ahead	Towards main road	E	303
2	300	0.3	At crossroads, turn right down the hill towards Siena on the SR2. Keep to the grass verge	Brown signpost ahead for Poggiolo	SE	293
3	1700	2.0	Turn right on strada del Pecorile direction Sovicille	Bar on right at junction	S	277
4	900	2.9	Turn left and then left again on strada del Pian del Lago		E	279
5	1100	4.0	T-junction turn right direction Siena, SR2	VF sign	E	337
6	90	4.1	Turn right direction Montalbuccio	Strada del Petriccio e Belriguardo	S	337
7	1200	5.3	Bear left at fork in road	Strada del Petriccio e Belriguardo	SE	323
8	400	5.7	Bear left at fork in road	Towards Autostrada and city	E	326
9	1500	7.2	At crossroads continue straight ahead, rejoin the official route Way Point #67			299

Alternate cycle route Monteriggioni to Siena 7.2 km

Useful Contacts

Tourist/Information Offices

Ufficio Informazioni e di Accoglienza Turistica, 5, Largo Fontebranda - 53100 SIENA
Tel: 0039 (0)577 304 810

Ufficio Informazioni e di Accoglienza Turistica, 56, piazza del Campo - 53100 SIENA
Tel: 0039 (0)577 280551 infoaptsiena@terresiena.it

Siena Internet Cafe

Cyber Pub, via Pasubio - 53100 SIENA

Porrione, 88/90, via del Porrione - 53100 SIENA

The Netgate, 12, Campo via Dupre - 53100 SIENA

Doctor

Centro Medico Il Giglio Di Bellucci Otello, 42, via Gigli Girolamo - 53100 Siena
Tel: 0039 (0)577 44174

Veterinary

Centro Cinofilo i Pioppi, str. Cassia Nord - 53100 TOGNAZZA
Tel: 0039 335 591 6354

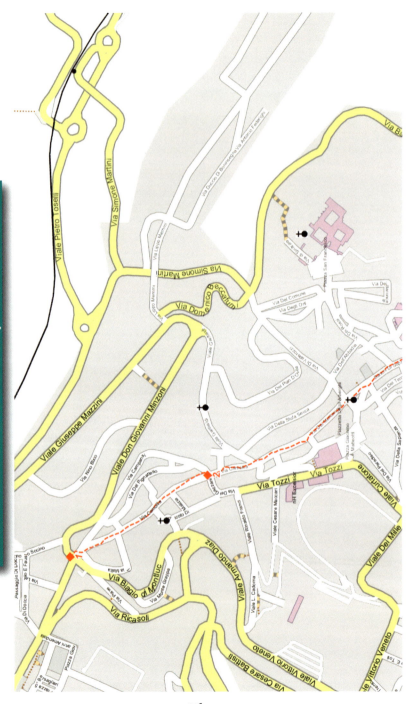

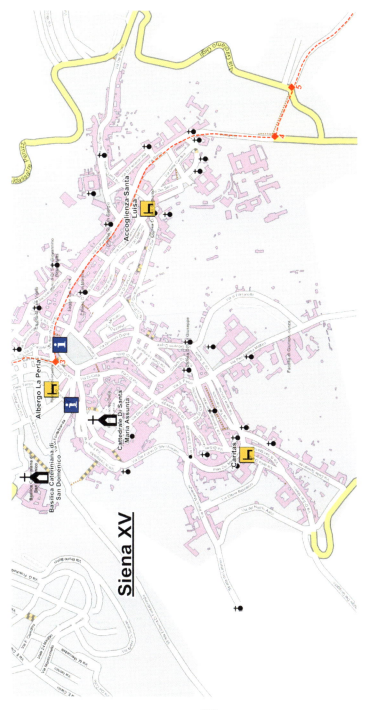

Siena XV

Basilica Caterniana di
San Domenico

Albergo La Perla

Accoglienza Santa
Luisa

Cattedrale Di Santa
Maria Assunta

Caritas

177

Hotel/B&B	Price
Agriturismo Il Colombaio, localita' il Colombaio - 53035 ABBADIA A ISOLA Tel: 0039 (0)577 306143 info@fattoriailcolombaio.com www.fattoriailcolombaio.com	B3
Villa i Cedri, via Carpineta, 2, Località Santa Colomba - 53035 MONTERIGGIONI Tel: 0039 0(5)77317078 **Note:** 1.5km off the route, Way Point #55	B3
Casanuova, 4, strada del Poggiolo - MONTERIGGIONI Tel: 0039 0577 318366	B2
Il Ceppo, via Cassia Nord, 3 53035 MONTERIGGIONI Tel: 0039 (0)577 593387 info@bedandbreakfastilceppo.it	B2
Arcobaleno Boutique, via Fiorentina 32/40 - 53100 SIENA Tel: 0039 (0)577-271092	B2
Albergo La Perla, via Delle Terme N. 25, piazza Indipendenza 25 - 53100 SIENA Tel: 0039 (0)577/47144 info@albergolaperla	B2

Religious Hostel	Price
Accoglienza Pellegrini ad Abbadia a Isola, Parrocchia di San Cirino (Contact: Don Doriano Carraro), località Abbadia a Isola, 3 - 53035 ABBADIA A ISOLA Tel: 0039 (0)577 304214 Mobile: 0039 335 6651581 casaferiesma@yahoo.it dondoriano@interfree.it	Donation
Casa Per Ferie s. Maria Assunta, piazza Roma, 23 - 53035 MONTERIGGIONI Tel: 0039 (0)577 304214 Mobile: 0039 335 6651581 dondoriano@interfree.it casaferiesma@yahoo.it	B2
Casa Sant'Anzano, Strada Statale Chiantiggiana 222, Località Montarioso, 35 - 53035 MONTERIGGIONI Tel: 0039 (0)577 596078	B2
Caritas, via della Diana, 4 - 53100 SIENA Tel: 0039 (0)577 280643 caritas@caritas-fiera.org www.caritas-siena.org	Donation
Accoglienza Santa Luisa, Via San Girolamo 8 - 53100 SIENA Tel: 0039 (0)577 284377	Donation

Youth Hostel	Price
Ostello Guidoriccio, 89 via Fiorentina, Stellino - 53100 SIENA Tel: 0039 (0)577 52212 siena.aighostel@virgilio.it	B1

Camping	Price
Camping Siena Colleverde, Strada di Scacciapensieri, 47 - 53100 SIENA Tel: 0039 (0)577 280044 campingsiena@terresiena.it www.terresiena.it **Note:** 2km north of the town (bus #3 or #)	B1

Equestrian
Il Lucherino, str. del Lucherino - 53100 SIENA Tel: 0039 335 6267582

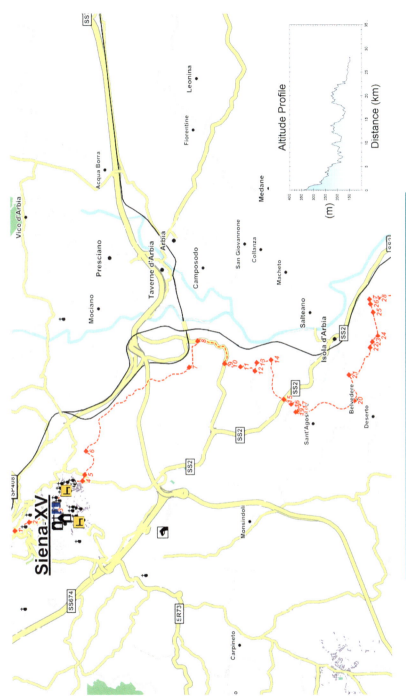

Altitude Profile

(m)

Distance (km)

Siena-XV

Vico d'Arbia
Presciano
Taverne d'Arbia
Mociano
Arbia
Camposodo
Acqua Borra
Fiorentine
Leonina
San Giovannone
Collanza
Medane
Macheto
Salteano
Isola d'Arbia
Sant'Agosti
Belvedere
Deserto
Monsindoli
Carpineto

SS674
S.R73
SS2

Siena to Ponte d'Arbia 29.4 km

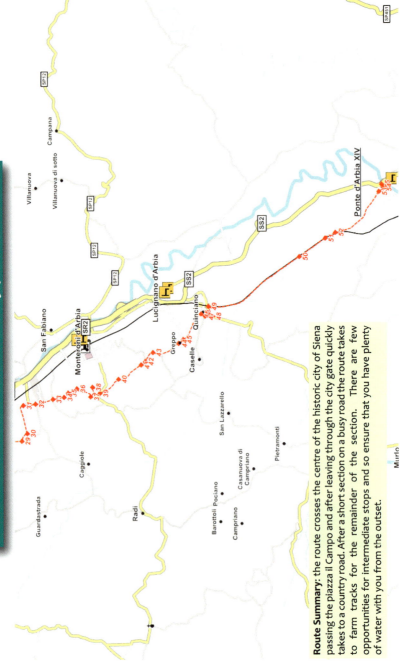

Siena to Ponte d'Arbia 29.4 km

Route Summary: the route crosses the centre of the historic city of Siena passing the piazza il Campo and after leaving through the city gate quickly takes to a country road. After a short section on a busy road the route takes to farm tracks for the remainder of the section. There are few opportunities for intermediate stops and so ensure that you have plenty of water with you from the outset.

Distance from Canterbury: 1799km   **Distance to Rome:** 284km

Ascent: 213m   **Descent:** 430m

Way Point Nº	Way Point Distance (metres)	Total Distance (kilometres)	Directions	Verification Point	Compass	Altitude (metres)
65.001	0	0.0	Enter Porta Camollia cross the piazza and take via Camollia straight ahead	Pass bike shop on the left	SE	343
65.002	400	0.4	At crossroads continue straight ahead on via Camollia	Direction Porta Romana	SE	345
65.003	700	1.1	Immediately before reaching the piazza Il Campo, turn left down via di Citta and then proceed to via Banchi di Sotto	Direction Porta Romana	SE	340
65.004	1200	2.3	Having passed through the Porta Romana, immediately turn left through the archway and take the narrow road down hill	VF sign	E	301
65.005	160	2.5	Cross the main road (SR2) and go straight ahead on strada di Certosa		E	277
65.006	700	3.2	Turn right remaining on strada di Certosa	VF sign	SE	266
65.007	3700	6.9	Road becomes a gravel track continue straight ahead	VF sign	E	220
65.008	700	7.6	Track comes down to a T-junction with a major road turn right, direction strada Cassia		SW	200
65.009	1100	8.7	Turn left from the main road towards the Fattoria	Equestrian centre	S	194
65.010	130	8.8	Bear right though the Fattoria		S	196
65.011	300	9.1	At crossroads go straight ahead and then right down a small slope over a stream	Houses on your left, progress towards trees	S	197
65.012	500	9.6	At T-junction in track turn left	Red-and-white VF sign and arrow	E	200

Way Point N°	Way Point Distance (metres)	Total Distance (kilometres)	Directions	Verification Point	Compass	Altitude (metres)
65.013	200	9.8	Fork right	Metal gate on the left	S	197
65.014	400	10.2	At T-junction turn right on strada di Borgo Vecchia	Line of tall thin conifers on your left as you turn	W	193
65.015	1200	11.4	Cross the main road (SR2) and continue straight ahead on the gravel road	VF sign, pass fir tree on the left	SW	221
65.016	200	11.6	Bear left in front of the house	Downhill	S	209
65.017	200	11.8	Turn right on the track	Beside greenhouses	W	187
65.018	200	12.0	Shortly after a bend to the left in the track, turn right	Over the bridge	NW	185
65.019	100	12.1	At the T-junction with a road turn left on the road	Strada di Murlo	S	185
65.020	1700	13.8	Shortly before reaching a farmhouse surrounded by trees, turn left on the track	Track passes between fields	E	220
65.021	600	14.4	At the end of the field turn right on the track	Track continues between fields	SE	215
65.022	900	15.3	Bear left on the track		E	218
65.023	150	15.4	Take the right fork towards Ponte a Tressa	VF sign	SE	213
65.024	200	15.6	At the top of the ridge fork left down the hill and away from the tree and crucifix	VF sign, via dei Poggio	E	215
65.025	600	16.2	Straight ahead passing equestrian centre		E	188
65.026	200	16.4	Continue straight ahead into Ponte a Tressa	House directly on the left	E	187
65.027	110	16.6	In Ponte a Tressa turn right	Via di Villa Canina	S	187
65.028	200	16.8	Fork right onto a less well-defined track, at the end of the housing development	Direction Il Canto del Sole	S	174

Way Point N°	Way Point Distance (metres)	Total Distance (kilometres)	Directions	Verification Point	Compass	Altitude (metres)
65.029	600	17.4	At T-junction on the top of the ridge turn left to Villa Canina	VF sign	SE	179
65.030	200	17.6	Turn left	Towards Cuna	E	172
65.031	700	18.3	At the entrance to Cuna turn right on the track	Beside the wall	S	173
65.032	300	18.6	At the crossroads in the tracks continue straight ahead	VF sign and metal cross	S	177
65.033	400	18.9	Fork right up the hill	VF sign	S	172
65.034	300	19.3	Fork left	Avoiding strada della Fornacina	SE	181
65.035	150	19.4	Track forks in three directions take middle track straight up the hill	VF sign	SE	181
65.036	200	19.6	Fork right just before reaching the top of the hill	VF sign	SW	199
65.037	400	20.0	Turn sharp left up onto the ridge	VF sign	E	223
65.038	200	20.2	T-junction turn right up the hill	VF sign and farm on left	SW	211
65.039	200	20.4	Track comes to T-junction with a minor road cross straight over and turn immediately left and follow the gravel track. Cyclists should turn left on the road and then bear right on the track in 70 metres		SE	211
65.040	600	21.0	Fork right up the hill	VF sign	SE	217
65.041	600	21.6	Fork left to pass farm on the right		SE	218
65.042	130	21.7	Continue straight ahead to the top of the ridge		SE	217

Way Point Nº	Way Point Distance (metres)	Total Distance (kilometres)	Directions	Verification Point	Compass	Altitude (metres)
65.043	300	22.0	Fork right in the direction of another farm on the ridge		S	222
65.044	600	22.6	Track comes onto small tarmac section and then runs between two houses	White arrow	SE	208
65.045	150	22.8	Fork right direction Quinciano - Lucignano d'Arbia is to the left	VF sign	SE	211
65.046	700	23.5	After entering Quinciano on a tarmac road, turn right onto a gravel track, via del Casello		SW	199
65.047	120	23.6	Fork left down the hill	VF sign	S	187
65.048	200	23.8	At T-junction with main road turn left uphill	VF sign	NE	165
65.049	200	24.0	Turn sharp right down a gravel track	VF sign, continue beside railway track	SE	177
65.050	2600	26.6	Continue straight over crossroads	VF sign and bridge on left	SE	159
65.051	800	27.4	Turn left over level crossing and bear right parallel and close to the railway track - metal barrier but passable with care	VF sign	SE	156
65.052	300	27.7	After crossing small ditch continue straight ahead on the track		SE	154
65.053	1500	29.2	Track comes out onto a tarmac road on the edge of Ponte d'Arbia, fork right on via degli Stagni towards river	VF sign, direction Piana	SE	147
65.054	150	29.4	T-junction turn left	VF sign, river on right	NE	146
65.055	90	29.4	Arrive in Ponte d'Arbia at T-junction with the SR2 beside the bridge over the river Arbia	Café to the left		146

Hotel/B&B	Price
Albergo Bella Napoli, 55/R , via Roma - 53014 MONTERONI D'ARBIA Tel: 0039 (0)577 375225	B2
Hotel Borgo Antico, 405, via Lucignano - 53014 LUCIGNANO D'ARBIA Tel: 0039 (0)577 374 888	B2
Monaci, via Di Lucignano - 53014 LUCIGNANO D' ARBIA Tel: 0039 (0)577 375245 **Note:** This is a self-catering apartment	B3

Religious Hostel	Price
Casa di Accoglienza Parrocchia di S. Giusto e S. Donato, 13, via Roma - 53011 MONTERONI D'ARBIA Tel: 0039 (0)577 3751 52 Contact: Don Roberto Pialli	Donation
Centro Cresti , via Arbia - 53014 PONTE D'ARBIA **Note:** Just over bridge from last Way Point The hospital, built in the 12 C, offered shelter to pilgrims and travellers passing along the Via Francigena. In the court-yard there is a I6 C well and a small loggia, partly blocked in, with three elegant columns. Contact: Patrizia Lotti Tel: 0039 (0)577 3700 96	Donation

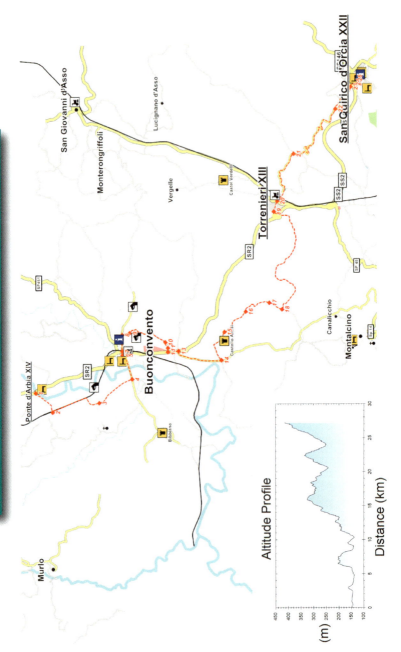

Altitude Profile

Distance (km)

(m)

Route Summary: the route continues over the Tuscan hills interleaving stretches of gravel and white roads with long stretches on the tarmac.

Distance from Canterbury: 1828km   **Distance to Rome:** 255km

Ascent: 605m   **Descent:** 338m

Way Point Nº	Way Point Distance (metres)	Total Distance (kilometres)	Directions	Verification Point	Compass	Altitude (metres)
66.001	0	0.0	From the junction beside the bridge in Ponte d'Arbia return along via del Magistrato beside the river	River on the left	SW	146
66.002	900	0.9	After crossing railway bridge turn left onto a gravel track	Not turning to Saltemmano	S	149
66.003	2000	2.9	Take left fork	VF sign and large farm on left	SE	162
66.004	1600	4.5	At T-junction with major road turn left	VF sign, via di Bibbiano	E	139
66.005	900	5.4	At the crossroads in Buonconvento, turn left on via Roma	Pass café terrace on the right, No Entry	N	146
66.006	110	5.5	Take the first turning to the right, smallroad via di Tercena	Sign - Roma 201km and VF sign just before the turning	E	147
66.007	140	5.7	Cross the main road (SR2) and continue straight ahead	Over level crossing	E	147
66.008	600	6.3	At the top of the hill turn right on the track		S	184
66.009	300	6.5	Bear left along the ridge	Pass industrial zone below on the right	S	201
66.010	1700	8.3	At the end of the ridge bear right down the hill	Pass farm on the left	SW	181
66.011	200	8.4	Bear right towards the main road	House on the left, row of conifers to the right	W	158

Way Point N°	Way Point Distance (metres)	Total Distance (kilometres)	Directions	Verification Point	Compass	Altitude (metres)
66.012	140	8.6	At the T-junction with the busy main road, cross over and turn left on the grass verge	Via Cassia – SR2	S	146
66.013	400	9.0	Turn right on the road	Direction Montalcino	S	143
66.014	1800	10.8	Just before the road bends to the left turn sharp left	Direction Castello Altesi and towards conifers	E	151
66.015	1500	12.3	After passing the castello take the left fork		SE	191
66.016	1200	13.5	Bear left to skirt the buildings on the right	Tree lined road	S	203
66.017	1200	14.7	Keep left on the white road		SW	266
66.018	500	15.2	Just before reaching a large farm on the right, turn left	Follow the road to Torrenieri	E	264
66.019	5000	20.2	At the T-junction in Torrenieri turn right on the main street	Via Romana	E	274
66.020	400	20.6	Continue straight ahead over crossroads in the centre of Torrenieria (XIII)	VF sign and church directly in front	E	257
66.021	2400	23.0	Right fork to continue on the main road	VF sign	SE	335
66.022	2800	25.8	For some relief from the road it is possible to fork left on the clay track and then bear right beside the cemetery to rejoin the road in 500metres. However, in wet weather the clay makes for impossible going on bikes and difficulties for all		SE	325

Way Point N°	Way Point Distance (metres)	Total Distance (kilometres)	Directions	Verification Point	Compass	Altitude (metres)
66.023	1000	26.8	Turn right over road bridge. **Note:** caution, crash barriers and no pavement on the roadside	VF sign	SE	383
66.024	180	27.0	After crossing the bridge turn right at the T-junction		S	394
66.025	50	27.0	Turn right onto the ramp	Via Dante Alighieri	E	393
66.026	180	27.2	Arrive in San Quirico d'Orcia beside the church	Piazza Chigi		413

Hotel/B&B	Price
Roma Giovanni, 14, via Soccini - 53022 BUONCONVENTO Tel: 0039 0577806021	B2
Hotel Palazzuolo, 43, via Santa Caterina - 53027 SAN QUIRICO D'ORCIA Tel: 0039 (0)577 897080 info@hotelpalazzuolo.it	B2
PR La Casa di Giacco, 70/A , via d' Alighieri - 53027 SAN QUIRICO D'ORCIA Tel: 0039 (0)577 897106 giacco@dedaloclick.it	B2
Albergo il Garibaldi, S.S. Cassia - 53027 SAN QUIRICO D'ORCIA Tel: 0039 (0)577 898315	B2
Maramai- Sra Lucrezia, P.za Chigi 18 - 53027 SAN QUIRICO D'ORCIA Tel: 0039 (0)577 897278/0577 897587 Mobile: 0039 347 7748732 Giorgio.ma ramai@tele2.it	B1

Religious Hostel	Price
Casa di Accoglienza Parrocchia di S. Giusto e S. 13, Donato - via Roma - TORRENIERI Tel: 0039 (0)577 375152	Donation
Parrocchia di s. Quirico d'Orcia, via Dante Alighieri - 53027 SAN QUIRICO D'ORCIA Tel: 0039 (0)577 897236	B1

Equestrian

Club Ippico Val D'Arbia, Loc. Pian delle Noci - 53022 BUONCONVENTO Mobile: 0039 340 2399106   quattroa@supereva.it

Pieve a Salti, str. Prov. Pieve a Salti - 53022 BUONCONVENTO Tel: 0039 (0)577 807244

Casali di Bibbiano, loc. bibbiano - 53022 BUONCONVENTO Tel: 0039 (0)577 809093

Useful Contacts

Tourist/Information Offices

piazzale Garibaldi, 2 (CAP:53022) BUONCONVENTO Tel: 0039 0577807181 www.terresiena.it buonconvento@crete.siena.it

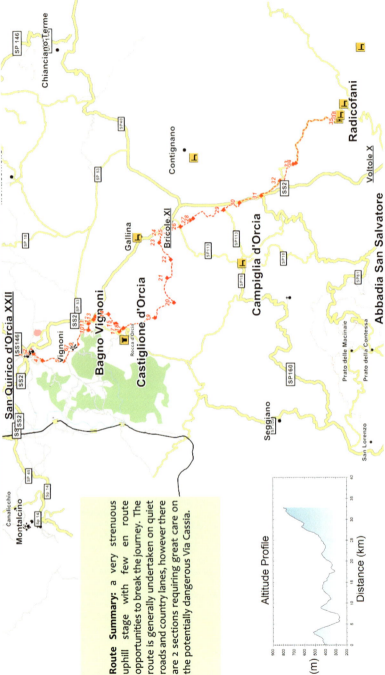

San Quirico d Orcia to Radicofani 32.9 km

Route Summary: a very strenuous uphill stage with few en route opportunities to break the journey. The route is generally undertaken on quiet roads and country lanes, however there are 2 sections requiring great care on the potentially dangerous Via Cassia.

Altitude Profile

(m)

Distance (km)

Distance from Canterbury: 1856km   **Distance to Rome:** 227km

Ascent: 978m   **Descent:** 598m

Way Point N°	Way Point Distance (metres)	Total Distance (kilometres)	Directions	Verification Point	Compass	Altitude (metres)
67.001	0	0.0	From the church in San Quirico d'Orcia on piazza Chigi continue ahead on via Dante Aligheri	Pass through piazza della Libertà	SE	413
67.002	300	0.3	Turn right at crossroads on the edge of the old town	Via Giacomo Matteotti	SW	410
67.003	180	0.5	At crossroads continue straight ahead	Via Giuseppe Garibaldi	SW	419
67.004	700	1.2	Tarmac road leads onto a track, take left fork	VF sign, towards Vignoni e Ripa d'Orcia	S	426
67.005	1400	2.6	Take the left fork	Towards Vignoni	SE	498
67.006	900	3.5	Bear left	Towards tower in Vignoni Alto	E	483
67.007	200	3.7	Turn right onto the pathway	Under the arch	SW	475
67.008	80	3.8	Turn left on the broad track	Downhill, strada di Bagno Vignoni	SE	476
67.009	400	4.2	Take the left fork		SE	443
67.010	1400	5.6	At T-junction in Bagno Vignoni turn left		E	297
67.011	400	6.0	At T-junction with the via Cassia turn right over the river bridge and continue on the via Cassia. **Note:** a footbridge is to be constructed here and is to be preferred over the dangerous road bridge		SE	264
67.012	500	6.5	Bear left at the junction onto the track that runs parallel to the via Cassia	Direction Roma 179, track on the right side of the road	SE	279

Way Point N°	Way Point Distance (metres)	Total Distance (kilometres)	Directions	Verification Point	Compass	Altitude (metres)
67.013	200	6.7	Cross the stream and turn right	Proceed with the stream on the right and fields on the left	S	267
67.014	900	7.6	At the junction in tracks, turn right and then take the second turning to the left	Across the stream	SW	279
67.015	700	8.3	Take the left fork	Beside farmhouse towards second farm	SE	362
67.016	120	8.4	Turn right	Beside second farmhouse	W	367
67.017	700	9.1	At the T-junction with the road turn sharp left onto the road	Hairpin bend to the right at the junction	SE	434
67.018	300	9.4	At the next junction bear left	Strada del Pozzo	S	448
67.019	2100	11.5	In the valley bottom, cross the bridge and continue straight ahead		SE	344
67.020	1700	13.2	At junction after passing woods on the right, turn sharp left along the ridge	Via delle Querciole	E	417
67.021	1600	14.8	Turn right on the track	Pass farm on the left	E	429
67.022	1200	16.0	Continue straight ahead on the white road	Farmhouse on the left	NE	384
67.023	1300	17.3	Turn right, downhill on the track	Pass Agriturismo on the left	E	366
67.024	600	17.9	Bear right on the track and cross the stream	Main road close on the left before the turn	S	311
67.025	400	18.3	At the junction with the white road turn right and quickly bear left	Towards Briccole (XI), pass farm on the left after the fork	S	323

Way Point N°	Way Point Distance (metres)	Total Distance (kilometres)	Directions	Verification Point	Compass	Altitude (metres)
67.026	900	19.2	Cross the main road to Campiglia d'Orcia and continue straight ahead on the track	Across the stream	SE	336
67.027	600	19.8	At the intersection with the old via Cassia turn right on the road		SE	338
67.028	300	20.1	Take the left fork	Tarmac road, uphill	S	344
67.029	2100	22.2	Take the left fork	Returning towards the new via Cassia SR2	SE	439
67.030	1200	23.4	At the T-junction with the SR2 turn right and proceed with care on the main road		S	400
67.031	1400	24.8	Turn left on the road across the river	Towards Radicofani, Strada Provinciale di Sarteano, VF sign, Roma 161	SE	420
67.032	1500	26.3	Shortly after a curve to the right turn right onto a track		SE	465
67.033	1400	27.7	Rejoin the Strada Provinciale di Sarteano and turn right		S	588
67.034	170	27.9	Bear left on the road	Towards Radicofani, Strada Provinciale di Sarteano	SE	599
67.035	4600	32.5	Turn left towards the centre of Radicofani	Viale Odoardo Lucchini	SE	765
67.036	200	32.7	At the crossroads, go straight ahead and then bear right	Viale del Maccione	SE	791
67.037	50	32.7	Bear left	Via Renato Magi	SE	797
67.038	150	32.9	Arrive in the centre of Radicofani	The church of San Pietro is to the right off the main street		792

Hotel/B&B	Price
Tre Rioni, 3, via Campotondo - 53020 CAMPIGLIA D'ORCIA Tel: 0039 (0)577 87 20 15	B3
Il Parallelo - Capitani Cassia, 3, loc. Gallina - 53020 CASTIGLIONE D'ORCIA Tel 0039 (0)775 880125	B2
Fattoria La Palazzina, 33, Località Le Vigne - 53040 RADICOFANI Tel: 0039 (0)578 55771	B3
Salvatore Albergo Ristorante La Torre , via della Croce, Nocchi Siro - 53040 RADICOFANI Tel: 0039 (0)578 55943	B3
Agriturismo Casa Tonietti, localita' Le Vigne - 53040 RADICOFANI Tel: 0039 (0)578 55876	B3
Agriturismo, La Selvella Di Kim Marina, 30, localita' Pod. Salvella - 53040 RADICOFANI Tel: 0039 (0)578 55555	B3
Religious Accommodation	Price
Casa D'Accoglienza San Jacopo di Compostela, via Magi Tel: 0039 (0)578 55614 Mobile: 0039 338 9240307 doneliasantori@libero	Donation

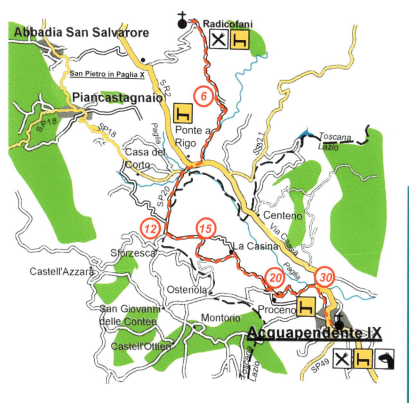

Altitude Profile

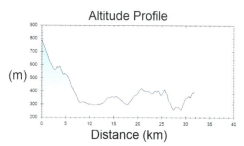

Route Summary: the long descent from Radicofani is followed by another exposed stretch over the the hills on broad country tracks. This makes for easy going for cyclists and riders.

195

Distance from Canterbury: 1889km   **Distance to Rome:** 195km

Ascent: 484m   **Descent:** 886m

Way Point N°	Way Point Distance (metres)	Total Distance (kilometres)	Directions	Verification Point	Compass	Altitude (metres)
68.001	0	0.0	From the church of San Pietro turn right and continue along the main street	Via Roma	E	792
68.002	300	0.3	On leaving the historic centre bear left on the road downhill	Viale Giacomo Matteotti	SE	763
68.003	500	0.8	Cross the main road and continue straight ahead	Direction Roma	S	718
68.004	200	1.0	On the apex of the bend to the right continue straight ahead	Old via Cassia	S	699
68.005	2800	3.8	Take the left fork	Towards the Pantano agriturismo	SE	586
68.006	1500	5.3	Take the right fork		S	521
68.007	2900	8.2	Take the right fork	Keep river Rigo to the left	SW	310
68.008	2200	10.4	At the T-junction with the main road turn right, cross the road and continue to the right on the track parallel to the road	SR2, pass bar on the right	W	294
68.009	600	11.0	Exit Ponte a Rigo, and continue straight ahead on the track	SR2 bends to the right, continue beside the smaller road	SW	294
68.010	300	11.3	At the end of the track turn right and then left to follow the road	Cross river on the road	SW	294
68.011	500	11.8	Take the next road to the left	Direction Sovana	S	298
68.012	3800	15.6	Turn left onto a gravel track direction Lavalle	VF sign	SE	360
68.013	700	16.3	Fork right down the hill	VF sign at end of farmyard	E	337

Way Point N°	Way Point Distance (metres)	Total Distance (kilometres)	Directions	Verification Point	Compass	Altitude (metres)
68.014	700	17.0	Continue straight ahead over crossroads in track	VF sign on telegraph pole	E	312
68.015	900	17.9	At T-junction in track turn right	VF sign, junction shortly after crossing river	S	300
68.016	1200	19.1	Take the left fork		E	358
68.017	1300	20.4	Continue straight ahead	Towards la Casina	NE	407
68.018	1000	21.4	At the T-junction turn right	VF sign	SE	398
68.019	3400	24.8	Road comes down to T-junction turn left up the hill	Direction Proceno	SE	367
68.020	130	24.9	Take the right fork	VF sign, via di Porta Fiorenta	SE	369
68.021	500	25.4	In the piazza in Proceno bear left	Viale Marconi	E	413
68.022	90	25.5	At the T-junction turn left and continue downhill	Skirting the village on via Belvedere	NE	399
68.023	300	25.8	On the crown of the sharp bend to the left, continue straight ahead	Via della Pace	E	385
68.024	300	26.1	Take right fork	Downhill	NE	334
68.025	100	26.2	At the T-junction turn left and continue downhill		NE	321
68.026	400	26.6	At the T-junction turn right on the SP	Beside sports ground	SE	294

Way Point N°	Way Point Distance (metres)	Total Distance (kilometres)	Directions	Verification Point	Compass	Altitude (metres)
68.027	300	26.9	Bear right on the disused road		SE	269
68.028	200	27.1	Return to the strada Provinciale and bear right		SE	257
68.029	200	27.3	Remain on the strada Provinciale	Bend to the left	NE	265
68.030	1500	28.8	At the bottom of the hill, shortly before T-junction with the via Cassia turn right on the small road	Strada Viccinale di San Giglio, VF sign	S	254
68.031	1700	30.5	At the T-junction with the via Cassia turn right	Enter Aquapendente on the via Cassia	S	361
68.032	170	30.7	Turn left across the car park and take the track to the left of the Albergo	"Aquila d'Oro"	SE	365
68.033	140	30.8	Cross the orchard and take the footpath downhill and to the left		SE	350
68.034	60	30.9	Turn right on the track		SE	345
68.035	150	31.0	In front of the albergo "la Ripa" turn left	Continue along via Cesare Battisti and then to the end of via Roma	SE	362
68.036	800	31.8	Arrive in Aquapendente beside the church of Santo Sepulcro	Piazza del Duomo		390

Hotel/B&B	Price
Oasis, Loc. Poggio Bernaglia - 01021 PROCENO Tel: 0039 (0)763 710127 Mobile: 0039 333 2271806 clactus@libero.it	B3
Agriturismo Poggio Porsenna di Paoletti Moira Fabio Paolo, località Boschetto - 01020 PROCENO Mobile: 0039 339 18 69 544 info@poggioporsenna.it	B3
Casina Centeno, Podere Casina Centeno, Via Cassia - 01020 PROCENO Tel: 0039 333 4798958 info@casinacenteno.it	B2
Castello di Proceno, 153-155 corso Regina Margherita - 01020 Proceno Tel: 0039 (0)763 710072	B3
La Ripa, 161, via C. Battisti - ACQUAPENDENTE Tel: 0039 (0)763730136 info@coop.elce.it	B3
Il Borgo, 1/3/5, via Porta S. Angelo - ACQUAPENDENTE Tel: 0039 (0)763711264 torre_gr@libero.it	B3
Agriturismo Sant'Angelo, S.S. Cassia - 01021 ACQUAPENDENTE Tel: 0039 (0)763 734738 Mobile: 0039 338 7271044 info@agriturismosantangelo.it	B3
Aquilla d' Oro, Strada Statale Cassia - AQUAPENDENTE Tel: 0039 (0)763 734175	B2
La casa del pellegrino, Via Roma- AQUAPENDENTE Mobile: 0039 339 8499965	Donation

Religious Hostel	Price
Caritas Diocesana, Via Cassia - PONTE A RIGO Mobile: 0039 339 8999610 Tel: 0039 (0)578 50016	Donation
Associazione Casa di Lazzaro, Via Cappuccini 2 - AQUAPENDENTE Tel: 0039 (0)763 730177	Donation

Useful Contacts

Doctor

Mansour Dr. Imad, 20, VICOLO DEL FIORE - 01021 ACQUAPENDENTE
Tel: 0039 (0)763 734766

Veterinary

VFratangeli Dr. Claudio, localita' LE GRAZIE - 01021 ACQUAPENDENTE
Tel: 0039 (0)763 733032

Radicofani to Aquapendente 31.8 km

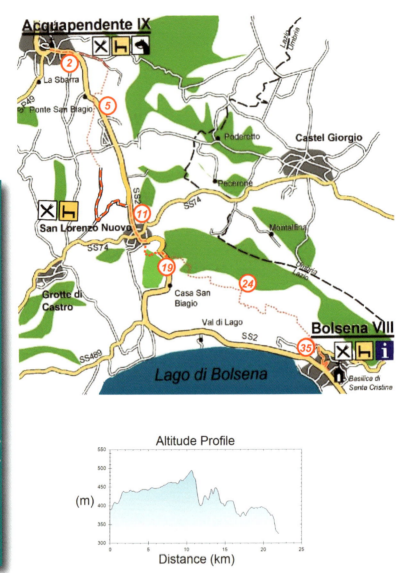

Acquapendente to Bolsena 22.1 km

Altitude Profile

Route Summary: initially the route meanders on farm and sheep tracks to avoid the Via Cassia, then it proceeds in the lower slopes of the hills overlooking lake Bolsena. The latter half includes paths over broken ground with some short steep ascents making for difficult progress for cyclists.

Distance from Canterbury: 1920km   **Distance to Rome:** 163km

Ascent: 260m   **Descent:** 326m

Way Point N°	Way Point Distance (metres)	Total Distance (kilometres)	Directions	Verification Point	Compass	Altitude (metres)
69.001	0	0.0	From the Basilica del Santo Sepolcro turn left on the main road	Via Cassia, towards San Lorenzo, Roma – 132	E	390
69.002	700	0.7	Turn left direction Torre Alfina	VF sign, shrine on the apex of the bend	E	410
69.003	1300	2.0	After a large factory building turn right onto gravel track	VF sign, strada di Lutinano	SE	439
69.004	300	2.3	At fork bear right on gravel track	VF sign and line of trees to your left	SW	436
69.005	1400	3.7	At junction with via Cassia cross straight over onto the small road	VF sign	S	436
69.006	1900	5.6	At T-junction with a minor road, turn left and then immediately right	VF sign and farmhouse on your left as you turn	SE	446
69.007	600	6.2	Take right fork	Strada del Podere del Vescovo	S	445
69.008	2000	8.2	At the T-junction turn left and left again at the next T-junction	Strada della Salcinella	NE	461
69.009	200	8.4	At the next junction fork right and keep left at the next two junctions		NE	461
69.010	900	9.3	At the T-junction turn sharp right	Track quickly bends to the left after the junction	E	463
69.011	500	9.8	At the T-junction with the main road turn right	Via Cassia, towards San Lorenzo Nuovo	S	466
69.012	1100	10.9	At crossroads with traffic lights in the centre of San Lorenzo Nuovo continue straight ahead	Direction Bolsena, Roma 124	SE	495

Acquapendente to Bolsena 22.1 km

Way Point Nº	Way Point Distance (metres)	Total Distance (kilometres)	Directions	Verification Point	Compass	Altitude (metres)
69.013	190	11.1	Take the right fork down the hill, parallel to main road	VF sign	S	491
69.014	90	11.2	At the next junction bear left	Returning towards the main road	E	481
69.015	200	11.4	At the break in the metal fence, bear right on the tarmac and then right again on the concrete road	Steeply downhill, house on the right on corner	S	474
69.016	500	11.9	Continue straight ahead across the clearing, then turn left to follow track		E	403
69.017	150	12.0	Skirt the house and bear left on the white road		E	400
69.018	600	12.6	At the T-junction cross the road with great care and turn right	Via Cassia	SE	429
69.019	160	12.8	Almost at the bottom of the hill turn left onto a gravel track. **Note:** the route ahead is generally off-road and while the conditions for walkers and horse-riders are good it is strenuous for bike riders, who can remain on the via Cassia rejoining the main route in Bolsena	VF sign, km 122,7, direction Agriturismo Pomele	SE	421
69.020	1500	14.3	At fork in the track continue straight ahead down the hill	VF sign	SE	446
69.021	200	14.5	Fork left parallel to lake-shore	VF sign, vocabolo Pomele	E	427
69.022	500	15.0	Fork right down the hill	Quarry on left	SE	410
69.023	800	15.8	At fork keep right	VF sign	E	412
69.024	500	16.3	At T-junction turn right	VF sign	S	413
69.025	400	16.7	Fork left	VF sign, strada della Roccaccia	E	377
69.026	600	17.3	Fork left up the hill	Line of posts on right and line of cultivated trees on left	SE	377

Way Point Nº	Way Point Distance (metres)	Total Distance (kilometres)	Directions	Verification Point	Compass	Altitude (metres)
69.027	200	17.5	At T-junction with another track, turn right down the hill	Entrance to large house on left	SE	376
69.028	150	17.6	Take the left fork	VF sign	NE	370
69.029	600	18.2	Fork right onto a smaller track	VF sign	SE	391
69.030	600	18.8	Fork right down the hill	Quarry to your left	E	393
69.031	400	19.2	Fork left through a line of trees		SE	391
69.032	1000	20.2	Fork left onto the track leading higher up the hill		SE	391
69.033	200	20.4	Straight ahead onto a minor tarmac road		SE	388
69.034	200	20.6	T-junction turn left and continue straight on, do not take the left indicated by the via Francigena sign, but go down the hill into Bolsena	VF sign and shrine on the corner	SE	375
69.035	300	20.9	T-junction with main road turn right down the hill	Via Orvieto, SP53	S	375
69.036	500	21.4	Bear right to leave the main road as it begins to bend to the left. Take the small road downhill	Alongside the church, chiesa Nuova	SW	351
69.037	70	21.5	At the T-junction turn left	Under the arch	S	339
69.038	30	21.5	Turn right	Via delle Piagge	SW	336
69.039	60	21.6	At the end of the road in piazza Primo Maggio, turn left	Corso Cavour	SE	327
69.040	300	21.9	Cross piazza Guglielmo Matteotti and continue straight ahead on Corso della Repubblica		SE	326
69.041	150	22.1	Arrive in the centre of Bolsena in piazza Santa Cristina	The church of Santa Cristina ahead		324

Hotel/B&B	Price
Italia, 3, via L. Turchetti - 01020 SAN LORENZO NUOVO Tel: 0039 3392774533	B3
Italia, corso Cavour, 53 - 01023 BOLSENA Tel: 0039 (0)761799193	B2
Nazionale, 50, via Gramsci - 01023 BOLSENA Tel: 0039 (0)761799006	B3
PR Bolsena Hotel, Royal piazza Dante Alighieri - 01023 BOLSENA Tel: 0039 (0)761 797048	B3
Al Castello, 11, via Castello - 01023 BOLSENA Tel: 0039.0763.78011 Mobile: Tel: 0039 339.8605166 info@santacristina.it **Note:** also equestrian centre	B3
Bed and Breakfast Francigena, 0039, corso della Repubblica - 01023 BOLSENA Tel: 0039 (0)761 798453	B3

Religious Hostel	Price
Ostello Francigena, Via Cassia Vecchia - 01020 SAN LORENZO NUOVO Tel: 0039 (0)763 7268211 info@comunesanlorenzonuovo.it www.comunesanlorenzonuovo.it	B2
Suore s.s. Sacramento, 14, p.zza Santa Cristina - 01023 BOLSENA Tel: 0039 (0)761 799058	B1
Foresteria ex-Convento Santa Maria del Giglio, 49, via Madonna del Giglio - 01023 BOLSENA Tel: 0039 (0)761 799066 puntidivista@pelagus.it www.conventobolsena.org	Donation

Camping	Price
Mario, 700, della Cassia - 01020 SAN LORENZO NUOVO Tel: 0039 (0)76377485	B1
Cappelletta, 500, della Cassia - 01023 BOLSENA Tel: 0039 (0)761799543	B1
Massimo, 600, della Cassia - 01023 BOLSENA Tel: 0039 (0)761798738	B1
Pineta, via A. Diaz - 01023 BOLSENA Tel: 0039 (0)761799801	B1
Val di Sole, della Cassia, 800 - 01023 BOLSENA Tel: 0039 (0)761797064	B1
Blu International Club, 650, della Cassia sul Lago di Bolsena - 01023 BOLSENA Tel: 0039 (0)761798855	B1

Useful Contacts

Doctor

Patri Dr. Maurizio, via a. Gramsci - 01023 BOLSENA Tel: 0039 (0)761 798869

Farrier

Coletti Ottavio & Tofanicchio Enzo Fabbri, Via Cassia - 01023 BOLSENA Tel: 0039 (0)761 799421

Bolsena VIII

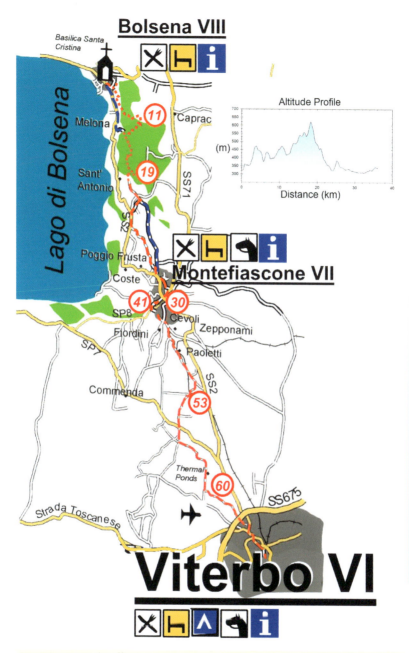

Basilica Santa
Cristina

Lago di Bolsena

Altitude Profile

(m)

Distance (km)

Melona

Caprac

SS71

⑪

Sant'
Antonio

⑲

SS2

Poggio Frusta

Montefiascone VII

Coste

⑪

㉚

SP8

Cevoli

Fiordini

Zepponami

SP7

Paoletti

SS2

Commenda

㊾

Thermal
Ponds

㉠

SS675

Strada Toscanese

Viterbo VI

Route Summary: the official route climbs into the hills overlooking the lake and progresses on farm and forest tracks to the hilltop town of Montefiscone. The route then descends and become easier on farm tracks and ancient roads passing the thermal springs before entering the large town of Viterbo on very busy roads.

Bolsena to Viterbo 36.2 km

Way Point N°	Way Point Distance (metres)	Total Distance (kilometres)	Directions	Verification Point	Compass	Altitude (metres)
70.001	0	0.0	Leave piazza Santa Cristina by Porta Romana	Basilica and cafe on left	SE	325
70.002	200	0.2	Take the first turning to the left. **Note:** - the official route returns quickly to the hills overlooking the lake. Unfortunately there are a number of barriers on the route and in order to avoid these carefully follow the Alternate Route straight ahead following the potentially busy via Cassia	Via Acqua della Croce, small park to the right of the junction	E	321
70.003	100	0.3	Turn to the right, and immediately take the left fork	Via Caio Rufo Musunio	SE	324
70.004	140	0.4	At the T-junction turn left uphill	Località Vigna	NE	323
70.005	90	0.5	Continue straight ahead on the track		E	332
70.006	180	0.7	Bear right on the track		E	355
70.007	180	0.9	Turn sharp right over the stream	Continue uphill	SW	363
70.008	300	1.2	At the T-junction turn right and immediately left	Parallel to the lake shore	SE	356
70.009	600	1.8	Turn right and then right again at the T-junction		SW	351
70.010	200	2.0	Turn left	On the straight tarmac road that eventually deteriorates into a track	SE	347
70.011	1900	3.9	Beside 2 pine trees turn right onto a track	Downhill between fields	SW	473

Way Point N°	Way Point Distance (metres)	Total Distance (kilometres)	Directions	Verification Point	Compass	Altitude (metres)
70.012	1500	5.4	Continue straight ahead	Across barrier	W	421
70.013	400	5.8	At the T-junction with the tarmac road turn left – Alternate Route rejoins from the right	Parallel to the lake shore	SE	370
70.014	800	6.6	Fork right onto the gravel track direction Parco di Turona	VF sign	S	436
70.015	600	7.2	Fork right down the hill	VF sign	W	420
70.016	300	7.5	Turn left up a gravel track just before you pass a small white chapel	VF sign	SE	386
70.017	1000	8.5	Fork right through a thin band of trees and proceed into an open area		E	399
70.018	90	8.6	After crossing the stream bear right	Derelict house to your left	SE	398
70.019	30	8.6	After passing the derelict house, at a junction of three tracks take the furthest right up the hill	Towards the house on the ridge	W	402
70.020	500	9.1	Turn left on to a paved road	The old via Cassia	S	419
70.021	800	9.9	Fork left	VF milestone	SE	450
70.022	600	10.5	Proceed straight over crossroads	VF sign	SE	474
70.023	300	10.8	The official route turns right - a dangerous section on the via Cassia may be avoided and total distance reduced by 1km by continuing straight ahead on the minor road to Way Point #26	Pilgrim milestone	SW	465
70.024	900	11.7	At the T-junction with the via Cassia turn left and proceed on the on the main road with great care	Direction Montefiascone	S	414

Way Point N°	Way Point Distance (metres)	Total Distance (kilometres)	Directions	Verification Point	Compass	Altitude (metres)
70.025	700	12.4	Bear left off the main road onto an unmade road	Barn to the right at the junction	SE	422
70.026	3000	15.4	At the junction with the tarmac road turn right		S	535
70.027	300	15.7	Turn left at T-junction with major road, direction Viterbo	Via Cassia, hotel on the left at the junction	SE	533
70.028	200	15.9	Turn left beside the modern office building	Towards Orvieto on via Cardinal Salotti, pass car wash on the right	SE	533
70.029	800	16.7	Bear left	Towards Orvieto on via Santa Maria delle Grazie	E	545
70.030	200	16.9	At the junction with the SS71 turn right	Direction Viterbo	SW	532
70.031	200	17.1	Take the left fork	Via Orvietana, SS71	S	538
70.032	200	17.3	Turn right onto via San Flaviano	Beside church	SW	553
70.033	190	17.5	Continue straight ahead up the ramp to enter the historic centre	Corso Cavour	SW	572
70.034	300	17.8	Continue straight ahead through the arch	Uphill towards la Rocca	SW	602
70.035	90	17.9	Turn left into the alley uphill - to avoid a flight of steps, take via 24 Maggio to the left and rejoin the main route just before exiting the old town at Way Point #39	Beside Tourist Office	SW	612
70.036	70	18.0	Enter the gardens and go straight ahead		W	620

Bolsena to Viterbo 36.2 km

Way Point N°	Way Point Distance (metres)	Total Distance (kilometres)	Directions	Verification Point	Compass	Altitude (metres)
70.037	120	18.1	Continue straight ahead through the gardens of Rocca dei Papi and descend on the steps before turning left	Pass beside the Torre del Pellegrino	SW	622
70.038	120	18.2	From the parking area behind la Rocca go straight ahead in the narrow street	Via della Rocca	S	613
70.039	70	18.3	At the T-junction turn right	Via 24 Maggio	W	614
70.040	60	18.3	Pass through the arch and turn left	Via Bandita	S	601
70.041	300	18.6	At the intersection with the busy SP8 turn left and immediately right right	Steep descent	SE	578
70.042	100	18.7	Take the left fork on the unmade road		SE	575
70.043	800	19.5	At crossroads continue straight ahead direction Viterbo	VF sign	SE	487
70.044	200	19.7	At fork bear right onto a dirt track	VF milestone and VF sign	S	482
70.045	300	20.0	Bear left on the paved section	VF sign	S	466
70.046	200	20.2	Bear right	VF sign	S	453
70.047	190	20.4	Turn left onto the paved track with a shrine directly to your right	VF sign	SE	451
70.048	500	20.9	Fork left down the hill	VF sign, via Paoletti	SE	436
70.049	1500	22.4	Turn left under the railway	VF sign	E	355
70.050	30	22.4	Turn right immediately after coming out of the tunnel		SE	355
70.051	600	23.1	Bear right	VF sign	SE	347
70.052	200	23.3	Bear right to continue on the main track	Strada Montejugo	SW	336
70.053	600	23.9	Turn left after going under second railway tunnel	VF sign	S	321

Way Point Nº	Way Point Distance (metres)	Total Distance (kilometres)	Directions	Verification Point	Compass	Altitude (metres)
70.054	60	23.9	Fork right remaining on the main track	Strada Montejugo	S	320
70.055	2300	26.2	At crossroads with major road (SP7), go straight ahead	VF sign, strada Casetta	S	340
70.056	500	26.7	At crossroads in the track continue straight ahead with farms on either side	VF sign	S	339
70.057	300	27.0	Fork left after passing the house on the right	VF sign	SE	332
70.058	1500	28.5	Fork left beside a fence and a line of trees	VF sign	SE	331
70.059	600	29.1	At T-junction in tracks turn right towards the thermal ponds	VF sign	S	320
70.060	1600	30.7	Turn left direction Vicinale San Lazzaro	VF sign	SE	311
70.061	3000	33.7	Track comes out onto a tarmac road continue straight ahead	VF sign and factory buildings on your right	E	319
70.062	400	34.1	At T-junction turn right onto strada Cassia Nord	VF sign and large Cemetery on your right	S	324
70.063	300	34.4	Pass under fly-over and bear left	Strada Cassia Nord, No Entry, towards petrol station	SE	325
70.064	400	34.8	At roundabout cross straight over towards Viterbo centre	Via della Palazzina, pass bank offices on the left	SE	322
70.065	700	35.5	Pass through the arched Porta Fiorentina into the old town of Viterbo and continue straight ahead	Via Matteotti, pass large piazza della Rocca on the right	SE	343
70.066	300	35.8	Cross piazza Verdi and take the second right	Corso Italia and via Roma, pass Banca di Roma on the right	SW	339
70.067	400	36.2	Arrive in the centre of Viterbo (VI)	Piazza del Plebiscito, beneath bell tower		335

Note: the Alternate Route allows cyclists, riders and those not wishing to deal with additional hillside tracks to proceed on the generally level main road.

Way Point N°	Way Point Distance (metres)	Total Distance (kilometres)	Directions	Verification Point	Compass	Altitude (metres)
1	0	0.0	Continue straight ahead and at the T-junction turn left onto the via Cassia	**Note:** the via Cassia can be very busy, without pavements in some sections. Proceed with caution	S	321
2	2600	2.6	After passing strada di Melona on the right turn left onto the small tarmac road, uphill	VF sign, shortly after crossing bridge over stream	SE	319
3	600	3.2	After a long curve to the right the official route rejoins from the left at Way Point #13 and continues straight ahead	VF sign		370

Alternate Route from Bolsena to Melona 3.2 km

Useful Contacts

Tourist/Information Offices

Ufficio Informazioni e di Accoglienza Turistica, 4/A, piazza Verdi - 01100 VITERBO
Tel: 0039 (0)761226666
Azienda di Promozione Turistica, 5, piazza san Carluccio - 01100 VITERBO
Tel: 0039 (0)761304795

Internet Cafes

Multidesk servizi viale Trento - 01100 VITERBO

Web and Coffee via Macel Gattesco - 01100 VITERBO

Last Planet, 7, via Pacinotti - 01100 VITERBO

Systemlink 7, via Pacinotti - 01100 VITERBO

Doctor

Bevilacqua Dr. Stefano, via Cattaneo Carlo - 01100 Viterbo Tel: 0039 (0)761 227242

Veterinary

Dr. Alessandro Clinica Veterinaria, piazzale Porsenna - 01100 VITERBO
Tel: 0039 (0)761 250546

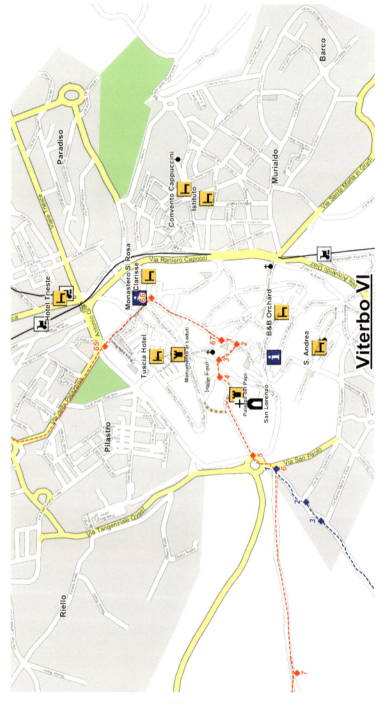

Viterbo Town Map

Hotel/B&B	Price
Rondinella, 800, della Cassia - 01027 MONTEFIASCONE Tel: 0039 (0)761 824995	B2
Dante, 2, via Nazionale - 01027 MONTEFIASCONE Tel: 0039 (0)761 826015	B2
Caminetto, 102, della Cassia - 01027 MONTEFIASCONE Tel: 0039 (0)761 826486	B2
Zi' giulia, 52, str. Tuscanese - 01100 VITERBO Tel: 0039 (0)761 250724	B2
PR Hotel tuscia, 41, via Cairoli - 01100 VITERBO Tel: 0039 (0)761 344400 info@tusciahotel.com	B3
Trieste, via N. Sauro, 32 - 01100 VITERBO Tel: 0039 (0)761 341882	B2
B&B Orchard, Via dell'Ortaccio 8 - 01100 VITERBO Tel: 0039 340 info@bborchard.it www.bborchard.it	B1
Mr Pietro Labate - 01100 VITERBO Tel: 0039 349 4409855 pietrusco58@hotmail.com	Donation

Religious Hostel	Price
Accoglienza Raggio di Sole, 3, via San Francesco - 01027 MONTEFIASCONE Tel: 347 5900953	Donation
Centro di Spiritualità s. Lucia Filippini, 11, via S. Maria in Arce - 01027 MONTEFIASCONE Tel: 0039 (0)761 826088	Donation
Domus la Quercia, 112, viale Fiume - 01030 VITERBO Tel:39 (0)761 33731 info@domuslaquercia.com	B1
Parrocchia Corpus Christi, Via Cassia - 01027 MONTEFIASCONE Tel: 0039 (0)761 826567	Donation
Monastero S. Rosa Clarisse, 33 via S. Rosa -01100 VITERBO Tel: 0039 (0)761 342887 www.monasterosantarosa.it	B1
S. Andrea, 31, via Fontana - 01100 VITERBO Tel: 0039 (0)761 347334 Mobile: 0039 339 8783818	Donation
S. Barbara, 31, piazzale dei Buccheri - 01100 VITERBO Tel: 0039 (0)761 250524 Mobile: 0039 339 3640935	Donation
Convento cappuccini, 16, via Iv Novembre - 01100 VITERBO Tel: 0039 (0)761 305564	B1
Istituto Adoratrici Sangue di Cristo, V.le 4 Novembre 25 - 01100 VITERBO Tel: 0039 (0)761 341900	B1

Camping	Price
Amalasunta, 98, della Cassia - MONTEFIASCONE Tel: 0039 (0)761 824151	B1
Camping Summerland, v. Cassia Nord - 01100 VITERBO Tel: 0039 (0)761/390017	B1

Equestrian

Quattranni, 154, v. del Lago - 01027 MONTEFIASCONE Tel: 0039 (0)761 820079

Club Roncone, Via Cassia Cimina - 01100 VITERBO Tel: 0039 (0)761 306230

Associazione Riding Club San Martino, Strada Sammartinese - 01100 VITERBO
Tel: 0039 (0)761 379057

Bolsena to Viterbo 36.2 km

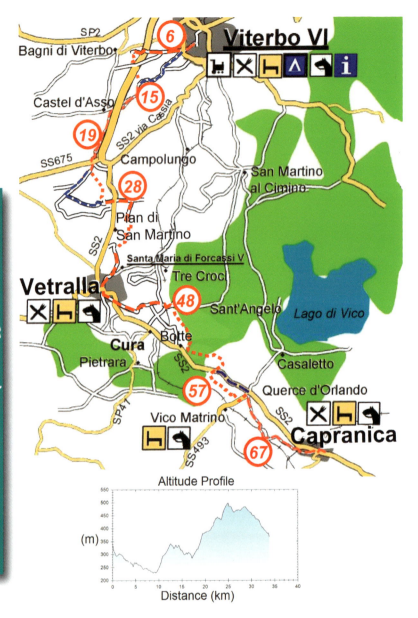

Altitude Profile

(m)

Distance (km)

Route Summary: the official route quickly leaves Viterbo and takes again to the country lanes and avoids the main roads. There is the opportunity to break the journey at Vetralla. The latter stages involve woodland tracks, before winding through hazel groves.

Distance from Canterbury: 1979km   **Distance to Rome:** 104km

Ascent: 436m   **Descent:** 406m

Way Point Nº	Way Point Distance (metres)	Total Distance (kilometres)	Directions	Verification Point	Compass	Altitude (metres)
71.001	0	0.0	From the piazza del Plebiscito bear left and leave the square on via San Lorenzo		S	335
71.002	90	0.1	Turn right	Via del Ganfione	NW	336
71.003	130	0.2	Turn left	Via Faul	W	323
71.004	90	0.3	Bear left remaining on via Faul	Pass through the Valle Faul with the Palazzo dei Papi on the left	SW	312
71.005	400	0.7	Exit the old town by Porta Faul, turn left at the roundabout and take the first road to the right direction Podere dell' Arco	Strada Signorino, red and white VF sign	SW	297
71.006	150	0.9	Take the first turning to the right - the official route requires crossing a number of barriers. Cyclists and riders can avoid these and reduce the route by 1.5km by continuing straight ahead on Alternate Route #1	Strada Freddano	W	294
71.007	1100	2.0	At the first junction bear right on the white road	Strada San'Ilario e Valentino, continue over the road bridge and into the farmland beyond	W	300
71.008	1500	3.5	At the T-junction after crossing the highway turn left	200m to the right is the ancient Ponte Camillario	S	274
71.009	60	3.5	Continue straight ahead	Through gate	S	274

Viterbo to Capranica 33.8 km

215

Way Point N°	Way Point Distance (metres)	Total Distance (kilometres)	Directions	Verification Point	Compass	Altitude (metres)
71.010	50	3.6	Continue straight ahead on the small path that quickly turns to the left and then right		SE	274
71.011	200	3.8	Continue straight ahead through gate and then bear right towards the small road	Beside Etruscan tomb	S	271
71.012	170	3.9	At the T-junction turn right on the road	Strada Freddano	W	272
71.013	130	4.1	Take the next turning to the left on the white road	Strada San Nicolao, returning under the highway	SE	270
71.014	300	4.4	Shortly after the tunnel under the highway bear right	Strada Asinello	S	264
71.015	700	5.1	At the T-junction turn right on the road – Alternate Route #1 rejoins from the left	Strada Signorino	SW	262
71.016	700	5.8	At fork bear left onto the gravel track, strada Risiere	VF sign and shrine on the corner	SW	260
71.017	900	6.7	Continue on the right fork under the highway	VF sign painted on the concrete	W	244
71.018	100	6.8	Take the left fork	Track close and parallel to the main road	S	241
71.019	1200	8.0	At crossroads in track continue straight ahead with the main road remaining on your left	Note: there are red and white signs that lead under the road and on towards the thermal ponds of Paliano. However, the signs quickly peter out. We advise those visiting the ponds to return here	SW	239

Way Point N°	Way Point Distance (metres)	Total Distance (kilometres)	Directions	Verification Point	Compass	Altitude (metres)
71.020	1000	9.0	After skirting the loop of the main road intersection turn left to go under the road	Red and white VF sign painted on wall just on left as you turn	E	228
71.021	130	9.1	At T-junction in track turn right	Strada Primomo	SW	230
71.022	150	9.3	At fork in the tracks keep right		SW	232
71.023	400	9.7	Turn left on the grassy track. **Note:** - this track can be overgrown. Alternate Route #2 continues on the white road to bypass the grass track	Beside large tree, VF sign painted on a rock to the right of the track	SE	233
71.024	1000	10.7	Bear right on the track	Uphill	S	276
71.025	400	11.1	Bear left. **Note:** Alternate Route #2 rejoins from the right		S	297
71.026	300	11.3	At T-junction turn left	Strada Quartuccio	E	302
71.027	500	11.8	At the junction with the via Cassia continue straight ahead	Strada Sasso San Pellegrino	E	314
71.028	800	12.2	Take the next turning to the right		S	344
71.029	800	12.9	At T-junction turn left	Strada Ciavalleta	E	325
71.030	300	13.3	Turn right on the track	Beside olive grove	S	336
71.031	300	13.6	Shortly after the track bends to the left turn sharp right on the path	Into the trees	W	327
71.032	140	13.7	Turn left on the track	Uphill	S	326
71.033	400	14.1	At T-junction turn right	Via Doganella	S	331
71.034	600	14.7	At T-junction turn right on the white road	Via Doganella	SW	319

Way Point N°	Way Point Distance (metres)	Total Distance (kilometres)	Directions	Verification Point	Compass	Altitude (metres)
71.035	300	15.0	At the junction bear right	Via Doganella	SW	305
71.036	200	15.2	At T-junction turn left	Strada Ponterello	S	298
71.037	1300	16.5	At the T-junction turn right on the road	Strada Forocassio	SW	306
71.038	200	16.7	Take the left fork towards Vetralla	Strada Volparo	SW	302
71.039	500	17.2	At the crossroads continue straight ahead	Via della Selvarella	S	297
71.040	200	17.4	Pass through piazza del Mattatoio, cross over the via Cassia and continue straight ahead	Towards the centre of Vetralla , via della Pletà	S	298
71.041	200	17.6	At the T-junction, turn left	Via Roma	SE	305
71.042	400	18.0	Shortly after the road bears right through piazza Marconi, take the left fork	Via San Michele	SE	319
71.043	300	18.3	Take the subway under the via Cassia and continue straight ahead	Via dei Cappuccini	SE	322
71.044	1100	19.4	T-junction turn left following the VF signs	Via del Giardino	NE	383
71.045	600	20.0	Take the left fork	Strada del Giardino	E	386
71.046	800	20.8	At the T-junction turn right on the road	Beside railway track	S	393
71.047	180	21.0	Turn left over the level crossing		NE	391
71.048	200	21.2	At the complex junction turn right across the car park onto the track towards the woods	Track proceeds on the edge of the woods with fields on the right	SE	401
71.049	1200	22.4	At the crossroads continue straight ahead		SE	437

Way Point N°	Way Point Distance (metres)	Total Distance (kilometres)	Directions	Verification Point	Compass	Altitude (metres)
71.050	700	23.1	Turn right on the track towards Botte	Strada Pian della Botte	SW	438
71.051	300	23.4	Turn left uphill on the road	VF sign	S	431
71.052	150	23.5	At the top of the hill and before entering Botte turn left onto a gravelled track into a woodland	White arrow on a tree further along the track	E	439
71.053	1700	25.2	Right fork down the hill	VF sign on tree	SE	497
71.054	400	25.6	At the T-junction turn right	VF sign hidden by brambles straight ahead	SW	486
71.055	500	26.1	At the intersection with the via Cassia, turn right and turn immediately left down a small track - the path ahead crosses cultivated hazel nut groves and may make for difficult going for cyclists who can turn left on the via Cassia to rejoin the official route at Way Point #64	VF arrows on the back of a signpost and once you have turned there are two VF signs painted on trees	S	469
71.056	400	26.5	At a large stone and a broken fence to the right go straight ahead between the trees with the road directly behind		S	462
71.057	90	26.6	At fence turn left and immediately right at the end of the fence	Parallel to the via Cassia	SE	465
71.058	200	26.8	At the T-junction turn left on the unmade road and immediately right through the gate	Continue across the fields parallel to the main road	SE	470
71.059	400	27.2	Turn left on the track and then immediately right	Beside hazel grove	SE	470

Way Point N°	Way Point Distance (metres)	Total Distance (kilometres)	Directions	Verification Point	Compass	Altitude (metres)
71.060	200	27.4	Continue straight ahead across the track		SE	470
71.061	130	27.5	Turn left and then right beside the hazel grove		SE	467
71.062	150	27.7	Turn sharp left and then right and right again beside the earthworks	After skirting the earthworks proceed parallel to main road	SE	469
71.063	300	28.0	At the T-junction with a broad tarmac road turn left on the SP493	Towards the via Cassia	NE	477
71.064	400	28.4	Just before reaching the via Cassia turn sharp right onto gravel track	Carved wooden VF sign and VF signs painted on electricity pylons	S	484
71.065	1000	29.4	At crossroads in track continue straight ahead on strada Doganale Oriolese		SE	466
71.066	800	30.2	Cross over railway and continue straight ahead	VF sign and hazelnut orchard on left	SE	450
71.067	500	30.7	Turn left to pass through tunnel under railway track		E	447
71.068	1700	32.4	At T-junction in tracks turn left	VF sign and crash barriers to your right	E	405
71.069	300	32.7	After passing through a tunnel under the railway continue straight ahead through a group of houses	Enter Capranica, via valle Santi	E	401
71.070	300	33.0	At the crossroads continue straight over on the Antica strada della Valle Santi	VF sign	E	390
71.071	400	33.4	At T-junction with a major road turn left down the hill		E	381
71.072	200	33.6	At T-junction with road running through the centre of the town turn right	SS2, via Nardini	SE	384
71.073	200	33.8	Arrive at the archway at the entrance to the historic the centre of Capranica			366

Alternate cycle and horse route from Viterbo on strada Signorino allows cyclists and riders to avoid obstacles on the official route and reduce overall route length by 1.5km. Total length 2.8km

Way Point N°	Way Point Distance (metres)	Total Distance (kilometres)	Directions	Verification Point	Compass	Altitude (metres)
1	0	0.0	Continue straight ahead on the road	Strada Signorino, red and white VF sign	SW	294
2	200	0.2	At fork in the road keep to the right	VF sign, strada Signorino	SW	310
3	130	0.3	Take right fork	Strada Signorino	SW	312
4	700	1.0	At crossroads continue straight ahead direction Bed & Breakfast Alcarre	Strada Signorino	SW	296
5	1800	2.8	Continue straight ahead to rejoin the official route at Way Point #15	VF sign on the crash barrier		262

Alternate cycle route using strada Quartuccio allows cyclists to avoid possible long grass on the official route, but increases overall route length by 1.7km. Total length 3.5km

Way Point N°	Way Point Distance (metres)	Total Distance (kilometres)	Directions	Verification Point	Compass	Altitude (metres)
1	0	0.0	Continue straight ahead on the white road, strada Primomo	VF sign painted on a large rock to the right of the track	SW	233
2	300	0.3	Take left fork		SW	232
3	1300	1.6	Turn left	Strada Quartuccio	E	216
4	1600	3.2	Turn right	Strada Quartuccio	E	287
5	300	3.5	Continue straight ahead to rejoin the official route at Way Point #26	VF sign on the crash barrier		302

Alternanate Routes

Hotel/B&B	Price
Vetralla Forum Cassii , 64, Strada Forocassio - 01019 VETRALLA Tel: 0039 (0)761 461394 colageo@alice.it	B2
Pino Solitario, Via Cassia, 299 - La Cura - 01019 VETRALLA Tel: 0039 (0)761 481045 alpinosolitario@libero.it	B3
Il Profeta, 3, viale Vico Matrino - 01012 VICO MATRINO Tel: 0039 (0)761 678865 Mobile: 0039 3382569932 **Note:** takes horses	B3
Monticelli, loc. Monticelli - 01012 CAPRANICA Tel: 0039 (0)761 678270 Mobile: 0039 348 0813421	B3
Al Casale Giallo, S.S. Cassia Km. 61,200, loc. Campo Spinella - 01012 CAPRANICA Tel: 0039 (0)761 660480 Mobile: 0039 338 1099072 alcasalegiallo@tele2.it www.infoviterbo.it/alcasalegiallo	B2
Ai dueCedri, 1, località Campo Padella - 01012 CAPRANICA Tel: 0039 (0)348 8235792	B2

Religious Hostel	Price
Monastero Regina Pacis, 4, via del Giardino - 01019 VETRALLA Tel: 0039 (0)761 481519	B2
Sala Nardini, Piazzetta Corte degli Anguillara - 01012 CAPRANICA Tel: 0039 (0)761 66791	Donation

Equestrian

Societa` Agricola Forestale Paternostro di Vetralla, localita' Paternostro - 01019 VETRALLA   Tel: 0039 (0)761 477605

Campo Data Di Fabbrini P, localita' Poggio Sambuco - 01012 CAPRANICA
Tel: 0039 (0)761 660414

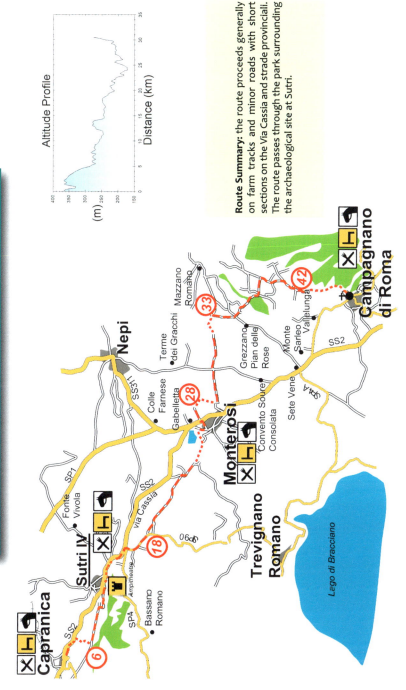

Capranica to Campagnano di Roma 30.5 km

Altitude Profile

(m)

Distance (km)

Route Summary: the route proceeds generally on farm tracks and minor roads with short sections on the Via Cassia and strade provinciali. The route passes through the park surrounding the archaeological site at Sutri.

Capranica

SS2

Sutri IV

Fonte Vivola

SP1

Nepi

SS311

Colle Farnese

Gabelletta

Terme dei Gracchi

Mazzano Romano

Amphitheatre

SP4

Bassano Romano

Via Cassia

SS2

SP90

Monterosi

Convento Source Consolata

Grezzano Pian delle Rose

Monte Sarleo

Sete Vene

Vallelunga

SS2

SPAA

Campagnano di Roma

Trevignano Romano

Lago di Bracciano

6

18

28

33

42

Capranica to Campagnano di Roma 30.5 km

Way Point N°	Way Point Distance (metres)	Total Distance (kilometres)	Directions	Verification Point	Compass	Altitude (metres)
72.001	0	0.0	Go straight ahead through the archway into the old town		E	366
72.002	190	0.2	Continue straight ahead. **Note:** the route ahead involves a flight of steps, cyclists and riders should turn left and follow via Romana to Way Point #4 just before the T-junction	Ponte dell'Orolgio, over the bridge towards the clock tower	E	363
72.003	500	0.7	After passing through the centro historico descend on the steps and turn right beside the town wall		SW	328
72.004	100	0.8	At the junction with the via Romana turn left and immediately right onto a track, strade Pogliere	VF sign, factory directly on your left as you turn	S	333
72.005	900	1.7	Bear right remaining on the main track		SW	357
72.006	300	2.0	At T-junction with a tarmac road turn left onto strade Capranichese		E	368
72.007	1800	3.8	At fork, bear right remaining on the main road	VF sign	E	332
72.008	1300	5.1	Shortly before reaching the via Cassia on the approach to Sutri take the footpath to the right		SE	282
72.009	300	5.4	Pass a gate and turn left on the road	Strada Capo Ripa	NE	268
72.010	200	5.6	At T-junction turn right to skirt Sutri on the via Cassia		E	276

Way Point N°	Way Point Distance (metres)	Total Distance (kilometres)	Directions	Verification Point	Compass	Altitude (metres)
72.011	200	5.8	Beside the park turn right towards the Mithraeum		S	279
72.012	70	5.9	In front of the Mithraeum turn left on the footpath	Pass beside the excavations in the volcanic rock	E	279
72.013	200	6.1	Continue straight ahead beside the Ampithetre on the footpath	Towards the Necropolis	SE	271
72.014	110	6.2	Turn right	Over the bridge	S	268
72.015	40	6.2	Turn left	Downhill through the trees towards the via Cassia	SE	268
72.016	200	6.4	At the junction with the via Cassia bear right and proceed straight ahead with care		SE	275
72.017	600	7.0	Take the second turning to the right	SP90, direction Bracciano, Roma – 52	SE	267
72.018	1500	8.5	On the apex of a bend to the right, turn left on the broad track	Strada Campo la Pera	SE	274
72.019	600	9.1	At the T-junction turn left		SE	264
72.020	3000	12.1	At the T-junction in front of the golf academy turn right to skirt the golf course on strada per Monterosi		SE	250
72.021	700	12.8	At fork bear left on the unmade road remaining beside the golf course	VF sign	SE	270
72.022	1300	14.1	Take the left fork	Section of Roman road	NE	275
72.023	400	14.5	Bear right on the track	Lago Monterosi to the left, merges with tarmac road via Papa Leone	E	249

Way Point N°	Way Point Distance (metres)	Total Distance (kilometres)	Directions	Verification Point	Compass	Altitude (metres)
72.024	300	14.8	At T-junction turn right	Via Cimina	S	243
72.025	400	15.2	Turn left and keep left beside building supplies yard	Via Dante and then via Prato della Fontana	NE	246
72.026	500	15.7	Pass under the highway and turn left beside the dual-carriageway and then take the second turning on the right	Via Gabelletta	NE	243
72.027	700	16.4	At the end of the straight section of road fork right beside the field		SE	245
72.028	200	16.6	At the junction with the track turn right	Towards the farm buildings	SE	240
72.029	300	16.9	Follow the track as it turns right		S	238
72.030	900	17.8	At the T-junction turn sharp left	White road	E	247
72.031	1600	19.4	Cross over the road (SP38) and continue straight ahead and then bear right at the fork	Pass wire fence on the left	E	230
72.032	2200	21.6	At T-junction with the road turn right		E	209
72.033	500	22.1	Turn sharp right		S	218
72.034	1200	23.3	At the crossroads with the SP37 continue straight ahead into Parco Regionale Valle del Treja	Strada Monte Gelato, sign Cascate Monte Gelato	SE	184
72.035	1000	24.3	Shortly after crossing the bridge turn left	Strada Monte Gelato, pass Cascate Monte Gelato on the left	SE	176
72.036	500	24.8	Take the left fork	Strada Monte Gelato	E	177

Way Point N°	Way Point Distance (metres)	Total Distance (kilometres)	Directions	Verification Point	Compass	Altitude (metres)
72.037	900	25.7	At the T-junction turn right		SW	213
72.038	400	26.1	Take the right fork		S	187
72.039	300	26.4	Pass between houses and continue straight ahead	On the white road	S	192
72.040	500	26.9	At the T-junction turn right		SW	197
72.041	500	27.4	Take the right fork	Beside farm building	S	209
72.042	200	27.6	Bear left and continue straight ahead towards Parci di Veio		S	207
72.043	2000	29.6	Bear right towards the town	Via Santa Lucia	SW	218
72.044	500	30.1	Bear right onto the ramp leading up to the town		NW	241
72.045	70	30.2	At the T-junction turn left on the main street through the high town	Via Sant'Andrea, pass bell tower on the left	SW	248
72.046	300	30.5	Arrive in the piazza in the centre of Campagno di Roma	Beside the church, piazza Cesare Leonelli		276

Hotel/B&B	Price
Sutrium, 1, p.zza S. Francesco - 01015 SUTRI Tel: 0039 (0)761 600468 info@sutriumhotel.it	B2
L'Amaca, 8, via Pietro Salvatori - 01030 MONTEROSI Tel: 0039 (0)761 699921	B3
Le Cese, 9, via strada delle cese - 00063 CAMPAGNANO DI ROMA Tel: 0039 (0)69042869	B2
Ristorante Albergo Benigni, 13, via della Vittoria - 00063 CAMPAGNANO DI ROMA Tel: 0039 (0)6 9041760	B2
I Platani, 33, via Monterazzano - 00063 CAMPAGNANO DI ROMA Tel: 0039 (0)329 1812301	B2
Hotel il Postiglione, 15, Via Cassia Antica - 00063 CAMPAGNANO DI ROMA Tel: 0039 (0)6 9041214	B3
Agriturismo il Casale di Martignano, str. Di Martignano - 00063 CAMPAGNANO DI ROMA Tel: 0039 (0)6 99802004 info@martignano.com	B3

Religious Hostel	Price
Casa d'Accoglienza, "Oasi di PacE", 15, via delle Viole - 01015 SUTRI Tel: 0039 (0)761 659175 www.oasidipace.it	B2
Monache Carmelitane, di Clausura, 1, via Garibaldi - 01015 SUTRI Tel: 0039 (0)761 609082	Donation
S. Giovanni arrocchia, Loc. Fontevivola - 01015 SUTRI Tel :39 (0)761 669053	Donation
Oratorio san Giovanni Battista, 7, via Dante Alighieri - 01015 SUTRI Tel: 0039 (0)6 9041094 Mobile: 0039 333 9381576 donrenzotanturli@virgilio.it	Donation

Equestrian

Scuderia Monte Brianzo s.r.l, v. della Cornacchia - 01015 SUTRI Tel: 0039 (0)761 600895

Poscolieri Salvatore, via Del Fontanile - 01030 MONTEROSI Tel: 0039 (0)761 699431

Centro Ippico Fattoria Del Sorbo, 63, via Monte Lupoli - 00063 CAMPAGNANO DI ROMA Tel: 0039 (0)6 9043008

Capranica to Campagnano di Roma 30.5 km

Campagnano di Roma
Baccano III
SP13a
SP10a
Poggio dell'Ellera
Sorbo
SS2
Cesano
via Cassia
Castelli
Formello
Monte Aguzzo
La Selviata
via Veientana Nuova
Prato
La Corte
via Cassia
Monte Michele
Isola Farnese
SP49
La Storta II

Altitude Profile

(m)

Distance (km)

Route Summary: despite the proximity to Rome this section remains surprisingly rural on farm and woodland tracks and small roads. There are some tricky descents and climbs between Monte Michele and Isola Farnese with a potentially dangerous river crossing.

Distance from Canterbury: 2043km **Distance to Rome: 40km**

Ascent: 402m **Descent: 509m**

Campagnano di Roma to La Storta 24.4 km

Way Point N°	Way Point Distance (metres)	Total Distance (kilometres)	Directions	Verification Point	Compass	Altitude (metres)
73.001	0	0.0	From the church in piazza Cesare Leonelli, continue straight ahead on the main street	Towards the arch, Corso Vittorio Emanuele, No Entry	SW	276
73.002	300	0.3	Pass through the arch and turn left in piazza Regina Elena	Towards Formello, via San Sebastiano	S	282
73.003	900	1.2	On the Apex of a sharp bend to the left, continue straight ahead on the more minor road	Via di Maria Bona, pass sports ground on the right. **Note:** caution on the winding road ahead where there are no pavements	SE	314
73.004	400	1.6	Turn right up the hill	Strada di Follettino, painted sign on kerb	SE	348
73.005	180	1.8	Turn sharp right up the hill	Via di Monte Razzano, woodland on the right	SW	363
73.006	200	2.0	Take the left fork	Strada delle Piane, pass house with roof terrace on the left at the junction	S	377
73.007	200	2.2	Take the right fork on the unmade road	Strada delle Piane, view over roof tops on the left at the junction	S	378
73.008	1100	3.3	At the T-junction turn left	Strada delle Pastine, VF sign painted on pole	SE	281
73.009	500	3.8	Take the left fork on the tarmac road	Strada del Sorbo, VF sign painted on electricity pole	SE	267
73.010	1700	5.5	Continue straight ahead on the road into the Valle del Sorbo	Pass the Santuario della Madonna del Sorbo on the left	S	202

Way Point N°	Way Point Distance (metres)	Total Distance (kilometres)	Directions	Verification Point	Compass	Altitude (metres)
73.011	1100	6.6	Cross the bridge and continue straight ahead	Towards the trees and climbing the hill	S	189
73.012	1600	8.2	On entering Formello bear right and right again	VF sign, via Antonio Angelozzi	SW	278
73.013	140	8.3	Take the right fork	Via di Grottefranca	W	272
73.014	600	8.9	Turn sharp left	Via delle Spinareta	S	251
73.015	180	9.1	Take the right fork	Remaining on the ridge, via delle Spinareta	S	253
73.016	700	9.8	At the crossroads continue straight ahead	Via delle Spinareta	S	217
73.017	1500	11.3	At the crossroads continue straight ahead	Via Baccanello	S	171
73.018	400	11.7	Take the left fork	Via Monte Lavatore, towards the highway, VF sign	SE	162
73.019	2000	13.7	At the crossroads with via Formellese Sud, turn right and cross the flyover with caution	Petrol station ahead at the junction	S	129
73.020	300	14.0	After crossing the flyover turn sharp left betwee the slip road and the parking area. **Note:** the official route ahead includes a river crossing that can be dangerous in times of flood. There are very limited alternatives beyond this point If in doubt remain on the via Formellese until reaching the via Cassia where you should turn left to enter La Storta and rejoin the Official Route at Way Point #32	VF sign. Via Monte dell'Ara, a small road close beside the slip road and then the highway before bearing right	SE	124

Way Point N°	Way Point Distance (metres)	Total Distance (kilometres)	Directions	Verification Point	Compass	Altitude (metres)
73.021	1500	15.5	At the crossroads turn right	Between fields on via Monte Michele	SE	111
73.022	1300	16.8	Turn right and right again to pass through a gap in a line of trees and continue with the trees on the right		W	124
73.023	100	16.9	Take the first turning to the left	Between fields	SE	127
73.024	200	17.1	Bear right towards the hamlet		SW	111
73.025	300	17.4	Pass through the gate and bear left	Hamlet on the right, via del Prato delle Cotte	S	122
73.026	1200	18.6	Take the right fork on the track through gate	The track winds downhill between trees. VF sign on tree	S	105
73.027	700	19.3	Bear right to ford the river with care and bear right again on the far side	Torrente Valchetta	W	56
73.028	700	20.0	Cross the bridge and turn right	Via del Prato della Corte	NW	53
73.029	800	20.8	At the junction bear right up the hill	Football field on the left before the junction	NW	58
73.030	600	21.4	Enter Isola Farnese and bear left on the road at the T-junction		W	96
73.031	1100	22.5	At the junction bear left up the hill	VF sign, via dell'Isola Farnese	SW	142
73.032	500	23.0	At the T-junction turn left on the via Cassia	Brow of the hill. Roma – 17	SE	158
73.033	1400	24.4	Arrive in the centre of La Storta(II)	Beside the elevated church on the right		169

Hotel/B&B	Price
Hotel Tempio di Apollo, 8, piazza della Colonnetta - 00123 ISOLA FARNESE Tel: 0039 (0)6 308 90515	B3
Hotel Cassia, 1736, Via Cassia - 00123 ROMA Tel: 0039 (0)6 30891772 info@hotelcassia.com www.hotelcassia.com **Note:** just outside La Storta	B3
Bela Motel, via Giuseppe Adami - 00123 TORRIONE CERQUETTA, ROMA Tel: 0039 (0)6 30891016 **Note:** just outside La Storta	B3
Hotel Residence La Cerquetta Di Bozza, 27, via Giovaninetti Silvio - 00123 ROMA Tel: 0039 (0)6 30860357 **Note:** just outside La Storta	B3

Religious Hostel	Price
Suore di Santa Brigida, 2040 , Via Cassia - 00100 LA STORTA Tel: 0039 (0)6 30880272	Donation
Stituto Suore delle Poverelle, 5, via Baccarica - 00100 LA STORTA Tel: 0039 (0)6 30890495	Donation
Cattedrale s.Cuore di Gesù e Maria, 43 , via del Cenacolo - 00100 LA STORTA Tel: 0039 (0)6 30890267 parrcatt.scgm@libero.it	Donation
Istituto Figlie di Nostra Signora del SacroCuore, 1826, Via Cassia - 00100 LA STORTA Tel: 0039 (0)6 30890863 fnssc_curiageneralizia@inwind.it	B2
Centro spiritualità Sg lourdes , 19 Campagnano. Il Postiglione, - 00100 LA STORTA segreteria@ilpostiglione.it. curiageneralizia@inwind.it	B2

For those of you who may not want to complete the last section through Rome, on foot, some information about other options

Transport Info Helpline - 0039 (0)657003
Information and services for public and private transport systems, timetables and routes for public transport systems, travel passes and tickets, permits (limited traffic areas, blue line areas, special badges for disabled persons), tourist bus plan, car-repair garage blue tickets, car sharing, traffic light and parking meter signs.

For Tourist Bus services, also Sundays and holidays (Monday to Saturday 8:00 am - 8:00 pm) Tel: 0039 (0)646952087
info@atac.roma.lt (private transport services)
clienti@atac.roma.it (public transport services)
infopagososta@atac.roma.it
bollinoblu@atac.roma.it
Tourist bus services: infobusturistici@atac.roma.it
Car sharing services: carsharing@atac.roma.it

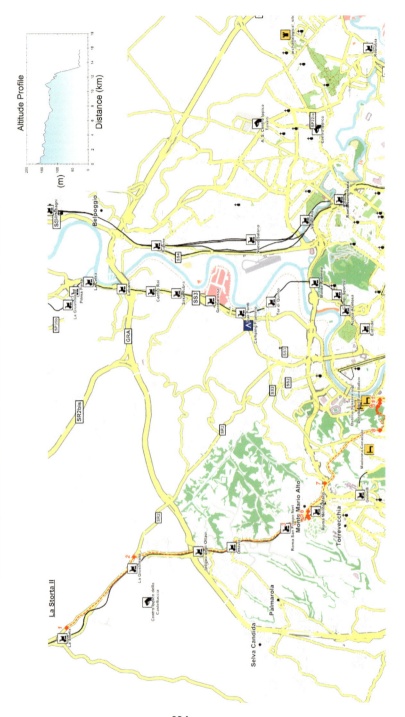

La Storta to Saint Peter's Basilica 15.8 km

Altitude Profile

Distance (km)

In order to receive the testimonium - certificate of authentication - you can present your passport/credential in one of two places:

Opera Romana Pellegrinaggi - piazza San Pietro) - 00193 Roma.
Standard Opening Hours: April - Sept Monday - Friday 09.00 - 13.00 15.00 - 19.00
October - March Monday - Friday 09.00 - 13.00 15.00 - 18.00
Closed Saturdays and holidays.
The centre also provides news and catalogues, suggests guides and other useful publications.
Sacristy of St Peter's Basilica - 09.00 - 12.00 except Sundays, Public Holidays and Papal Audience days.

Route Summary: the route into Rome initially uses the very busy Via Cassia and via Trionfale, there is brief relief on the pathways through the Monte Mario park before returning to the broad city boulevards for the final approach to the Vatican.

Distance from Canterbury: 2067km   **Distance to Rome:** 16km

Ascent: 90m   **Descent:** 234m

Way Point N°	Way Point Distance (metres)	Total Distance (kilometres)	Directions	Verification Point	Compass	Altitude (metres)
74.001	0	0.0	On the via Cassia below the church in La Storta continue with great care on the road towards Roma	Church on the right and petrol station on the left	SE	169
74.002	2700	2.7	Take the right fork following the flow of traffic	Via Trionfale, pass motor car sales showrooms on the right	S	148
74.003	4800	7.5	At the traffic lights, just beyond the railway station, turn right on via Giuseppe Barellaia, pass under the railway and immediately turn left	Via Eugenio di Mattei, keep railway close on the left	S	116
74.004	600	8.1	In piazza Santa Maria della Pietà turn left and cross over the railway	Via Vincenzo Chiarugi, direction via Trionfale	NE	124
74.005	80	8.2	Bear right at the next turning	Via Franco Basaglia	E	124
74.006	130	8.3	Rejoin the via Trionfale, carefully cross the road, turn right and then keep left	Pass petrol station on the right	SE	124

La Storta to Saint Peter's Basilica 15.8 km

235

Way Point N°	Way Point Distance (metres)	Total Distance (kilometres)	Directions	Verification Point	Compass	Altitude (metres)
74.007	1000	9.3	At the complex intersection with the underpasses bear right with great care	Remain on via Trionfale	SE	122
74.008	2400	11.7	Turn left up the steps and through the archway into the walled Monte Mario park and follow the footpath as it crosses the viale del Parco, passes through the gate in the metal fence, skirts the hill, with the observatory on the left and zigzags downhill through the park	Archway is shortly after pedestrian crossing with traffic lights. **Note:** to avoid the obstacles in the park remain on via Trionfale to the crossroads with the tree lined via Andrea Doria, where you should bear right on via Leone IV to rejoin the official route in piazza del Risorgimento at Way Point #12	E	117
74.009	1500	13.2	At the bottom of the hill pass through the gate and continue straight ahead		SE	39
74.010	120	13.3	After leaving the park, take the pedestrian crossing over the road and continue straight ahead	Via Novenio Bucchi	E	24
74.011	90	13.4	At the T-junction, cross the broad road and go straight ahead through the gardens in piazza Maresciallo and turn right	Viale Angelico	S	23
74.012	2000	15.4	Continue straight ahead across piazza Risorgimento towards the Vatican	Via di Porta Angelica, dome of St Peter's to the right	S	23
74.013	400	15.8	Arrive in Saint Peter's Square (I)			24

The Rome subway network is relatively simple. As a rough guide, it's basically a cross-shaped intersection of two train lines, one running north-west to south-east ('Linea A'), and the other north-east to south-west (the 'Linea B'). intersecting at the 'Termini' station which is in the centre of the city.

TRAINS
Regular trains from both the central Railroad Station, Stazione Termini, and the Tiburtina Station connect to the major cities in Italy and Europe. The Eurostar trains are the most rapid, next are the Intercity trains and last are the local trains. For the Eurostar trains you must buy a ticket and reserve a seat before boarding. Tickets may be purchased at the stations, at most travel agencies (there is no extra fee) or online at the TrenItalia web site. On the Internet you need to register and pay with a credit card and your tickets will be waiting for you at the station. Remember to validate your tickets at the yellow electronic boxes located in the boarding areas before boarding the train.

BUSES TO OTHER CITIES IN ITALY
Buses to other Italian cities and to European destinations leave from in front of the Tiburtina train station.

AIRPORTS
The main airport, Leonardo da Vinci (also known as Fiumicino), is located 26km southwest of the city center. A train runs between the airport and the central railroad station, Stazione Termini. It operates every 30 minutes between the hours of 5:52 am and 10:52 pm. The trip takes approximately 30 minutes.

The other airport is Ciampino, about 20 km southeast of the city centre. Ciampino mainly serves domestic flights and charter flights. COTRAL buses run every 40 minutes from the ANAGNINA stop of Subway Line A (price 1 Euro) to Ciampino.

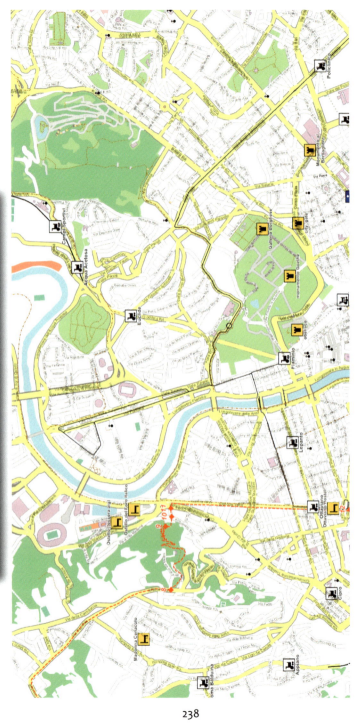

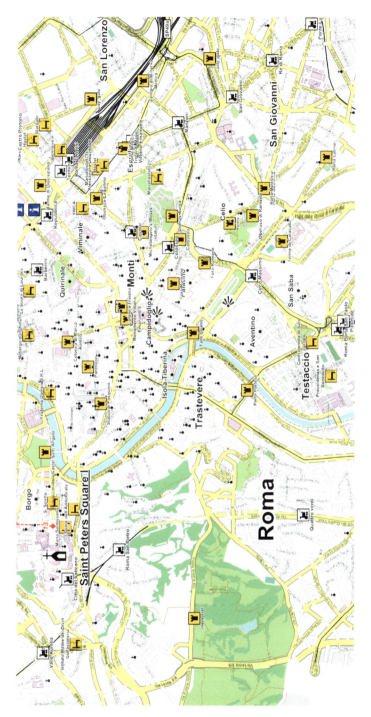

Rome City Map

239

Hotel/B&B - Many options available in Rome, list below selected on price and recommendation	Price
Viennese, 64, via Marsala - 00100 ROME Tel: 0039 (0)6 4456357 www.hotelviennese.it hotelviennese@tin.it	B2
PR D'Inghilterra Hotel, 14, via Bocca di Leone - 00187 ROME Tel: 0039 (0)6 699 81204	B2
Stargate, 88, via Palestro - 00100 ROME Tel: 0039 (0)6 4457164 www.stargatehotels.com informa@stargatehotels.com	B2
Mariahostel (1), Via Principe Amedeo - 00100 ROME Maria49@tin.it	B2
Mariahostel (2), Via Mecenate, 27- 00100 ROME Maria49@tin.it	B2
Religious Hostel	**Price**
Figlie dei Sacri Cuori di Gesù e Maria, 28, via Pio VIII - 00100 ROME Tel: 0039 (0)6 636825 info@casaravasco.it www.casaravasco.it	B2
Confraternita di San Jacopo di Compostella, 51, via Galvani (zona Testaccio - fermata Piramide, oppure Bus 75) - 00100 ROME Tel: 0039 (0)755736381 www.confraternitadisanjacopo.it santiago@ unipg.it	Donation
Foyer Phat Diem, 45, v. Pineta Sacchetti - 00100 ROME Tel: 0039 (0)6 6638826	B2
Istituto Madre del Divin Pastore, 16 , via Pio VIII - 00100 ROME Tel: 0039 (0)6 39366582 fdproma@tiscali.it	B2
Istituto Suore dell'Addolorata, 41, Borgo S.Spirito - 00100 ROME Tel: 0039 (0)6 6861076 ssmsanpietro@libero.it	Donation
Ostello (tessera aig), viale delle Olimpiadi, 61, Foro Italico - 00100 ROME Tel: 0039 (0)6 3236267 roma@ostellionline.org www.highhostels.com www.ostellionline.org	B1
Madonna Cenacolo, 9, via Vincenzo Ambrosio - 00100 ROME Tel: 0039 (0)6 35401142 cenacolopellegrini@hotmail.com	Donation
Istituto Madri degli Abbandonati, 88, viale Vaticano - 00100 ROME Tel: 0039 (0)6 39723807	B2
PR Casa d'Accoglienza s. Spirito, 41, Suore Francescane dell'Addolorata Borgo S. Spirito - 00193 ROME Tel: 0039 (0)6 686 1076 ssmsanpietro@libero.it	B2
PR Istituto Maria SantissimaBambina, 21, via Paolo VI - 00120 CITTÀ DEL VATICANO Tel: 0039 (0)6 6989 3511 imbspietro@mariabambina.va	B2
PR Le Suore di Lourdes, 113, via Sistina - 00187 ROME Tel: 0039 (0)6 474 5324	B2
PR Fraterna Domus, 62, via del Monte Brianza - 00186 Rome Tel: 0039 (0)6 6880 2727 domusrm@tin.it	B2
Spedale della Provvidenza e San Benedetto Labre, c/o Instituto Suore Figlie della Divina Provvidenza, 51, Via Galvani - 00153 ROME Tel: 0030 338 4340 072 santiago@unipg.it **Note:** about two and half miles from St Peter's Basilica, by bus, take No. 75 from the Termini raliway station, by underground, take the Laurentino direction and stop at Piramide	Donation

Camping - all Rome's campsites are some way out of the city, but easy enough to get to.	Price
Camping Flaminio (8km north of centre), 821, via Flaminia Nuova - 0189 ROMA Tel: 0039 (0)63332604 info@villageflaminio.com www.villageflaminio.it	B1
Camping Tiber, via Tiberina - ROMA Tel: 0039 (0)633610733 **Note:** free shuttle service to and from nearby Prima Porta station, for the Roma-Nord train service to piazzale Flaminio www.campingtiber.com info@campingtiber.com	B1

Youth Hostel	Price
YWCA, 4, via C. Balbo - 00100 ROME Tel: 0039 (0)6 4880460	B1
Ottiviano, 6, via Ottiviano - 00192 ROMA Tel: 0039 (0)639738138 info@pensioneottaviano.com www.pensioneottaviano.com **Note:** near the Vatican and popular with backpackers, English spoken - book well in advance.	B1
Ostello del foro Italico, 61, viale delle Olimpiadi - 00194 ROMA Tel. 06 3236267 roma@ostellionline.org www.ostellionline.org	B1
Allessandro Palace Hostel, 42, via Vicenza - 00185 ROME Tel: 0039 (0)649380534 palace@hostelsalessandro.com www.hostelsalessandro.com **Note:** voted one of the top hostels in Europe for its creative style	B1
Alessandro Downtown Hostel, 23, via C. Cattaneo -00185 ROME Tel: 0039 (0)644340147 downtown@hostelsalessandro.com **Note:** partner to the above	B1

Equestrian
Centro Ippico della Castelluccia, via Giuseppe Clemente - 00123 ROMA Tel: 0039 (0)6 30366179
A.S. Equestre Kappa, 1939, v. Portuense - 00050 ROMA Tel: 0039 (0)6 65000249
Centro Ippico, via Nomentana - 00137 Roma   Tel: 0039 (0)6 41400108
A. S. Centro Ippico Talenti, 38, via Dario Niccodemi- 00137 ROMA Tel: 0039 (0)6 87133209
Centro Ippico Castel Di Guido, via Aurelia - 00100 Roma   Tel: 0039 (0)6 6689302
Centro Ippico Cinque Stelle, via Giuseppe Lazzati - 00166 ROMA Tel: 0039 (0)6 61908109

Information Kiosks in Rome	
Castel Sant'Angelo, Piazze Pia	Tel: 0039 (0)6 68809797
Fontana di Treviv via Minghetti	Tel: 0039 (0)6 6782988
Fori Imperial, piazza del Tempio della Pace	Tel: 0039 (0)6 69924307
Piazza Navona, piazza delle Cinque Lune	Tel: 0039 (0)6 8809240
Santa Maria Maggiore, via dell'Olmata	Tel: 0039 (0)6 4740955
Trastevere, piazza Sonnino	Tel: 0039 (0)6 58333457
via del Corso, Largo Goldoni	Tel: 0039 (0)6 8136061
via Nazionale, Palazzo delle Esposizioni	Tel: 0039(0)6 47824525

Tourist/Information Offices

Ufficio Informazioni della Provincia di Roma, 26, via XX Settembre - 00186 ROME
Tel: 0039 (0)6 42138221

Azienda di Promozione Turistica, 11, via Parigi - 00185 ROME   Tel: 0039 (0)6 4819316
www.romaturismo.it info@aptroma.com

Azienda di Promozione Turistica, 5, via Parigi -ROME 00185 Tel: 0039 (0)6 4819316
Note: Visitor's Centre

Rome Internet Cafes

VirtualWorldNetwork via Mazzini 18 - 53 Civitavecchia

TheNetgate - Pantheon piazza Firenze, 25

Excape Internet Café viale Somalia, 227

Internet Café (Stargate) via Marrucini, 12

Internet Point Rome corso Vittorio Emanuele II, 312/305A

The Net al Nuovo Pasquino piazza S.Egidio, 10

Nauta Cafè via Fiume delle Perle, 114

infonet via valle corteno 10/12

Music All via Manlio Torquato, 21

Rimanet Internet Cafes via del Portico d'Ottavia, 2/a

Xplore via dei Gracchi, 85

TheNetgate - Termini Stazione Termini, c/o Drug Store

TreviNet Pl@ce Internet Point via in Arcione, 103 (fontana di Trevi)

Embassies in Rome

United States Embassy, 119/A, via Vittorio Veneto - 00187 ROME
Tel: 0039 (0)6 4674 2356

Australian Embassy, 215, via Alessandria - 00198 ROME   Tel: 0039 (0)6 852 721

South African Embassy, 14, via Tanaro - 00198 ROME   Tel: 0039 (0)6 8419794
or 0039 06 852 541

British Embassy, 80a, via XX Settembre - 00187 ROME   Tel: 0039 (0)6 482 5441
or 0039 (0)6 482 5551   Night emergencies: 0039 (0)6 482 5400/8893
ConsularRome@fco.gov.uk

New Zealand Embassy, 28, via Zara - 00198 ROME   Tel: 0039 (0)6 441 7171
nzemb.rom@flashnet.it

Canadian Embassy, 27, via Giovanni Battista De Rossi - 00161 ROME
Tel: 0039 (0)6 445 981

Irish Embassy, 3, piazza di Campitelli - 00186 ROME   Tel: 0039 (0)6 697 9121

Doctor

Abu Eideh Dr. Ibrahim, via Cola di Rienzo - 00192 ROME Tel: 0039 (0)63201634

Veterinary

Dr. Fiore Mark, v. Romagnoni - 00125 ROME   Tel: 0039 (0)6 5215398

ROUTE	Map References	Number	Description
	Carta topografica d'Italia serie 1:50,000	Foglio 136	SANTHIA Edizione/aggiornamento anno 1974
	Carta topografica d'Italia serie 1:50,000	Foglio 137	VERCELLI currently out of print
Vercelli to Mortara	Carta topografica d'Italia serie 1:50,000	Foglio 137	VERCELLI Edizione/aggiornamento anno 1996
	Carta topografica d'Italia serie 1:50,000	Foglio 058	MORTARA Edizione/aggiornamento anno 1996
Mortara to Garlasco	Carta topografica d'Italia serie 1:50,000	Foglio 058	MORTARA Edizione/aggiornamento anno 1996
Garlasco to Pavia	Carta topografica d'Italia serie 1:50,000	Foglio 058	MORTARA Edizione/aggiornamento anno 1996
	Carta topografica d'Italia serie 1:50,000	Foglio 059	PAVIA Edizione/aggiornamento anno 1996
Pavia to Santa Cristina	Carta topografica d'Italia serie 1:50,000	Foglio 059	PAVIA Edizione/aggiornamento anno 1961
Santa Cristina to Piacenza	Carta topografica d'Italia serie 100/V e 100/L	Foglio 059	PAVIA Edizione/aggiornamento anno 1961
Piacenza to Fiorenzuola d'Arda	Carta topografica d'Italia serie 100/V e 100/L:	Foglio 060	PIACENZA Edizione/aggiornamento anno 1959
	Carta topografica d'Italia serie 1:50,000	Foglio 072	FIORENZUOLA D'ARDA Edizione/aggiornamento anno 1961
Fiorenzuola D'Arda to Fidenza	Carta topografica d'Italia serie 1:50,000	Foglio 072	FIORENZUOLA D'ARDA Edizione/aggiornamento anno 1961
	Carta topografica d'Italia serie 1:50,000	Foglio 073	PARMA Edizione/aggiornamento anno 1961

ROUTE	Map References	Number	Description
Fidenza to Fornovo di Taro	Carta topografica d'Italia serie 1:50,000	Foglio 073	PARMA Edizione/aggiornamento anno 1961
Fornovo di Taro to Berceto	Carta topografica d'Italia serie 1:50,000	Foglio 085	CASTELNOVO NE' MONTI Edizione/aggiornamento anno 1951
Berceto to Pontremoli	Carta topografica d'Italia serie 100/V e 100/L	Foglio 085	CASTELNOVO NE' MONTI Edizione/aggiornamento anno 1951
	Carta topografica d'Italia serie 100/V e 100/L	Foglio 073	PONTREMOLI Edizione/aggiornamento anno 1951
Pontremoli to Aulla	Carta topografica d'Italia serie 100/V e 100/L:	Foglio 084	PONTREMOLI Edizione/aggiornamento anno 1951
	Carta topografica d'Italia serie 100/V e 100/L:	Foglio 096	MASSA Edizione/aggiornamento anno 1951
Aulla to Sarzana	Carta topografica d'Italia serie 1:50,000	Foglio 096	MASSA Edizione/aggiornamento anno 1951
Sarzana to Pietrasanta	Carta topografica d'Italia serie 1:50,000	Foglio 096	MASSA Edizione/aggiornamento anno 1951
	Carta topografica d'Italia serie 1:50,000	Foglio 104	PISA Edizione/aggiornamento anno 1952
Pietrasanta to Lucca	Carta topografica d'Italia serie 100/V e 100/L:	Foglio 104	PISA Edizione/aggiornamento anno 1952
	Carta topografica d'Italia serie 100/V e 100/L:	Foglio 105	LUCCA Edizione/aggiornamento anno 1954
Lucca to Ponte a Cappiano	Carta topografica d'Italia serie 100/V e 100/L:	Foglio 105	LUCCA Edizione/aggiornamento anno 1954
Ponte a Cappriano to Gambassi Terme	Carta topografica d'Italia serie 100/V e 100/L:	Foglio 105	LUCCA Edizione/aggiornamento anno 1954
	Carta topografica d'Italia serie 100/V e 100/L:	Foglio 112	VOLTERRA Edizione/aggiornamento anno 1953
	Carta topografica d'Italia serie 100/V e 100/L:	Foglio 113	CASTELFIORENTINO Edizione/aggiornamento anno 1953

ROUTE	Map References	Number	Description
Gambassi Terme to Gracciano d'Elsa	Carta topografica d'Italia serie 100/V e 100/L:	Foglio 113	CASTELFIORENTINO Edizione/aggiornamento anno 1953
Gracciano d'Elsa to Siena	Carta topografica d'Italia serie 100/V e 100/L:	Foglio 113	CASTELFIORENTINO Edizione/aggiornamento anno 1953
	Carta topografica d'Italia serie 100/V e 100/L:	Foglio 120	SIENA Edizione/aggiornamento anno 1953
Siena to Ponte d'Arbia	Carta topografica d'Italia serie 100/V e 100/L:	Foglio 120	SIENA Edizione/aggiornamento anno 1953
	Carta topografica d'Italia serie 100/V e 100/L:	Foglio 121	MONTEPULCIANO Edizione/aggiornamento anno 1953
Ponte d'Arbia to San Quirico d'Orcia	Carta topografica d'Italia serie 100/V e 100/L:	Foglio 121	MONTEPULCIANO Edizione/aggiornamento anno 1953
San Quirico d'Orcia to Radicofani	Carta topografica d'Italia serie 100/V e 100/L:	Foglio 121	MONTEPULCIANO Edizione/aggiornamento anno 1953
	Carta topografica d'Italia serie 100/V e 100/L:	Foglio 129	SANTA FIORA Edizione/aggiornamento anno 1953
San Quirico d'Orcia to Radicofani	Carta topografica d'Italia serie 100/V e 100/L:	Foglio 129	SANTA FIORA Edizione/aggiornamento anno 1953
Acquapendente to Bolsena	Carta topografica d'Italia serie 100/V e 100/L	Foglio 129	SANTA FIORA Edizione/aggiornamento anno 1953
	Carta topografica d'Italia serie 100/V e 100/L	Foglio 137	VITERBO Edizione/aggiornamento anno 1953
Bolsena to Viterbo	Carta topografica d'Italia serie 100/V e 100/L:	Foglio 137	VITERBO Edizione/aggiornamento anno 1953
Viterbo to Capranica	Carta topografica d'Italia serie 100/V e 100/L:	Foglio 137	VITERBO Edizione/aggiornamento anno 1953
	Carta topografica d'Italia serie 100/V e 100/L:	Foglio 143	BRACCIANO Edizione/aggiornamento anno 1953
Capranica to Campagnano di Roma	Carta topografica d'Italia serie 100/V e 100/L:	Foglio 143	PIACENZA Edizione/aggiornamento anno 1953
Campagnano di Roma to La Storta	Carta topografica d'Italia serie 100/V e 100/L	Foglio 143	BRACCIANO Edizione/aggiornamento anno 1953

The list below gives details of the churches and religious organisations either in or near towns along the route. These have not specifically stated that accommodation is provided for pilgrims, but it is likely that a phone call will put you in contact with someone who will be able/willing to help. * indicates that there are more churches than could be listed in this limited space

VERCELLI *

Basilica Di Sant'Andrea, 35, PIAZZA ROMA 13100 Vercelli (VC)   Tel: 0039 (0)161 255513

Chiesa Cattedrale Di S. Eusebio? PIAZZA S. EUSEBIO 13100 Vercelli (VC) Tel: 0039 (0)161 252930

Parrocchia Dello Spirito Santo, VIA ERITREA 13100 Vercelli (VC) Tel: 0039 (0)161 212041

Parrocchia Di S. Agnese, 7, VIA BORGOGNA ANTONIO 13100 Vercelli (VC) Tel: 0039 (0)161 252768

MORTARA

Centro Sociale Padre Francesco Pianzola, 2, VIA MAZZA PRIMO 27036 Mortara (PV) Tel: 0039 (0)384 296585

3 Parrocchia S. Lorenzo Casa Parrocchiale? 1, CONTRADA S. DIONIGI 27036 Mortara (PV) Tel: 0039 (0)384 99772

PAVIA *

Basilica S. Pietro In Ciel D'Oro, 2, PIAZZA S. PIETRO IN CIEL D'ORO 27100 Pavia (PV)   Tel: 0039 (0)382 303040

Basilica S. Pietro In Ciel D'Oro? 2, PIAZZA S. PIETRO IN CIEL D'ORO 27100 Pavia (PV) Tel: 0039 (0)382 303036

Parrocchia Dei Santi Primo E Feliciano Martiri, 1, PIAZZA S. PRIMO 27100 Pavia (PV) Tel: 0039 (0)382 26677

PIACENZA *

Chiesa Cattolica Parrocchiale Borgotrebbia, 89, VIA TREBBIA 29100 Piacenza (PC) Tel: 0039 (0)523 480298

Chiesa Cattolica Parrocchiale Corpus Domini, 24 STRADA FARNESIANA 29100 Piacenza (PC) Tel: 0039 (0)523 592321

Chiesa Cattolica Parrocchiale della Ss. Trinita' Alessandrini Don Riccardo, 30, VIA MANFREDI GIUSEPPE 29100 Piacenza (PC) Tel: 0039 (0)523 458204

Parrocchia Di San Fiorenzo Gestione Scuola Infanzia, VIA PELLICO SILVIO 29017 Fiorenzuola D'Arda (PC)   Tel: 0039 (0)523 98317I

Fiorenzuola D'Arda

Parrocchia Di San Fiorenzo Suore Pastorelle, VIA CAVALIERE 29017 Fiorenzuola D'Arda (PC) Tel: 0039 (0)523 241038

List of churches and religious organisations continued.

FORNOVO DI TARO	1 Parrocchia Di S.Margherita Abitazione Del Parroco, 18, localita' SIVIZZANO CENTRO 43045 Fornovo Di Taro (PR) Tel: 0039 (0)525 56258
BERCETO	Santuario Di Berceto, VIA SEMINARIO 43042 Berceto (PR) Tel: 0039 (0)525 60071
PONTREMOLI	Parrocchia Cattedrale, 54027 Pontremoli (MS) Tel: 0039 (0)187 830572
	Parrocchia Ss. Giovanni E Colombano, 3, VIA REISOLI 54027 Pontremoli (MS) Tel: 0039 (0)187 830511
SARZANA	Cattedrale Basilica S. Maria, 5, VIA NICOLO' V 19038 Sarzana (SP) Tel: 0039 (0)187 620017
	Parrocchia Di S. Venanzio? 33, VIA CROCIATA 19038 Sarzana (SP) Tel: 0039 (0)187 621036
PIETRASANTA	Circolo Anspi Renzo Tognetti, 163, VIA DUCA DELLA VITTORIA 55044 Marina Di Pietrasanta (LU) Tel: 0039 (0)584 267049
	Parrocchia Di S. Antonio? 161, VIA DUCA DELLA VITTORIA 55045 Marina Di Pietrasanta (LU) Tel: 0039 (0)584 20866
	Parrocchia S. Maria Assunta, 9, VIA MALTA 55044 Marina Di Pietrasanta (LU) Tel: 0039 (0)584 21312
LUCCA	Chiese Cattoliche Parrocchiali, 53, VIA TOGLIATTI PALMIRO 55100 Lucca (LU) Tel: 0039 (0)583 510933
	Chiese Cattoliche Parrocchiali Parrocchia Di S. Anna, 367, VIALE PUCCINI G. - S. ANNA 55100 Lucca (LU) Tel: 0039 (0)583 587593
GAMBASSI TERME	Caritas Parrocchiale, 50050 Gambassi Terme (FI) Tel: 0039 (0)571 638242

List of churches and religious organisations continued.

Parrocchia Di S. Maria A Le Grazie, 53034 Colle Di Val D'Elsa (SI) Tel: 0039 (0)577 959068

Parrocchia S. Caterina, 35, VIA DEL CAMPANA 53034 Colle Di Val D'Elsa (SI) Tel: 0039 (0)577 920647

Parrocchia S. Marziale, 1, LOCALITA' S. MARZIALE 53034 Colle Di Val D'Elsa (SI) Tel: 0039 (0)577 928677

SIENA * Chiesa Cattolica Parrocchiale Maria Ss. Immacolata Abitazione Del Parroco,104, STRADA DEI CAPPUCCINI 53100 Siena (SI) Tel: 0039 (0)577 287240

Parrocchia Beata Anna Maria Taigi Abitazione Del Parroco, 6, VIA LIGURIA 53100 Siena (SI) Tel: 0039 (0)577 593562

Parrocchia Di S. Spirito Abitazione Del Parroco, 2, PIAZZA S. SPIRITO 53100 Siena (SI) Tel: 0039 (0)577 284353

BOLSENA 1 Parrocchia Basilica S. Cristina Pp. Sacramentini, 1, VIA MAZZINI 01023 Bolsena (VT) Tel: 0039 (0)761 799067

VITERBO * Parrocchia della Crocetta, 4, PIAZZA DELLA CROCETTA 01100 Viterbo (VT) Tel: 0039 (0)761 343170

Parrocchia S. Giovanni Battista? 22, PIAZZA XX SETTEMBRE 01100 Viterbo (VT) Tel: 0039 (0)761 289826

Parrocchia S. Maria Dell'Edera, 5, VIA ZARA 01100 Viterbo (VT) Tel: 0039 (0)761 340925

CPSIA information can be obtained
at www.ICGtesting.com
Printed in the USA
254074LV00001BA

9 782917 183120